D1298314

CHICAGO PUBLIC LIBRARY

R00725 14758

Economic Development in Seven Pacific Island Countries

Christopher Browne
With Douglas A. Scott

International Monetary Fund
Washington, D.C.
1989

HC
681
·B76
1989

The regional map was reproduced with the permission of the Hawaii Geographic Society. Individual country maps were prepared by the Graphics Section of the International Monetary Fund, using national sources and World Bank material. The boundaries shown on these maps do not imply, on the part of the International Monetary Fund, any judgment on the legal status of any territory or any endorsement or acceptance of such boundaries.

© 1989 International Monetary Fund
Reprinted January 1990

Library of Congress Cataloging-in-Publication Data

Browne, Christopher, 1944–
   Economic development in seven Pacific island countries.
   "January 1989."
   1. Oceania—Economic conditions—Case studies. I. Scott,
Douglas A., 1934–   II. Title.
HC681.B76   1989   338.99   88-29660
ISBN 1-55775-035-1

Price: US$18.00

Address orders to:
International Monetary Fund, Publication Services
700 19th Street, N.W., Washington, D.C. 20431, U.S.A.
Telephone: (202) 623-7430
Telefax: (202) 623-7491
Cable: Interfund

Foreword

The seven Pacific island countries that are members of the International Monetary Fund have made impressive economic progress since attaining independence. Growth has accelerated and living standards have steadily improved. Extensive public investment has strengthened health, education, transport, communication, power, and water facilities. The traditional way of life has been preserved even as the processes of development have created modern institutions and helped to meet changing aspirations. Economic prosperity has generally been attained in politically stable environments.

Prospects for continued advancement appear favorable. Governments are taking decisive measures to overcome structural impediments to more broadly based and rapid development, including diversification of the productive base, training of skilled workers, and modification of land ownership patterns. They are also expected to pursue cautious and flexible financial policies. However, in view of the island nations' limited natural resources and the openness of their economies, assurances are needed that world markets will remain open to them and that the assistance programs of major donors will be maintained. The Fund believes that continued strong international support is merited and reaffirms its own commitment to help the member countries of the region meet their development objectives.

Michel Camdessus
Managing Director
International Monetary Fund

Preface

Fund association with the Pacific island economies dates back almost two decades. Initial contacts were with Fiji and Western Samoa, which joined the Fund in 1971. Between 1975 and 1986, membership broadened to include Papua New Guinea, Solomon Islands, Vanuatu, Tonga, and Kiribati. As with all other members, the Fund has held frequent discussions with policymakers in these countries. The Fund has also provided technical experts on short- and long-term assignments, participated in aid groups and seminars, and has enabled officials to participate in training courses at headquarters in Washington, D.C. The Fund has made financial resources available to these members on numerous occasions, particularly in periods of low export earnings. This close and continuing collaboration has certainly enriched our experience with different national economic situations.

During the process of working with these countries, it became clear to us that ample information on their economies existed which, if suitably developed and systematically presented, could be of interest to a wide audience. This information is the main source material for this book. The first chapter surveys the history of the Pacific islands in the years leading up to independence and analyzes topical economic issues in a regional perspective. Each of the following seven chapters is a country study that describes geographic and demographic features, outlines the economic structure and institutions, and traces the evolution of the economy. Comprehensive statistics are presented in a manner that is intended to facilitate intercountry comparisons. Medium-term projections are not discussed in detail, because they can quickly become dated. We hope, however, that this volume will help those readers who wish to reflect on the challenges that these nations face as they prepare for the 1990s.

Many members of the Asian Department staff contributed to this publication. Bruce Smith initiated and shaped the project but was reassigned to another area department before he could implement it. Chris Browne then undertook the work and, with the help and advice of Douglas Scott, saw it through to its conclusion. For both of them, this was certainly a labor of love performed with devotion and perseverance, and the book is largely their work.

Other colleagues also made substantial contributions. Willem Evers, Padma Gotur, Emine Gürgen, Richard Hemming, Richard Hides, Michio Ishihara, Reza Kibria, Francoise Le Gall, Susan Schadler, and Sukhdev Shah assisted in drafting the country chapters and provided helpful comments on the text. Rosanne Heller edited the many drafts through which the work passed. Amber Martini typed and coordinated the manuscript. Sheila Meehan of the External Relations Department edited and prepared the book for publication. The Graphics Section was responsible for production; Philip Torsani designed the cover and produced the individual country maps. To all of them, sincere thanks are due.

P. R. Narvekar
Director
Asian Department
International Monetary Fund

Contents

Regional Perspectives

The Pacific region was settled thousands of years ago, predominantly by Melanesian people in Papua New Guinea, Solomon Islands, and Vanuatu; Micronesians in Kiribati; both Melanesians and Micronesians in Fiji; and Polynesians in Tonga and Western Samoa. Most of the inhabitants resided in closely knit coastal communities, which were governed by powerful local chiefs. Fertile soil, except on coral atolls, and plentiful fish enabled living standards to be kept above subsistence levels in these economies. An ample diet, in terms of calories and protein, and a generally equable climate contributed to relatively long life expectancy. Explorers from Spain and Portugal in the sixteenth century, from the Netherlands in the seventeenth century, and from the United Kingdom in the eighteenth century were primarily interested in trade in precious metals and spices. Except for the spread of diseases, against which local inhabitants lacked immunity, the life of the region was unaffected by these contacts.

During the first half of the nineteenth century, increased exposure to the rest of the world affected the islands' economic and social structure. The main sources of contact were calls by U.S. whaling vessels to replenish supplies; trade in sandalwood with Australia, New Zealand, and China; the establishment of British and German trading centers; and attempts by France to increase its political influence. This period also witnessed the arrival of missionaries from Europe and the United States. Although the various settlers initially received little support from their governments, the placement of consuls and warships to protect the interests of their citizens eventually became widespread.

During the second half of the nineteenth century, partly as a result of growing contact between the Western nations and China and Japan, the region became more integrated with the main international trade routes. As sailing ships gave way to steam power, several Pacific locations became important coaling stations. As they grew more urbanized, Europe and North America also focused their attention on the region as a source of foodstuffs and of coconut products that could furnish soap and edible oils. Increased copra and banana production was feasible with the preservation of traditional small-scale agriculture, but large-scale plantations offered the greatest potential for profits in many islands, especially for newly introduced crops such as sugar and cocoa. For this purpose, foreigners acquired land in Fiji, Solomon Islands, Papua New Guinea, and Western Samoa through transactions that frequently were of questionable legality. Since available labor was often unwilling to accept the discipline of the foreign-owned enterprises, indentured workers were procured. Many Indians recruited for the Fiji sugar fields settled permanently on completion of their contracts. At the same time, workers from Solomon Islands and Vanuatu were pressed into service in the sugar industry in Australia. Mining operations commenced in a few islands, including the extraction of gold in Fiji and Papua New Guinea, and phosphate in Kiribati.

Growing economic involvement, combined with political rivalries among the Western powers, resulted in extensive colonization. The British authorities were initially reluctant to become entangled because of the high administrative cost, but pressure from planters and traders for officials who would regularize their land acquisitions and protect their property, as well as the misgivings in Australia and New Zealand about the growing power of France and Germany, created sentiment for greater commitment. Following a petition from a powerful chief, the United Kingdom annexed Fiji in 1874 and added Solomon Islands, most of Kiribati, and the Territory of Papua to its possessions within the next 20 years. It also strengthened ties with Tonga, which remained independent, and took joint control with France of what is now Vanuatu. German interests centered on commercial plantations in Western Samoa and New Guinea.

After World War I, the United States and Japan strengthened their influence in the North Pacific, while the expropriated German properties of New Guinea were placed under Australian administration and those of Western Samoa under New Zealand administration. Subsequently, the economic affairs of the South Pacific became more interwoven with those of Australia and New Zealand. Trading and shipping services originated there, carrying a progressively wider range of goods to the islands and returning with agricultural and mining output. World War II underscored the strategic value of the region for the Western powers. With the ending of hostilities, which had devastated a wide area, the United States became more entrenched in the North

Pacific, while the other powers showed no disposition to retire from their dependencies in the South Pacific.

The degree of autonomy possessed by the island administrations was modest and indigenous political parties were almost nonexistent. Over the next few decades, in line with developments in dependent territories elsewhere, government functions were progressively entrusted to local officials. However, expatriates continued to exercise a major influence over political and economic affairs until independence, which was attained by Western Samoa in 1962 and by the other six Pacific island countries that are Fund members between 1970 and 1980. The close economic links with the metropolitan powers remained strong. Little regional integration occurred, despite the establishment in 1947 of the South Pacific Commission to promote that objective.

Economic Characteristics at Independence

Agriculture was the predominant activity throughout the region at the time of independence. Coconut products were a major source of food, fuel, clothing, and housing in most countries. Receipts to traders from sales of copra for export also provided a regular flow of cash income to smallholders. Plantations established in the previous century remained in operation under foreign management in several countries, producing copra, cocoa, and bananas in Western Samoa; copra, coffee, and cocoa in Papua New Guinea; and copra in Solomon Islands and Vanuatu. The commercial production of sugar was of major importance in Fiji, where marketing was undertaken by a foreign-owned enterprise, while production was largely in the hands of many farmers of Indian origin. No large-scale enterprises existed in Tonga, where foreigners were not granted land rights; nor in Kiribati, where the shortage of land and the poor quality of the soil of the coral atolls ruled out such exploitation.

Fishing was generally only undertaken on a subsistence level. Despite the abundance of deep-sea fish, especially tuna, the large-scale investment in vessels, storage, and transport facilities required to commercialize this activity was beyond local resources. Mineral deposits were not known to exist on most islands, except for gold in Fiji, gold and copper in Papua New Guinea, and phosphate in Kiribati. Forestry development was inhibited by poor transport and communications. Industry accounted for a small part of national production in all countries, comprising facilities for the export processing of primary products and the small-scale manufacture of a few basic consumer goods. With the notable exception of the Indian community in Fiji, there was no tradition of an entrepreneurial class. Skilled labor was in short supply, and wage costs were often high relative to the economy's maturity. The expatriate retail trading houses ensured the easy availability of most imported goods.

Government was the main source of employment in the services sector, although the universal desire of the colonial powers to contain administrative costs limited the number of jobs. The widespread use of foreign experts and the low levels of education and training also constrained opportunities for the indigenous work force. Tourism became a source of employment in some islands in the wake of improved sea and air transport, but the lack of infrastructure hampered growth. In all countries, the pace at which labor could be absorbed from the subsistence sector into the monetized economy was tightly circumscribed.

In these traditional societies, the rate of population increase exceeded 2 percent annually, reflecting high birth rates and declining mortality rates. Emigration served to abate population pressures in some cases, notably for citizens of Tonga and Western Samoa who had free access to New Zealand. Without emigration, the population flow from outlying districts to urban centers created a growing pool of unemployed labor. Extended family units shared income and thus helped overcome adversity without the introduction of elaborate public welfare structures. However, certain features of these societies were not conducive to rapid economic growth and employment creation. Land was communally owned and, in some areas, could be redistributed among families by local chiefs. Communal property rights and belief in egalitarian income distribution discouraged private sector savings and investment throughout the economies.

The narrow resource base and dependence on external trade increased the vulnerability of these economies to changes in world economic conditions. Movements in the terms of trade had a profound effect on national income, and fluctuations in export prices were particularly hard felt because of the lack of diversification in production. The islands were also subject to natural disasters, including cyclones, which caused extensive damage. Kiribati was sometimes affected by drought. In general, persistent swings in economic activity discouraged investment and retarded growth.

The range of policy instruments available to help alleviate structural impediments to growth and to conduct countercyclical policies was extremely limited. In the fiscal area, government services were restricted primarily to administration and law and order. Public investment was small and the scope for discretionary changes in taxation and current spending was restricted. In the monetary area, foreign-owned commercial banks provided few services and extended little credit either to the government or the private sector. Balance of payments surpluses were the main source of monetary expansion and the authorities could not effectively offset the impact of these impulses. Conversely, balance of payments deficits contracted the monetary base, resulting in a built-in external adjustment mechanism. Nevertheless, the approach to fiscal and monetary management ensured that the government budget was kept in balance, and the overall external position remained sound.

Development Strategy

The economic strategy adopted in each of the island countries has aimed at the establishment of a more dynamic framework to generate growth, while retaining the traditional structure of society to the maximum extent feasible. Broad statements of objectives have usually been conveyed through multiyear national development plans. In addition to pointing out the desire to strengthen cultural and national identities, these documents have invariably stressed the need to raise investment, diversify production, enhance foreign exchange earnings, and create employment opportunities. The conservative philosophy of policymakers and external concessional assistance have generally helped to ensure that demand management policies have been consistent with a stable financial environment and the preservation of an open economy.

While progress has been made toward sustained development through the creation of economic and social infrastructure, the supply side of the economies has remained relatively unresponsive to policy changes. The growth of agricultural productivity and the development of industry and private services has been slow. The main source of employment has usually been the public sector, but budgetary constraints have limited opportunities for job creation. In several countries rigidities in the labor market have also inhibited the pace at which labor could be absorbed into the formal economy. This has contributed to the coexistence of rapid growth in real wages and a high rate of unemployment, particularly among young people.

Investment and Savings

In view of the low investment expenditure prior to independence, and the high incremental capital-output ratio that typically existed because of the structure of the island economies, increased investment appeared to be the essential driving force in the development process. Most countries have substantially raised the rate of public investment. Attention has focused on transport, including roads, harbors, and shipping services, and airport and airline facilities; domestic and external telecommunications; public utilities, especially electricity, water, and sewerage; and education and health, notably the provision of schools and hospitals. Public enterprises have been created to undertake many of these industrial and commercial functions.

In addition to promoting social development, the buildup of infrastructure has been intended to facilitate private investment. To this end, most countries have maintained a favorable regulatory environment. Price controls have been seldom used; few barriers have existed to the establishment of business firms; and exchange and trade systems have usually been liberal and nondiscriminatory, with a general absence of controls on current payments. Nevertheless, private investment has remained sluggish in most countries, particularly in the agricultural sector, where a lack of clear access to land has been an inhibiting factor. Infrastructure remained rudimentary, transport costs high, and markets fragmented. The departure of expatriates has exacerbated shortages of skilled labor. Although a high degree of automaticity has usually permitted inward and outward capital movements, little foreign direct investment has been attracted since independence, except for mining enterprises in Papua New Guinea and plantations in Solomon Islands.

Public and private savings have financed a small part of investment throughout the region. Public resource mobilization has been constrained by the lack of activities on which domestic taxes could be imposed and by the high expectations of the population with respect to government services. Apart from the tradition of low rates of interest on bank deposits and the limited range of alternative financial savings instruments, private savings have been discouraged by social impediments to the acquisition of individual wealth. In view of the constraints on voluntary savings, most countries have introduced national provident funds to which wage and salary earners in both the public and private sectors have been required to contribute.

Concessionary assistance has financed the bulk of the public investment programs. Aid per capita from bilateral and multilateral sources has been generous relative to other parts of the world. In addition to important political and strategic considerations, donors have recognized that capital-output ratios are unusually high in this region and the effective minimum size of infrastructural projects is large in relation to the small population. The lack of skills and experience with the planning process, rather than the shortage of capital, has been the main constraint on the pace of initiating, appraising, and executing projects. To strengthen absorptive capacity, short-term expedients in aid programs have included the provision of foreign experts, simplified administrative procedures, greater local cost recovery, and allowances for maintenance. To correct the fundamental problems over the longer term, aid programs emphasize human resource development, institution building, and improvement of the statistical base. The success of programs has been enhanced when aid agencies have responded to the priorities of recipients, made medium-term commitments, and maintained close coordination with each other.

Agriculture

Agriculture has remained the mainstay of the seven Pacific island economies in this study. Both the subsistence and plantation sectors have potential to increase productivity by diversifying into nontraditional crops and exploitation of additional land, but gains in output have been limited. An increased supply response has usually characterized periods of favorable prices, although after the relatively buoyant conditions of the second half of the 1970s, lower export prices reduced incentives for expansion during most of the 1980s. Aging trees and disease have also adversely affected production in the tree crop sectors. While large-scale investment in new facilities might not have been appropriate, given long-term world market price projections, greater replanting and maintenance could have raised yields considerably. Attempts have been made in several countries to diversify production into such areas as tropical fruits and vegetables. Progress has often been difficult because of the lack of adequate transport and marketing facilities.

Communal land ownership has been a major impediment to agricultural investment and growth. Traditional practice and legislation have usually severely restricted the transfer and leasing of land. Frequent disputes have developed over boundaries and ownership, especially in cases where land appropriated by foreigners was returned to communal owners after independence. Where official bodies have had the authority to settle land tenure disputes, adjudication procedures have been complex and extremely slow. In view of the widespread social repercussions, few governments have been willing to contemplate radical changes in land reform.

Shortages of trained managers have limited the growth of commercial agriculture in the postindependence era. In Papua New Guinea and Vanuatu, production in the plantation sector has stagnated or declined with the departure of expatriate managers. In Western Samoa, management difficulties on public sector estates have inhibited agricultural revitalization. These difficulties have been compounded by the strong preference in rural areas for subsistence activities rather than wage employment on plantations. Solomon Islands consolidated the gains in production and diversification it achieved in the 1970s through the establishment of joint ventures between the Government and foreign private investors, but it has undertaken few additional projects.

Publicly owned commodity boards have been established to purchase and market the main export crops and, in most cases, to operate intervention schemes to counter the impact of fluctuations in world market prices on producer prices. A formula, based on a moving average of actual prices received for the past several years, has normally been applied to set procurement prices in relation to medium-term trends. In some countries, pressures from growers impeded the retention of funds to build up reserves when world prices were high in the late 1970s and 1983–84. The degree of downward adjustment to domestic prices was also inadequate when world prices declined in 1980–82 and 1985–86, thereby eroding reserves and ultimately necessitating budgetary support. However, these operations have led to greater stability in export earnings which, in turn, has helped to increase production incentives, particularly for copra. Fiji has been successful in helping to stabilize incomes in the sugar sector through the negotiation of long-term sales contracts at fixed prices with the European Community.

Nonagricultural Primary Production

Most countries have acted to exploit fish resources more comprehensively. In the subsistence sector, greater government assistance has been provided for boat-building, fishing gear, harbor facilities, marketing arrangements, and bank credit. Since the advent of 200-mile exclusive economic zones, several countries have established fishing fleets, mainly for tuna, with public funds or foreign investment. External aid projects and joint ventures have been undertaken to supply capital and technical expertise, enhance the knowledge of available fish resources, and provide onshore infrastructure. Processing canneries have been established in Fiji, Papua New Guinea, Solomon Islands, and Vanuatu. In recent years, the strong competitive position of fishing fleets from outside the South Pacific region has left prospects for expansion uncertain. In these circumstances, Kiribati and other nations have negotiated licensing arrangements to permit foreign-owned vessels to operate in their waters.

The mining sector has had a major impact on economic growth in the postindependence era only in Papua New Guinea, where two of the world's largest copper-gold mines are in operation. While the employment possibilities of these projects have been limited and their local purchases of materials and equipment small, they have made an important contribution to the country's budget and balance of payments. Kiribati, on the other hand, experienced the exhaustion of phosphate deposits in 1979, the same year that it achieved independence.

Industry and Services

The industrial sector is small in all seven countries. Although Fiji has a larger manufacturing sector than the other countries, its role as a regional center has evolved slowly. Opportunities for export-oriented production have been enhanced by the provision, since 1981, of duty-free access to the Australian and New Zealand markets under a South Pacific regional trade agreement. There has been scope for import substitution because of the relatively high degree of effective protection resulting from reliance on tariffs as a major source of government revenue. Fiscal incentives, including income tax holidays and duty drawbacks on imported materials, have been offered to motivate investors. Nevertheless, the structural features identified at independence, such as high transport costs, infrequent shipping, lack of marketing skills, and rigidities in labor markets, have continued to impede growth.

The public sector remains the main source of employment creation in all of these countries, reflecting increased current and capital spending by both the central government and the public enterprises, although relatively high wages have tended to limit employment growth. To ease budgetary pressures, several countries implemented policies in the early 1980s to leave existing vacancies unfilled, to freeze recruitment, and to impose retirement. However, the creation of positions commonly proved easier than the elimination of posts, and cutbacks in public sector employment were usually temporary. Fiji has developed a diversified private services sector that includes a large tourist industry and trade and financial services. Vanuatu has created jobs in tourism and its offshore financial center. However, throughout the region, the growth in demand for formal employment has outpaced the available opportunities. In Tonga and Western Samoa, pressures have been partially eased by emigration.

Wages Policy

Centralized wage-setting arrangements, especially de facto indexation for consumer price changes, have been prevalent. The use of such arrangements has limited the potential for real wage flexibility. Additional factors influencing wage determination have included the presence of strong labor unions, the dominant role of the public sector in establishing wage rates throughout the economy, and expectations of living standards on the scale of that enjoyed by expatriates. Such features of the labor market have been deeply entrenched in Fiji and Papua New Guinea and have also existed in Solomon Islands, Vanuatu, and Western Samoa. Strong demand for government services during the 1970s enabled trade unions in these countries to negotiate public sector wages that were high in relation to productivity and subsequently to secure regular increases in real wages. In some cases, the government has favored such a policy to attract and retain in the public sector those with managerial and technical skills who might otherwise have sought employment opportunities abroad. This level of wages has spread to the private sector, inhibiting the business investment needed to create job opportunities and promoting the adoption of labor-saving techniques, while at the same time enhancing the attractiveness of wage labor in village societies.

Downward real wage rigidity has been of particular concern when external adjustment has been required in response to a long-term deterioration in the terms of trade. Pressures for more flexible wage policies have also arisen because of the reservoir of underutilized labor in the rural economy. The need to strengthen competitiveness intensified following the weakening of the regional external payments position during the 1979–82 period of increased oil prices and world recession. In most of the seven countries, the initial response was slow and competitiveness was weakened, but greater wage flexibility was gradually introduced during 1983–87. Papua New Guinea introduced elements of flexibility into centralized wage determination beginning in 1983, when it gave only partial indexation for consumer price changes. Fiji discontinued the link between wages and prices when it implemented a 15-month wage freeze in late 1984. In 1986, it introduced wage fixation procedures that took into account changes in productivity and the terms of trade as well as price adjustments. Vanuatu and Western Samoa implemented more restrained wage policies in the public sector in 1983–87 as part of programs to secure external adjustment.

External Economic Relations

The region has generally avoided balance of payments difficulties. Owing to the narrow resource base, exports have remained concentrated in a small number of primary products. Import dependence has been pronounced for almost all types of commodities, including most development materials and a wide range of consumer goods. The trade deficits have normally been more than offset by net receipts from services and transfers, reflecting a combination of earnings from tourism, other private services, emigrants' remittances, and official concessional grant assistance. In most countries, the overall balance of payments has been persistently in surplus, except during 1980–82, and official international reserves equivalent to several months of imports have been maintained.

Historical links have dominated external economic relations. Aid flows and sometimes emigration have reinforced traditional trading routes. Export markets for traditional commodities in Europe and North America have remained relatively stable, but efforts to penetrate the large and faster growing markets of Asia have been limited. Australia and New Zealand have continued to be the main sources of imports. Regional integration in trade has been minimal, because of the low degree of complementarity in production among the economies, insufficiently developed transport facilities, and tariff barriers. In the absence of greater progress in economic diversification and in reducing dependence on external aid, the present pattern of relations with the rest of the world is expected to continue.

Export earnings have reflected the volatility of prices of primary commodities in world markets. In the upswing of the world trade cycle, a rise in export incomes has led to an improvement in the external current account, the accumulation of foreign reserves, and a surge in monetary growth. Subsequently, increased private and public spending has resulted in higher imports. With the consequent decline in net foreign assets, monetary and credit conditions have tightened. However, several governments have worried that such fluctuations discouraged private investment and had adverse consequences for medium-term growth. The operations of the commodity price stabilization boards have been designed to cushion the impact of variations in export receipts on producers. The relative stability of receipts from services, remittances, and official transfers has also reduced the vulnerability to adverse trends in the foreign trade accounts.

During the 1970s, with the exception of Western Samoa, most of the independent island countries enjoyed sound external positions reflecting buoyant export markets, plentiful concessional assistance, and cautious demand management policies. During 1980–82, adverse movements in the terms of trade associated with weak commodity prices and higher costs of energy and other imports caused a pronounced weakening in the external current accounts. In this period, the inherent difficulties in adjusting domestic demand management policies to offset the impact of changes in external economic conditions were clearly demonstrated. Initially, the main burden of adjustment fell on fiscal policy, because of the large public sector and its importance for the balance of payments. However, given real wage rigidities and political considerations, policymakers could not initiate bold new measures or sharp changes in direction. Moreover, the scope for monetary policy was limited because central monetary institutions and instruments were only beginning to take shape. During 1983–87, the required degree of external adjustment was achieved through the progressive tightening of fiscal, monetary, and wage policies. In several cases, greater flexibility in the management of interest and exchange rates played a useful supporting role.

Foreign Trade

The importance of merchandise exports has varied considerably among the island countries. Fiji has had a long-established and profitable export sector, which continued to be based on sugar after independence. By diversifying into cocoa, palm oil, fishing, and timber over the past two decades, Solomon Islands boosted exports to more than 50 percent of GDP during the 1970s. Papua New Guinea, through the exploitation of copper and gold, raised exports to 40 percent of GDP by the mid-1980s. Export growth was weak in the other four countries whose production base was dominated by coconut products, and their export sectors have accounted for only 10–15 percent of GDP in this decade. In Kiribati, exports declined sharply after the exhaustion of phosphate reserves in 1979. In Tonga and Western Samoa, production of bananas declined and output of other traditional crops was stagnant over the past two decades. In Vanuatu, exports were adversely affected by the departure of expatriate plantation managers after independence. In these cases, poor export performance restricted the growth of real GDP.

Imports have ranged between 40 and 70 percent of GDP in the island economies, apart from Fiji, which has had a smaller degree of import dependence. Typically, food and beverages have represented about one fourth of the total, and finished consumer goods an additional 10–15 percent, reflecting consumption standards that have been well above the poverty level. Despite the heavy dependence on imported energy, petroleum products have normally been equivalent to less than 15 percent of total imports. Most energy has been used for transport, commercial, and household purposes, in view of the small industrial demand. Materials and capital equipment, financed largely out of aid flows, have accounted for up to one half of total imports. This share increased substantially after independence as a result of higher investment in economic and social infrastructure.

Exports and imports have been of about the same magnitude for Papua New Guinea and Solomon Islands and the trade deficit of Fiji has been limited to about 10 percent of GDP. Trade deficits have ranged between 30 and 60 percent of GDP for Kiribati, Tonga, Vanuatu, and Western Samoa, and, in each of these cases, the proportion of exports to imports has declined considerably since independence. The viability of this situation has been preserved by the strong growth of receipts of services and transfers, including private remittances and concessional assistance.

Services and Transfers

Fiji has recorded net surpluses on its services account as a result of tourist receipts, as has Kiribati because of interest on its foreign asset portfolio and fees under fishing agreements with foreign countries. Interest earnings on official reserves have been an important item for several countries. Following natural disasters, in addition to higher aid flows, compensation has normally been received from foreign insurance companies. This made an important temporary contribution to the easing of balance of payments pressures in Fiji, following cyclones in 1983 and 1985, and in Solomon Islands after the cyclone of 1986. Papua New Guinea recorded a net deficit on its services account because of management and investment income payments by the mining sector, and Solomon Islands did so reflecting dividend payments. For all countries, freight and insurance have been major payment items in the services account, representing about one fourth of the import bill.

With regard to private transfers, Tonga and Western Samoa have received workers' remittances equivalent to about one third of GDP, well in excess of merchandise exports. Large numbers of citizens residing in Australia, New Zealand, and the United States have sent funds to relatives at home. The strength of family ties has encouraged the transmittal of a high proportion of earnings, even after long periods of absence abroad. While some funds have been sent as savings to facilitate the eventual return of emigrants to their own countries, the overwhelming proportion of remittances has financed imports of consumer goods by relatives at home. Although several recipient countries tightened their immigration laws during the 1980s, remittances have grown rapidly because additional emigrants have been able to join family members abroad and the earning capacity of those established abroad has continued to grow. Kiribati has received considerable receipts from private transfers through the employment of its citizens on foreign-owned ships.

Official transfer receipts have been large throughout the region, since most external concessional assistance has been provided in grant form. Fiji has been an exception, because, in view of its higher per capita income, aid flows have been smaller and much of the assistance provided in the form of low-interest loans. During the 1980s, receipts were equivalent to nearly 10 percent of GDP in Papua New Guinea; 15–20 percent in Solomon Islands, Tonga, Vanuatu, and Western Samoa; and 60 percent in Kiribati. Although cash budgetary support was gradually withdrawn after independence by the former colonial powers, these donors have been willing to provide additional funds for development projects. While the region has not been completely immune to the effects of budgetary constraints in the industrial world, most bilateral aid programs have expanded considerably during the 1980s. In addition to a willingness to help development, there have been regional and security considerations in the cases of Australia, Japan, New Zealand, and the United States; and assistance for former dependencies provided by France and the United Kingdom.

Capital Flows and External Debt

By comparison with official transfers, capital account transactions have been relatively small in most island countries. Multilateral financial institutions, especially the World Bank and the Asian Development Bank, have provided a limited amount of concessional loan finance. Several countries undertook extensive borrowing during 1980–82, when external conditions deteriorated sharply. Except for Papua New Guinea, which since the early 1970s has experienced a regular flow of private foreign capital into the mining sector, and Western Samoa, which during the late 1970s greatly expanded its public investment program, external commercial borrowing has not been undertaken on a continuing basis. The authorities have recognized that their ability to finance commercial loans is highly limited.

The ratio of outstanding debt to GDP in 1987 was 70–75 percent for Papua New Guinea, Solomon Islands, and Western Samoa, and 40 percent for Fiji. External debt service for Solomon Islands was about 7 percent of exports of goods, services, and private transfers in recent years. For the other three countries, external debt service was within 15–20 percent of receipts of goods, services, and private transfers. External borrowing has almost always been avoided by Kiribati, Tonga, and Vanuatu, except on highly concessional terms. For these three countries, external debt service was about 2 percent of current receipts in 1987. The island countries have not encountered problems in meeting their debt-service obligations, except for Western Samoa during 1980–82. In view of their vulnerability to external factors, most of these countries have maintained gross reserves equivalent to about 4–5 months of imports.

Exchange Rate Policy

At independence, the three island countries that possessed their own currencies pegged them at par to the currency of a metropolitan power. In this manner, the Fiji dollar was linked to the pound sterling; the Tongan pa'anga to the Australian dollar; and the Western Samoa tala to the New Zealand dollar. Other countries adopted similar arrangements when they issued their own currencies. Papua New Guinea and Solomon Islands fixed their currencies (the kina and the dollar, respectively) to the Australian dollar, and Vanuatu linked the vatu to the French franc. In view of the fluctuations in the value of the main currencies and a desire to secure greater stability in the overall value of their exchange rates, most island countries subsequently moved to a system of determining their exchange rate daily in relation to a weighted basket of currencies, usually those of their four or five main trading partners. All Pacific island member countries have established this system, except for Kiribati, which has not issued its own currency, and Tonga, which has continued to peg the pa'anga to the Australian dollar. Vanuatu pegged the vatu to the SDR between 1981 and early 1988 and then switched to a basket of currencies.

During the 1970s, little use was made of flexible exchange rate policy to strengthen competitiveness. In Fiji and Papua New Guinea, depreciation was considered to be of limited usefulness in view of the close link between wages and prices. In several countries, exchange rate appreciation was considered an appropriate means to counter inflationary pressures. Western Samoa was virtually alone in pursuing an active exchange rate policy, but the impact of several depreciations was quickly eroded by expansionary domestic demand policies. During the 1980s, most countries introduced greater exchange rate flexibility as part of their external adjustment policies in response to less favorable world economic conditions and to help develop the traded goods sector. Fiji and Vanuatu made several large discrete changes against their baskets, while Solomon Islands and Western Samoa made small, frequent adjustments against their baskets. Except for Papua New

Guinea and Tonga, the currencies of the other island economies depreciated considerably in real effective terms between 1984 and 1987.

Role of the Public Sector

A large and pervasive public sector has characterized all the island economies. Despite the limited domestic tax base, budgetary receipts in relation to GDP have been substantial, given the stage of economic development, often as a result of the extensive use of import levies and external grants channeled through the public sector. Current expenditure has also been large in relation to GDP, reflecting strong demand for public services and employment, high wage and salary rates, and financial support for agricultural marketing boards and public enterprises. Public investment programs have been almost entirely financed with external concessionary assistance. In most of these countries, fiscal policy has aimed at approximate budgetary balance over the medium term, influenced by the consideration that a more expansionary policy stance would contribute to balance of payments pressures. The avoidance of fiscal deficits has depended crucially on maintaining the buoyancy of revenue and tight control over expenditure. In most countries, success in these areas has been achieved with little government recourse to bank financing although, in a few cases, countries have experienced difficulties in attaining the required degree of expenditure control and restraint.

Budgetary Receipts

Budgetary receipts among the island countries have ranged from about 25 percent of GDP in Fiji to 85 percent of GDP in Kiribati. Tax revenue has averaged at least 17–20 percent of GDP. Higher ratios have been recorded in Solomon Islands, where the presence of large profitable foreign-owned companies in the plantation sector has helped to raise the ratio to 22 percent, and in Western Samoa, where revenue-raising measures implemented in recent years as part of external adjustment policies have raised the ratio to 30 percent. Nontax revenue in the island countries has averaged about 5 percent of GDP, except in Kiribati where interest earnings on foreign assets and fees under fishing agreements with foreign countries have increased the ratio to 33 percent. External grants have ranged from a negligible amount in Fiji to 35 percent of GDP in Kiribati, primarily reflecting differences in income levels. For Papua New Guinea and Vanuatu, which were unusually dependent on grant assistance during the colonial period, external aid has declined in relation to GDP since independence but, for most other countries, aid has risen substantially.

Import duties have been the largest single source of tax revenue in all of the island countries, except in Fiji and Papua New Guinea where they have represented about one third of taxes. Taxes on imports have been attractive because of the ease of collection, at relatively few points of entry into the country, and the need only for simple accounts, audits, and other procedures in order to secure compliance. Selective high taxes have been imposed to discourage consumption of luxury goods and to protect domestic producers against foreign competition. Generally, tariffs have been preferred to quotas and licensing as a means of limiting imports. Duty drawback schemes have often existed for materials used in export production, with exemptions granted on machinery and equipment in order to promote private investment.

Export levies have been modest, except in Solomon Islands where they have accounted for 13 percent of tax revenue as a result of duties on the exported output of commercial plantations. In the past, export taxes were used more commonly as a convenient means of obtaining revenue from the crops of small-scale farmers who were otherwise difficult to reach by income and land taxes. Over the years, rates have been reduced or taxes abolished in order to encourage agricultural production and exports. In circumstances of temporarily high world prices, several of the Pacific island countries have preferred to allow agricultural marketing boards to build up reserves rather than to levy additional export duties. Taxation of nontraditional exports has generally been avoided.

The main source of income tax has normally been wages and salaries of public employees, which could be easily deducted at the source by the government. Receipts from private businesses have usually been limited because of their small share in national income and the availability of incentives to reduce tax liability and encourage investment in manufacturing, hotels, and tourist activities. Public enterprises have usually been treated in the same manner as private companies but limited profitability has restricted the revenue yield from this source. Income tax has accounted for 50 percent of tax receipts in Fiji and Papua New Guinea, partly because of the importance of private corporations in these countries but primarily because of progressive personal tax rates. Income tax has not been imposed in Vanuatu.

Budgetary Expenditure

Budgetary expenditure has ranged from about 30 percent of GDP in Fiji to 85 percent of GDP in Kiribati. In most countries, current expenditure has varied between 22 and 30 percent of GDP, except for Kiribati where, although substantial cuts were made in real terms after the end of phosphate mining, the ratio has remained above 50 percent of GDP. Budgetary capital expenditure has ranged from 20 to 35 percent of GDP in those countries where investment by the public enterprises has been incorporated in the budget presentation. In Fiji, Papua New Guinea, and Solomon Islands, where this is not the case, development spending has been considerably smaller.

Efforts have been made to redirect current expenditure to areas that reflected more closely the priorities of the postindependence era. Increased attention has been given to health facilities, particularly since the age structure of the population is changing, including growing percentages of young and elderly people; and education, where intensified development efforts and the replacement of expatriate staff have demonstrated the shortage of trained workers. The traditional functions of defense and law and order have not imposed an unduly heavy burden on the budget. Most countries retained the structure of expenditure inherited from the colonial period for these purposes. With regard to administration, several countries have determined that the number of civil servants inherited from the preindependence era was beyond their resources and needs.

Wage and salary payments have comprised a large share of total expenditure. In most cases, real wages increased after independence, except in Kiribati, where repeated cuts in real wages were imposed to constrain expenditure to levels consistent with the more limited resources of the postphosphate era. In the context of economic adjustment programs, greater public sector wage flexibility has been introduced in Papua New Guinea and Western Samoa from 1983 and in Fiji from 1984.

Purchases of goods and services have represented about one fourth of total current expenditure in the island economies. When it was necessary to reduce fiscal deficits, this type of expenditure often bore a large share of the adjustment because of the difficulties of reducing spending in other areas. This has been of particular concern with respect to ensuring adequate funds for maintenance of the growing capital stock. Interest payments have been a small element of total spending, because domestic borrowing has been limited in most countries and foreign funds have been provided in grant form or on highly concessional terms.

The development of social welfare and fiscal transfers has been accorded low priority, partly because of the income-sharing ethic of the extended family system. Food subsidies for consumers have not been needed, because there is limited urbanization and large subsistence food production, even among wage earners, in most countries. Subsidies to public enterprises have often been a more substantial item. While the profitability of many enterprises has been modest, the need for budgetary support to cover operating expenses has been reduced by flexible pricing policies and investment capital provided out of aid funds on highly concessionary terms. When export prices were weak and the reserves of agricultural marketing boards needed replenishment, funds have usually been provided by the on-lending of compensatory grants received from the European Community.

Budgetary Framework and Implementation

Most countries have well-developed procedures for the formulation of annual budgetary estimates of central government revenue and current expenditure. Revenue projections, including the yield of new measures, have generally been predictable on the basis of expected domestic activity and international trade. Current expenditure estimates have been formulated from the submissions by the relevant ministries, on the basis of assumptions about overall economic trends given by the ministry of finance and interdepartmental discussion of these estimates. Although most countries have emphasized the desirability of a current budget surplus to meet a portion of development spending, increases in government revenue have been absorbed by an expansion of current spending.

The development budget, financed largely if not entirely by external aid, has normally been prepared as a separate exercise. The ministry of finance has often played a lesser role in this process, with greater influence accorded to the planning authorities. To maximize the adherence to multiyear national plans, overoptimistic assumptions have sometimes been made about the availability of funds and implementation capacity, with the result that an excessive number of projects have been included in the budget. Increased attention is being given to the integration of current and capital budgets to help achieve more reliable estimates of total expenditure; closer coordination between investment spending and future allocations for maintenance; and emphasis on the need to generate additional current savings.

In the short run, budgetary policy has been relatively inflexible. The narrow range of productive activity has made it difficult to devise new taxes. Countries have not always been able to contain current expenditure within approved limits. Efforts are being made to improve the administrative process by developing allocation systems under which the release of funds is controlled with sufficient regularity; adequate supervision is exercised over the cost and quality of goods and services acquired; accounting systems record government transactions in a framework appropriate for the analysis of their implications; and reporting systems provide data for the prompt periodic appraisal of the actual implementation of fiscal policy. When supplementary budgets have been introduced during the fiscal year, simple procedures to curb expenditure, such as across-the-board cuts in all programs or quarterly cash limits have tended to be favored. In these circumstances, resources have not always been used efficiently.

During the 1970s, growth in expenditure in relation to GDP did not create budgetary deficits in most of the countries, and fiscal policies did not add notably to external pressures. The major exception was Western Samoa where slow revenue growth, frequent wage and salary increases, higher transfers to public enterprises, and the financing of development spending in advance of aid receipts were major contributors to balance of payments pressures. In the early 1980s, continued strong growth in expenditure in most of the countries, despite declines in national income, resulted in larger budgetary deficits that exacerbated the external problems associated with the deterioration in world economic conditions. Subsequently, these countries generally pursued less expansionary fiscal policies for several years in order to achieve the required degree of adjustment.

These experiences have underlined the desirability of framing expenditure policy in a medium-term context. In periods of buoyant world demand and rising government revenues, vigilance has been needed to ensure the application of stringent criteria to new spending projects because excessive expenditure growth would prove difficult to trim back later, especially if it came in the form of an expanded wage bill. To strengthen revenue performance, several island countries have requested Fund technical assistance with tax reform. Measures may be examined to broaden the tax base, including the possibility of general sales taxes and hotel and other tourist taxes; moderate the disincentive effects of high marginal rates; promote private savings and improve resource allocation; strengthen collection and administration; and rationalize the tariff structure. In many cases, continued strong reliance on import duties has appeared inevitable. While these taxes do not differ fundamentally from the taxation of incomes, in view of the openness of these economies, difficulties could arise when imports have to be compressed.

Public Enterprises

Overall, public enterprises have added to budgetary pressures rather than contributed to resource mobilization. While some enterprises have earned considerable profits over a long period, including the corporations engaged in sugar production and distribution in Fiji and plantations in Solomon Islands, no country has been immune from these pressures. In the industrial and commercial fields, high wage costs, overstaffing, and management problems have been common. Additional difficulties in the fishing industry have arisen from weak foreign demand and external competition. In the transport sector, the largest losses have been incurred by the national airlines, especially where efforts were made to develop networks on highly competitive or sparsely traveled regional routes, and on interisland shipping services. Road transport has typically been provided by the private sector. In energy and housing, problems have been associated primarily with insufficiently flexible pricing policies.

During the 1980s, in the face of increased balance of payments pressures, several countries attempted to limit the creation of new enterprises and stem the losses of existing ones. To secure greater management efficiency in cost control and investment decisions, several countries instigated more detailed discussion within the government during annual budgetary preparations. Since few countries have had facilities for the systematic collection of annual data on enterprise performance, monitoring units have been created to strengthen the assessment of financial performance. A shortage of capital among potential buyers has hampered efforts to privatize selected enterprises.

Financial Structure

Most of the seven economies have established central monetary institutions, expanded commercial and development banking functions, and created national provident funds. The gradual introduction of monetary instruments has accompanied these steps, although the scope for monetary policy has remained limited. In most cases, the borrowing needs of the public sector and bank lending to the private sector have been small, and most commercial bank assets have been invested abroad. To preserve financial stability, the authorities have printed money sparingly. Liquidity growth has been closely related to balance of payments developments. Monetary targeting has been little used because money and credit growth have not been closely linked; the authorities have been relatively powerless to offset the swings in domestic liquidity associated with changes in the external position. Nevertheless, during the 1980s these countries have increasingly recognized the importance of discipline in credit policy in containing balance of payments pressures and promoting a more efficient allocation of resources.

Banking Structure

Central banks were established with Fund technical assistance in most of the island countries. In Papua New Guinea and Vanuatu, full-fledged central banks were established shortly after independence. In Fiji and Solomon Islands, central monetary authorities operating under the direction of their ministries of finance were first created as an intermediate step; these institutions were granted virtually all central banking functions and were transformed into central banks after several years. In Western Samoa, prior to the establishment of the Central Bank, a monetary board operated between 1974 and 1983 that was staffed by officials of the Ministry of Finance. In Kiribati, the Government decided that the present arrangement, whereby monetary authority functions were shared between the Ministry of Finance and a commercial bank, was adequate at this stage of economic development.

In most countries, there have been a relatively small number of commercial banks, usually branches of Australian, New Zealand, and other foreign-owned banking groups. The government has often been a minority shareholder in one or more of these banks. Given the banks' international connections and conservative attitude toward domestic private sector lending, the financial soundness of the banking system has usually not been in question. In these circumstances, the supervision of bank activities by the monetary authorities has been relatively underdeveloped. Reflecting the limited degree of competition, banking operations have generally been profitable. A concern in most of the island countries has been the disinclination of the banks to pursue domestic lending opportunities.

Evolution of Monetary Instruments

Prior to independence, domestic currencies had been issued for many years in Fiji, Tonga, and Western Samoa. The ministry of finance, a monetary board, or the local commercial bank undertook the automatic conversion of foreign notes and coins into domestic currency, which was normally issued at par with that of the metropolitan power. These arrangements did not permit control over credit creation; the maintenance of a rigid link between the volume of currency in circulation and balance of payments developments safeguarded the external position and the value of the domestic currency. Near independence, the authorities introduced domestic currencies in Papua New Guinea, Solomon Islands, and Vanuatu. A dual currency period of about one year was normally allowed, after which the foreign currency ceased to be legal tender. In view of the absence of exchange controls, few difficulties were experienced in securing local acceptance of these arrangements. Kiribati has retained the Australian dollar as its domestic currency for reasons of convenience and the costs associated with the introduction of its own currency.

The central monetary authorities of most countries took over the management of foreign exchange reserves shortly after their establishment, except in Vanuatu where the function was retained by a local commercial bank for several years. The substitution of domestic currency for foreign assets created the potential for large credit creation. To prevent balance of payments problems that could arise from a highly liquid banking system, the monetary authorities usually imposed reserve requirements to neutralize a substantial part of these funds. However, reflecting the absence of demand from the public sector for bank credit and the perceived lack of lending opportunities in the private sector, most of the assets of the commercial banks have been invested abroad.

The most commonly used instrument to influence bank liquidity has been variable reserve requirements in the form of a stipulated minimum liquid assets ratio for bank holdings of cash, deposits at the central bank, and government securities in relation to deposit liabilities. A minimum cash ratio has also sometimes been imposed. The main problem with this type of instrument has stemmed from the wide fluctuations in bank liquidity, which required frequent adjustments in the reserve ratio to maintain control over bank lending capacity. Some authorities have relied on direct credit ceilings applied to each bank to limit credit growth. The Western Samoan authorities followed this approach during 1983–86, but to avoid undue rigidity in credit allocation, that system was then replaced with a more flexible arrangement that tied the growth in lending of each bank to the growth of deposits, thereby promoting greater competition among banks for deposits.

The principal private sector credit operations of the commercial banks have consisted of short-term business financing, especially of foreign trade. Longer-term loans for the purchase of capital equipment and other investment goods in agriculture, tourism, and industry have been made, but borrowers have usually been able to obtain cheaper loans from the development finance institutions. In most countries, central banks can provide facilities for the rediscounting of trade bills and for short-term advances to commercial banks, but these have not been used as a major instrument of monetary policy. To promote domestic lending and the efficient allocation of resources, sparing use has been made of selective credit controls that favor priority areas.

The monetary authorities in most countries have not relied on intervention through open market operations in securities. Although it is recognized that the flexible and fast acting nature of these instruments could have been helpful in a monetary environment subjected to large swings in bank liquidity associated with external events, financial markets are not sufficiently broad and deep to permit their effective use. Where treasury bills and other short-term securities have been issued, notably in Fiji and Papua New Guinea, the initial purchasers normally held these until maturity; secondary and interbank markets generally have not developed. Secondary markets in longer-term government and public enterprise instruments remain undeveloped.

Conduct of Monetary Policy

Monetary targeting has been considered to be of limited usefulness in the island economies. Liquidity growth has been difficult to gauge accurately because of unpredictable export earnings and other large external shocks. Attempts to influence monetary growth were pursued most actively in Papua New Guinea during the 1970s, including the sterilization of a substantial part of the accumulated reserves of the agricultural stabilization funds during periods of high export demand. However, officials have seen little need to influence monetary growth that has arisen from other foreign transactions. At least in the short run, changes in demand have influenced imports more than domestic price movements, thereby weakening the link between monetary growth and inflation. While increased foreign exchange receipts have initially been reflected in higher external reserves and a surge in monetary growth, these trends have subsequently been reversed, as domestic demand strengthened and imports rose. If a weakening of the external position had been predicted, steps might have been implemented to tighten monetary policy in advance of the prospective loss of international reserves, but turning points in the balance of payments were usually difficult to determine.

The main aim of most of the monetary authorities has been to establish money and credit conditions that are consistent with the achievement of external objectives. In this regard, the determination of the appropriate rate of growth of domestic credit, irrespective of the possible existence of monetary targets, has been important. Occasionally, the public sector borrowing requirement, over which the monetary authorities have had little control, has dominated credit growth. In Western Samoa, an expansionary fiscal policy contributed to rapid monetary and credit growth and a deteriorating balance of payments during the late 1970s. In most of the other countries, where fiscal policy was less expansionary, monetary policy has been broadly successful in keeping the growth of domestic credit within acceptable limits, as evidenced by generally moderate price movements and the maintenance of liberal trade and payments systems.

The deterioration in external economic conditions in the early 1980s demonstrated the usefulness of influencing bank liquidity to moderate import demand and protect the balance of payments. During this period, private traders in several countries expanded their use of bank credit to finance imports. In Western Samoa, the authorities applied moral suasion to curtail credit expansion, but the absence of other instruments limited their ability to restrain lending. Credit growth was also rapid in Solomon Islands, partly because reserve requirements had not been imposed earlier on commercial banks. In other countries, including Fiji, where reserve requirements could be raised quickly, monetary policy was more effective in curbing private sector credit. In 1983–87, as part of adjustment policies, the authorities of most of the countries closely monitored developments in bank liquidity.

Interest Rates

Bank deposit and lending rates in the Pacific region have traditionally been determined administratively, and interest rate policy has not been actively employed as a tool of economic management. Nominal bank rates have generally been kept low and stable. Higher deposit rates have not been thought likely to influence savings since income sharing in traditional societies made it difficult for individuals to save. Deposit rates have also not been seen as a major factor in encouraging remittances from residents living abroad. Transfers have been prompted by the obligation to support the income and consumption levels of family members at home. With regard to lending rates, interest rates have not been thought to influence the allocation of resources, particularly since a large part of total investment has been undertaken by the public sector with financing obtained through external concessional assistance.

In 1980–82, most interest rates became negative in real terms, as nominal rates were not adjusted for higher rates of price increase. During 1983–87, most island countries introduced greater flexibility in interest rate policies to establish positive real rates for longer-term deposits and virtually all loans. In this period, increased weight was given to the possibility that higher deposit rates would encourage savings by the growing urban household sectors and the private business communities. Several countries raised ceilings on loan rates to encourage banks to more actively seek domestic lending opportunities. In other cases, higher rates were aimed at discouraging borrowers in order to reduce domestic demand and balance of payments pressures or investment in areas of relatively low profitability. The only country that did not move toward more market-oriented rates was Tonga, where legislation, in effect for 50 years, stipulated a 10 percent ceiling on lending rates and where deposit rates were kept commensurately low.

Market-determined rates were applied to virtually all transactions in Vanuatu after independence, because the authorities felt that the imposition of controls was inconsistent with the country's role as an offshore financial center. In Kiribati, the introduction of internationally competitive rates on large-scale time deposits in 1984 resulted in the transfer to that country of considerable funds that had previously been held abroad. Other countries that adopted higher nominal rates as part of external adjustment programs in the 1980s were sometimes reluctant to align rates fully with the markedly higher rates prevailing in regional centers, especially Australia and New Zealand.

Other Financial Institutions

Each of the island countries has established a development bank to provide longer-term finance for private sector investment, mainly in agriculture and industry. While the government has usually provided most or all of the equity, the loanable funds have generally been made available on concessional terms by multilateral financial institutions, notably the World Bank and the Asian Development Bank, by bilateral aid donors, and by the European Community. In several countries, the new institutions replaced agricultural and industrial loan boards that had been financed out of the government budget. Such budget allocations were on a smaller scale and subject to abrupt changes. The development banks have improved the availability of credit for small businesses, where high risk and administrative costs deterred commercial bank lending. However, the shortages of staff and lack of experience in processing loan applications have affected the quality of their loan portfolios in several countries. Loans have been made at below market rates, reflecting the low average cost of funds. This has increased the likelihood of the allocation of resources to unprofitable activities and has contributed to the growth of loan arrears.

All of the countries, except Tonga, have established national provident funds for wage earners in the public and private sectors. Rates for employers and employees together have ranged from 6 to 14 percent of the wage and salary bill, usually payable in equal proportions by the two groups. Given the social constraints on voluntary savings, compulsory and contractual schemes have been a useful means of raising private savings. Most funds have earned substantial surpluses, which proved to be an important source of financing for the public sector, especially in Fiji, Papua New Guinea, and Solomon Islands. With a lack of demand at home, the assets of the Kiribati institution have been almost entirely invested abroad.

Issues and Outlook

The seven Pacific island countries have made considerable economic progress since independence, despite deep-seated impediments to growth associated particularly with geographical location and difficult topography. High public investment has helped to create infrastructure, mainly in the fields of transport, communications, health, and education. Fiscal and monetary policies have served to ensure domestic financial stability and sound balance of payments positions. The island countries have initiated steps to broaden the tax base and increase the array of monetary instruments. Recourse to import restrictions has been modest and external commercial borrowing has been kept within manageable limits. To promote competitiveness and efficiency, most countries have progressively introduced flexibility in exchange rate, interest rate, and wage policies. However, diversification of production and penetration of new export markets have not proved to be easy.

The increased emphasis on economic development has not fundamentally changed the traditional values of these societies. As the size of the monetized economy has expanded relative to the subsistence sector, extended family units have continued their long-standing income-sharing functions that contribute to a more equitable distribution of income and reduce the need for governments to build extensive social welfare systems. While the authorities in several of the countries have simplified the formal procedures for the sale and lease of land and the resolution of boundary issues, customary land ownership rules have stayed largely intact. With the exception of Fiji in 1987, all countries have experienced political stability throughout the postindependence era, within a framework that has ensured regular general elections.

Over the medium term, the current stance of policies is expected to be maintained. Cautious domestic financial management remains crucial to the preservation of sustainable balance of payments positions. In addition, notwithstanding the importance attached to the ultimate goal of national self-reliance, these countries continue to depend heavily on external economic aid. The historical underpinnings of the relationship between Pacific island countries and aid donors provide a mature and stable environment for assistance. In several of the island countries, external viability also depends on the continued receipt of emigrants' remittances.

Policies in most of the island countries are oriented to bring about basic changes in the economic structure without disturbing the strength inherent in enduring social traditions. However, the willingness to pay and collect taxes sets an upper limit to the size of government, particularly to achieve the longer-term political aim in most countries of substantially reducing dependence on external aid and remittances. In order not to overburden the public sectors, more dynamic private sectors are being encouraged to evolve. The foundation for this process has been laid through investment in infrastructure, the lessening of administrative rigidities in the determination of real wages, and the development of financial systems. Although the productive base of most countries is expected to remain narrow, incentives are being put in place to stimulate the faster development of exports, including tourism. These steps to promote private investment, combined with measures to attract foreign capital in appropriate cases, should help to improve the employment outlook. Modifications to land ownership regulations could also generate agricultural investment.

While the outlook for the seven member countries is diverse in terms of income levels and resource endowment, the implementation of structural changes will create the potential for higher output growth and improved living standards throughout the region. However, dramatically higher rates of expansion of real GDP are not envisaged. In most cases, rapid population increase, limited capacity to absorb labor into the formal monetized sector, and deep-seated impediments to raising productivity in traditional activities are expected to hinder the pace of development of the monetized sectors. The main task will be to satisfy the rising aspirations and needs of societies in transition. Preserving the political tolerance and stability that has traditionally held together and served the interests of the island nations will be the fundamental requirement for meeting this challenge.

Table 1. Pacific Island Countries: Economic and Social Indicators[1]

	GDP (in millions of SDRs)	GDP per capita (in SDRs)	Area (in thousands of square kilometers)	Population (in thousands)	Population density (in persons per square kilometer)	Population growth (percent per annum)	Life expectancy at birth (in years)	Crude birth rate (per thousand)	Crude death rate (per thousand)	Infant mortality (per thousand live births)	Primary school enrollment (in percent)	Calories per day (per capita)
Fiji	1,100	1,200	18.3	710	39	2.1	68	30	7	38	100	2,900
Kiribati	20	275	0.7	66	91	1.9	53	38	14	82	100	2,515
Papua New Guinea	2,200	650	461.7	3,600	8	2.6	52	37	13	68	65	2,145
Solomon Islands	110	380	27.6	300	10	3.5	58	45	12	46	73	2,200
Tonga	65	650	0.7	95	127	0.6	64	29	8	58	77	2,845
Vanuatu	105	750	12.0	140	12	3.2	63	38	12	75	61	2,100
Western Samoa	75	500	2.8	160	57	0.3	65	34	8	51	91	2,400

Sources: Data provided by the national authorities; and the World Bank.
[1]Latest available data.

FIJI

▲ SUGAR MILLS
    MAIN ROADS
    TRAMWAYS

Fiji authorities;
and IMF Graphics Section.
April 1985

LAU GROUP

VANUA LEVU

TAVEUNI

KORO

GAU

OVALAU

SUVA

VITI LEVU

KADAVU

YASAWA GROUP

2
Fiji

Fiji covers a land area of 18,000 square kilometers in the South Pacific, midway between Hawaii and Australia. The country is made up of about 400 islands, of which the two largest comprise 90 percent of the total area and population. Owing to its volcanic origin, about four fifths of the land is mountainous and unsuitable for cultivation, but contains forests, mineral resources, and hydroelectric potential. Agricultural land is fertile with plentiful rainfall, although it is subject to drought and cyclones.

Fiji's population is about 700,000 and its growth rate averaged about 2 percent annually during the 1970s and 1980s. The population density of 26 persons per square kilometer is considerably below the regional average. Life expectancy is about 65 years and most health and education indicators are favorable by regional standards. The University of the South Pacific is located in the capital, Suva. Fijian society is unique in terms of its racial characteristics. The native Melanesians, who comprise 45 percent of the population, are engaged mainly in subsistence agriculture and public sector employment. The people of Indian descent, who comprise 50 percent of the total, are engaged in sugar cultivation and trading activities. The remaining population is composed of Chinese, Europeans, and other Pacific islanders.

Indian immigration started soon after the United Kingdom began to administer the islands in 1874, mainly as indentured labor for the sugar industry. On completion of their contracts, many of these people settled permanently and became independent small-scale sugar producers. Since most agricultural land is communally owned and may not be sold except to other Melanesians, these farmers rely on lease arrangements. Fiji became independent from the United Kingdom in 1970, with a parliament elected every four years. Until 1987, a political party dominated by native Fijians won all general elections and a party dominated by people of Indian descent constituted the opposition. In the April 1987 general election, an Indian-dominated party defeated the ruling Fijian party. During the remainder of 1987, there were two military coups d'etat. While control has been handed back to a civilian government, the political outlook is unclear.

Fiji is the most advanced economy in the region, with annual per capita GDP of SDR 1,200. Its prosperity is based on an efficient sugar industry, a profitable tourist sector, and a broadly based services sector. With good transport and communication links, the country serves as a regional center in a variety of fields. Economic and social infrastructure are well developed, following a large public investment program undertaken during the 1970s. There are many entrepreneurs who are experienced in small business operations. Shortages of skilled labor are less pronounced than in other Pacific island countries. Although industrial growth is constrained by an inefficient system of protection, production should benefit from the greater flexibility in wage and exchange rate policies that has been introduced recently. However, the pace of development is likely to remain constrained until stable political conditions are re-established.

Economic Structure

Production and Prices

The production and processing of sugarcane contributes about 15 percent of GDP. Sugar production of about 500,000 metric tons per year, with normal weather, is virtually all exported, both on long-term contracts to the European Community at relatively stable prices and on the volatile free world market. Cultivation is undertaken by about 22,000 smallholders. The harvesting, transportation, milling, and marketing of sugar is arranged by the Fiji Sugar Corporation, which is predominantly government owned. Under the present formula, the sales proceeds are divided between the growers and the Corporation on an approximate basis of 70:30.

A wide variety of other agricultural production accounts for about 10 percent of GDP. Copra is the second largest crop. Although its importance has declined over the years with the aging of trees, it remains the major source of cash income in the outer islands. The Copra Price Stabilization Scheme, established in 1975, has helped to stem the long-term fall in output by ensuring more stable prices to growers. Rice, an important crop for domestic consumption, is grown mostly as a second crop to sugarcane. Although priority is attached to increasing production in order to create rural employment opportunities, half of the domestic rice requirement continues to be met from imports. Among the smaller crops, ginger, cocoa, citrus fruits, and vegetables have growth potential and are contributing increasingly to export earnings. Nonagricultural primary production, which contributes another 10 percent of GDP, has been growing as a result of the commercialization of fishing activities, the exploitation of pine forests, and investment in gold mining and mineral prospecting.

The manufacturing sector contributes 10 percent of GDP. Excluding the processing of sugarcane, which continues to represent half of total value added, the focus traditionally was on import substitution, with considerable investment by foreign companies. In addition to the small domestic market and relatively high wages, trade barriers inhibited the development of an efficient industrial sector. The deficiencies in the system of incentives included a pronounced bias against export industries, a level of effective protection that in some cases resulted in low or negative value added, and a wide dispersion in tariffs that interfered with efficient resource allocation. More recently, the focus has shifted toward export-oriented production, assisted since 1981 by the commitment of Australia and New Zealand to provide long-term favorable access to their markets.

The services sector, which contributes half of GDP, is dominated by tourism, trading, government administration, finance, and insurance. The tourist sector alone contributes 15 percent of GDP, far greater than in any other country of the region, with 250,000 visitors in 1986 mainly from Australia, Japan, New Zealand, and North America.

Wage developments have traditionally reflected a tendency to compensate non-sugarcane cultivators to the full extent of any increases in consumer prices, which, in turn, are influenced strongly by import prices. Compensation for cane growers has been determined through the formula for sharing sales proceeds with the Sugar Corporation. During 1970–76, when wages were determined primarily by collective bargaining, compensation for price changes set a floor on wage settlements. Between 1977 and 1984, the Tripartite Forum— under the chairmanship of the Prime Minister with representatives of the Government, the trade unions, and the Employers' Association— established annual wage guidelines, which were closely based on the rate of consumer price increase in the previous year. Although adherence to the guidelines was voluntary, they were usually applied throughout the public sector and to most private sector employees in manufacturing, construction, and finance. However, wages were substantially reduced in real terms through a freeze in 1985, small nominal rises in 1986, and large nominal cuts in 1987.

Balance of Payments

The foreign trade account normally records a large deficit. Domestic exports are equivalent to 20 percent of GDP. Sugar accounts for two thirds of the total and the other main traditional exports are coconut oil and gold. In view of the varied markets for these products, the destination of exports is broadly based. Owing to Fiji's central location among the Pacific island countries and its access to air and sea transport, entrepôt trade is also an important source of foreign exchange. Imports are equivalent to 35 percent of GDP, comprising a large variety of raw materials and intermediate and final goods. Apart from consumer demand, a major determinant of imports is the capital projects of the Government and the public enterprises. Most of Fiji's imports originate from Australia and New Zealand, but Japan and other Asian countries have also become important suppliers in recent years.

The net surplus on services averages 10 percent of GDP. Tourism is the largest source of receipts, followed by shipping and insurance services. Private transfers show a net outflow, mainly because of the flow of payments from citizens of Indian origin. Official transfers are equivalent to only 3 percent of GDP, much smaller than in other Pacific economies, mainly reflecting the higher level of income in Fiji. The external current account (including grants) usually shows a small deficit. Private and official capital inflows are somewhat larger in relation to GDP than in most other countries of the region, including official concessional assistance from multilateral financial institutions, commercial borrowing for public investment projects, and limited foreign direct investment.

Policies relating to international reserves, external debt management, and the exchange rate have tended to be cautious. Official reserves are normally maintained at the equivalent of at least four months of imports. Outstanding external debt was reduced in terms of U.S. dollars in 1987. However, with lower GDP and exports, external debt rose to 40 percent of GDP and debt service reached 18 percent of current receipts. In 1971, Fiji introduced a policy of fixing the value of the Fiji dollar to a weighted basket of the currencies of five major trading partners. Between 1975 and 1984, the wage determination process served to make the active use of exchange rate policy largely ineffective. During this period, the exchange rate was kept broadly unchanged in nominal effective terms. During 1985–86, a modest degree of flexibility was introduced in exchange rate management. In 1987, the exchange rate was depreciated in two large steps by more than 30 percent and exchange controls on capital transactions were put in place.

Public Sector

The public sector consists of the central government, local authorities, and 14 nonfinancial public enterprises. The central government budget, prepared on a calendar year basis, covers current and capital transactions in an integrated and comprehensive framework. The relatively small expenditure of the provincial, town, and rural councils is financed by local property taxes, fees and charges, grants from the central government, and domestic borrowing primarily from the National Provident Fund. The public enterprises are engaged primarily in the production, processing, and marketing of certain primary commodities, including sugar and timber; the supply of housing, electricity, and other utilities; and the provision of transportation services, including domestic and international air and shipping facilities. Several government departments engage in commercial undertakings including the provision of post and telegraph, water and sewerage, and inter-island shipping services. The Government is a shareholder in the foreign-controlled fish canning and international telecommunications companies.

Budgetary receipts were equivalent to about 25 percent of GDP during 1980–87, with tax revenue accounting for four fifths of the total. The tax structure places greater reliance on income tax than most countries in the region, while foreign trade taxes have correspondingly less weight. Personal income tax collections, which account for about one third of revenue, increased in relation to GDP over the past decade as most taxpayers moved into higher brackets. Corporate income taxes were less buoyant, reflecting tax incentives to encourage industrial development. Import duties, which represent one fourth of revenue, were adjusted frequently in order to increase their yield. Nontax revenue includes earnings from participation in UN peacekeeping operations in the Middle East. External grants account for only 3 percent of total receipts.

Budgetary expenditure was relatively stable in relation to GDP during 1980–87. Current expenditure gradually rose to 25 percent of GDP, with wage and salary payments accounting for over 40 percent of the total. However, capital expenditure and net lending have fallen considerably since major hydroelectric and other infrastructure projects were completed in the early 1980s. The overall deficit, which averaged about 4 percent of GDP during 1980–87, is financed mainly by borrowing from the National Provident Fund. The public enterprises operate on commercial principles and deficits are generally avoided, except for the airline following an expansion of regional services in the early 1980s and the sugar corporation during periods of unusually low international prices.

Financial Sector

The banking system includes the Reserve Bank of Fiji and six commercial banks, five of which are branches of foreign banks. The Reserve Bank was established in 1984, replacing the Central Monetary Authority of Fiji which, since 1973, had performed most central banking functions. Prior to that, a currency board had issued or redeemed currency automatically against foreign exchange. From its early days, the central monetary institution acted as banker, fiscal agent, and depository for the central government; managed the foreign exchange reserves; introduced reserve requirements and refinancing facilities for commercial banks; set minimum deposit rates and maximum loan rates for the banking system; and supervised the operations of nonbank financial institutions. Commercial bank operations are carried out through a wide network of branches and agencies, making service easily accessible even in remote areas.

The largest nonbank financial institutions are the National Provident Fund and the Fiji Development Bank. The National Provident Fund, to which all public sector and many private sector employers and employees each contribute 7 percent of gross wages and salaries, has large investable surpluses. Under its lending guidelines, at least 50 percent of surpluses are lent to the central government and the Housing Authority, 20 percent to the public enterprises, and 30 percent to the private sector. The Development Bank is the main source of long-term finance to the private sector in agriculture and industry. Its resources comprise equity subscribed by the Government (25 percent) and domestic bonds issues and concessional external loans (75 percent). The surpluses of the insurance companies, which have grown rapidly in recent years, are mainly invested in public sector securities.

Developments in the 1970s

During the 1970s, a satisfactory rate of real GDP growth averaging 4–5 percent annually was maintained, employment opportunities expanded steadily, and financial policies contributed to a stable environment. Major contributors to development were tourism, particularly in the early 1970s when foreign investment was substantial; the sugar industry from the mid-1970s through an expansion of the area under cultivation; and public investment in the late 1970s, mainly in hydro-electric and water services. The central government budget deficit averaged less than 3 percent of GDP, and most public enterprises operated profitably. The credit needs of the private sector were met without excessive monetary expansion. Assisted by the growth in sugar exports, tourist receipts, and concessional assistance, overall balance of payments surpluses were recorded in most years. The external current account deficit averaged below 5 percent of GDP, which was more than matched by private and official capital inflows.

From 1970 to 1973, the increase in real GDP averaged 10 percent annually, led by an unprecedented growth in tourism and the associated boom in the construction sector. The sugar industry also prospered because of the strong rise in export prices. Reflecting the improvement in the terms of trade, national income grew faster than output. With large real wage increases in the public sector, the distribution of income between wages and profits was relatively stable. The underlying budgetary position improved because of buoyant revenue from income and foreign trade taxes, while the pace of credit expansion was moderate. With the strong growth in current receipts, the balance of payments position was comfortable and official reserves remained equivalent to about five months of imports.

In 1974–75, the growth in economic activity was halted by the world recession. However, in contrast to the experience of most other countries in the region at this time, the balance of payments did not deteriorate. While tourist activity slackened because of the downturn in the industrial economies, the boom in world sugar prices associated with supply shortages in major producing countries offset the effect of high petroleum import prices. In 1975, following the first round of oil price increases, the terms of trade was 25 percent above its level at the beginning of the decade, the external current account was almost in balance, and gross official reserves rose to the equivalent of nine months of imports. Nevertheless, with a projected decline in sugar prices when world supply conditions returned to normal, there was concern about the fragility of the external situation. Even though the demand for labor weakened, strong trade unions succeeded in obtaining wage increases that were substantially in excess of the trend in productivity, with adverse consequences for competitiveness.

In order to lay the foundation for a stronger external position over the medium term, the public expenditure program was designed to stimulate the traded goods sector. Efforts were concentrated on the provision of infrastructure for the expansion of the sugar sector, where the response in output was highly favorable. The cultivated area was increased by one third and yields were improved by investment in drainage facilities, greater use of fertilizer and other inputs, and more efficient harvesting techniques during the second half of the decade. Steps to diversify export earnings included the establishment of a publicly owned deep-sea fishing fleet and a tuna canning factory. Major investment projects were commenced to exploit forestry resources for export and hydroelectric resources for import substitution.

Accompanied by strong growth of current expenditure, mainly wage and salary payments, total central government budgetary spending rose from 21 percent of GDP in 1975 to 26 percent in 1979. However, to minimize the impact of higher spending on domestic prices and the balance of payments, the coverage and rates of other tax and nontax revenue items were frequently raised. Budgetary receipts increased from 20 percent of GDP in 1975 to 23 percent in 1979. The overall budgetary deficit was held to an average of 4 percent of GDP during the latter half of the 1970s. Most of the deficit financing was obtained from the National Provident Fund. Public enterprise and private sector credit demand was strong. The central monetary authority introduced a series of instruments to influence bank liquidity, including specified minimum ratios of cash and holdings of government securities to deposit liabilities. While credit growth remained rapid, the effect on prices appeared to be limited.

Wage policy was broadly consistent with the preservation of internal and external balance. The guidelines issued by the Tripartite Forum resulted in more modest wage increases than the earlier system of collective bargaining. The growth of nominal wages was kept closely in line with the rate of consumer price increase of the previous year. Since the inflation rate was gradually decelerating, employees secured persistent real wage and salary increases. With the expansion of sugar output contributing to fast growth in national income, profits also increased steadily. Industrial relations were harmonious; inflationary expectations were reduced; and incentives for private investment were preserved.

Despite the growth in export volumes and higher tourism receipts, the external current account deficit widened from 1 percent of GDP in 1975 to 7 percent in 1979. This principally reflected the higher imports associated with the public investment program for which capital inflows were secured mainly in the form of external concessional assistance. Although official reserves were gradually drawn down, they still exceeded the equivalent of four months' imports. Outstanding external debt remained relatively stable at 18 percent of GDP during 1975–79 and the debt service ratio declined to only 5 percent of current receipts.

Developments in the 1980s

Fiji was initially protected from the full impact of the second round of oil price increases by a dramatic rise in sugar prices triggered by a temporary shortage of world supplies. However, disquieting economic trends began to emerge in 1981–82. Sluggish growth in real GDP and a 30 percent decline in the terms of trade caused national income to fall considerably. Although demand management policies gradually became more restrictive, the overall external adjustment effort was slow to adapt to the fall in the terms of trade and real incomes. In particular, real wage increases in the public sector contributed to a weakening of the fiscal accounts, excessive credit growth, and pressure on the balance of payments. During 1985–86, more decisive action, including financial restraint, a reduction in public sector real wages, and exchange rate flexibility, enabled considerable progress to be made in correcting domestic and external imbalances. Real GDP growth averaged only 1–2 percent annually during 1980–86, well below that in the previous decade. Conditions favorable to the resumption of faster medium-term growth were re-established by the beginning of 1987. Following the change in the political situation during the year, real GDP fell sharply and severe adjustment measures had to be implemented.

Unfavorable Trends During 1980–82

In 1980–82, as the pace of private sector economic activity slackened, with real GDP growth averaging only 1 percent annually, financial policies became more expansionary. Government expenditure increased to more than 30 percent of GDP, mainly because of the rapidly rising wage and salary bill and the large public investment program. Coupled with sluggish revenue performance, the budget deficit widened to 6 percent of GDP. The financial position of the public enterprise sector weakened; lower world prices reduced the profits of the Sugar Corporation; and rising fuel costs contributed to losses in fishing and airline operations. The public sector made greater use of bank credit and, although increases in real interest rates helped to limit private sector demand, the rate of growth of domestic credit was high. However, with less imported inflation, the rate of price increase abated.

An exceptionally large balance of payments surplus was recorded in 1980, because of high export earnings and strong capital inflows associated with public investment projects. However, the overall balance of payments moved into substantial deficit in 1981–82, when the terms of trade deteriorated because of lower export prices. While the net surplus on services and transfers remained largely unchanged, the external current account deficit rose to an unsustainable level that averaged 10 percent of GDP. Although part of the increase reflected unusually high imports of capital equipment, the demand for consumer goods rose strongly because of wage increases. Substantial external commercial borrowing was undertaken and outstanding debt increased to 32 percent of GDP in 1982.

Beginnings of Recovery in 1983–84

During the period 1983–84, trends in the real sector and the balance of payments remained disappointing. Real GDP fell by 4 percent in 1983, when cyclones and drought compounded the problems of weak world demand for sugar and a fall in tourism. With the recovery of activity in these sectors, real GDP rose by 8 percent in 1984, but real national income was little changed because of the further deterioration in the terms of trade. The narrowing of the external current account deficit was related mainly to large inflows of insurance receipts and emergency grants following the cyclones. Imports were reduced because of the completion of major public investment projects. However, this resulted in smaller external concessional assistance and further commercial borrowing was required to rebuild official reserves.

Much of the reduction in the central government budget deficit to 3 percent of GDP in 1984 reflected the cutbacks in capital spending. While the high buoyancy of the tax system enabled budgetary receipts to reach 26 percent of GDP, current spending also rose further in relation to GDP, led by wages and salaries. In order to prevent a resurgence of imports, monetary policy was tightened in late 1984, mainly through higher reserve requirements. Nominal interest rates on bank deposits and loans remained virtually unchanged, so that rates became progressively higher in real terms which helped to stimulate private savings and reduce credit demand.

The growth in wages remained an area of concern because the procedures for centralized wage fixing did not take account of the impact of adverse external factors on the economy's capacity to pay. The most important determinant of the annual guidelines remained the rate of consumer price increase, which ensured that wage earners received full compensation for higher import prices. No provision existed in the arrangements to moderate the wage increases to reflect the deterioration in the terms of trade and declining prosperity in the export sector. Moreover, the guidelines did not take into account the adverse impact of exogenous factors, including cyclones and drought, that also reduced export income. The real effective exchange rate index was kept broadly unchanged in this period by making small, discrete adjustments against the basket of currencies. If wages had moved in line with real national income adjusted for the terms of trade during 1981–84, they would have been about 15 percent lower at the end of 1984.

Progress in Adjustment in 1985–86

A consensus emerged in late 1984 among economic policymakers that, in addition to continued financial restraint, structural measures were needed to reduce cost-price distortions and encourage private savings and investment in order to promote external equilibrium. As a first step toward correcting the problem, an economy-wide wage freeze was put into effect through the end of 1985. In 1986, the method of setting wage guidelines was changed to take into account recent changes in productivity and the terms of trade, in addition to the past year's inflation rate. The result was a relatively restrictive recommendation for wage increases. With these changes, more flexible exchange rate management became practical and the effective exchange rate was gradually depreciated by about 15 percent during 1985–86. The combination of these policies reversed the sharp growth in real wages that had occurred in 1981–84.

Real GDP was again affected by adverse weather in 1985, which reduced sugar output and tourist arrivals, but the economy rebounded strongly in 1986. More buoyant economic conditions and higher public capital spending contributed to the recovery in gross investment to 21 percent of GDP, the highest ratio since 1983, although still well below that of 1980–82. The recovery was accompanied by a further deceleration in the rate of consumer price increase. With a pronounced improvement in the terms of trade, mainly because of the drop in petroleum import prices, the external current account registered a surplus. Gross official reserves increased to the equivalent of six months' imports.

In these circumstances, the authorities decided that fiscal and monetary policies could be eased. Direct tax concessions were implemented that reduced the budget receipts to 24 percent of GDP. Notwithstanding a marked decline of current expenditure to less than 23 percent of GDP, mainly because of reduced wage and salary payments, the budget deficit widened to nearly 5 percent of GDP in 1986. The financial position of the public enterprises improved, particularly that of the domestic airline, following the introduction of a management contract with a foreign airline, and that of the Sugar Corporation in view of stronger world market conditions. With adequate official reserves and private savings at a historically high rate in relation to GDP, bank lending rates were lowered to stimulate private investment, but most rates remained positive in real terms.

Renewed Need for Adjustment in 1987

The buoyant economic conditions were abruptly changed by the military coup d'etat in May 1987, which led to a sharp deterioration in business and consumer confidence, a precipitous fall in tourist arrivals, and pronounced rises in the emigration of skilled labor and capital outflows. The subsequent gradual return to normalcy was interrupted by a second military takeover in September 1987. The renewed uncertainty about economic prospects was compounded by severe drought, which considerably reduced the projected size of the sugar crop. In light of these developments, the policy stance was shifted from one of supporting continued growth to one of protecting foreign exchange reserves.

Fiscal measures were aimed at containing the increase in the budget deficit in 1987, stemming from weak revenue, especially lower customs duty and company tax collection, and higher military expenditure. Discretionary spending was cut deeply, including wage and salary reductions of 15 percent in the civil service and 25 percent in the military. Undisbursed grants and transfers to public enterprises were curtailed and lower priority investment projects were deferred. Despite these measures, the budget deficit rose to 6 percent of GDP, requiring a sharp increase in bank financing, partly because of the cessation of some external concessionary assistance.

To contain the expansion of private credit, the monetary authorities relied mainly on market mechanisms. The interest rate ceilings on bank lending were abolished; the lending rate to commercial banks was raised; and the penalties for using central bank credit were stiffened. With the change in the external situation, banks' excess reserves plunged and interest rates increased. However, private sector credit demand remained strong as import payments were brought forward, export credit facilities from foreign banks were withdrawn, and branches of foreign companies attempted to repatriate dividends and retained earnings and repay loans. Direct credit controls were introduced as a precautionary measure, but for the most part were nonbinding.

While the main defense against foreign exchange outflows was the tightening of credit policies, additional measures were needed. The Fiji dollar was devalued by 18 percent in June 1987 and by a further 15 percent in October, which proved effective in discouraging outflows through both current and capital transactions. The inflationary consequences appeared manageable; although the price level jumped with higher import prices, weak domestic demand and the real wage cuts limited the secondary impact. Foreign exchange controls were also tightened on emigration transfers, dividend remittances, overseas travel allowances, gifts, overseas investments by residents, and prepayment of foreign borrowings. These restrictions, which represented a departure from Fiji's past practice of maintaining a high degree of freedom for capital flows, were seen as a short-term expedient.

Table 1. Fiji: Gross Domestic Product by Sectoral Origin, 1975–87

(In millions of Fiji dollars at 1977 prices)

	1975	1976	1977	1978	1979	1980	1981	1982	1983	1984	1985	1986	1987
Agriculture, forestry, and fishing	126	131	141	128	163	153	172	176	144	181	156	186	174
Sugar	49	53	62	56	81	68	81	83	48	83	59	86	67
Other	77	78	79	72	82	85	91	93	96	98	98	100	107
Mining and quarrying	1	1	1	1	1	1	1	1	1	1	1	1	1
Manufacturing	59	64	69	77	88	80	89	86	77	91	79	95	85
Sugar	20	22	24	25	31	26	31	32	18	32	22	33	27
Other	39	42	45	52	57	54	58	54	59	59	57	62	58
Electricity and water	5	5	6	6	6	7	7	7	7	8	8	9	9
Building and construction	49	47	49	47	51	60	54	53	51	40	41	47	35
Distribution (including tourism)	108	108	105	109	125	117	125	113	122	122	124	134	117
Transport and communication	53	54	55	49	67	67	70	77	78	87	90	90	88
Finance and insurance	74	75	77	79	83	84	86	91	94	96	98	100	96
Community and other services	118	118	118	135	126	129	127	128	131	138	139	131	126
Less: bank service charges	-18	-18	-16	-18	-19	-19	-20	-20	-21	-23	-23	-24	-22
GDP at factor cost	575	585	605	613	691	679	711	712	684	741	707	769	709
Memorandum item:													
Change in real GDP (in percent)	—	1.8	3.5	1.3	12.7	-1.7	4.7	0.1	-3.9	8.3	-4.7	8.8	-7.8

Sources: Data provided by the Fiji authorities; and Fund staff estimates.

Table 2. Fiji: Gross Domestic Product by Expenditure, 1975–87

(In millions of Fiji dollars at current prices)

	1975	1976	1977	1978	1979	1980	1981	1982	1983	1984	1985	1986	1987
Consumption	450	519	578	573	664	744	861	888	980	1,039	1,089	1,133	1,183
Private sector	382	434	481	458	520	587	688	684	748	794	842	873	923
Government	68	85	97	115	144	157	173	204	232	245	247	260	260
Investment	116	134	150	160	234	294	376	296	224	250	227	291	177
Private sector	59	62	67	86	111	135	146	113	112	124	147	162	137
Public sector[1]	45	57	67	64	86	112	142	149	127	92	76	112	62
Change in stocks[2]	12	15	16	10	37	47	88	34	–15	34	4	17	–22
External balance[3]	–3	–30	–21	–31	–46	–49	–150	–71	–62	–14	–5	32	55
Exports	242	235	289	300	386	470	458	481	498	546	584	609	640
Imports	245	265	310	331	432	519	608	552	560	560	589	577	585
GDP at market prices	563	623	707	702	852	989	1,087	1,113	1,142	1,275	1,311	1,456	1,415
						(In percent of GDP)							
Memorandum items:													
Investment	20.6	21.5	21.2	22.8	27.5	29.7	34.6	26.6	19.6	19.6	17.3	20.0	12.5
Domestic savings	20.1	16.7	18.2	18.4	22.1	24.8	20.8	20.2	14.2	18.5	16.9	22.2	16.4
Foreign savings[4]	0.5	4.8	3.0	4.4	5.4	5.0	13.8	6.4	5.4	1.1	0.4	–2.2	–3.9

Sources: Data provided by the Fiji authorities; and Fund staff estimates.

[1] Includes public enterprises.
[2] Includes statistical discrepancy.
[3] Goods and nonfactor services.
[4] Equivalent to the external balance on goods and nonfactor services.

Table 3. Fiji: Output of Main Commodities, 1975–87

(In thousands of metric tons)

	1975	1976	1977	1978	1979	1980	1981	1982	1983	1984	1985	1986	1987
Sugarcane	2,126	2,284	2,700	2,800	4,100	3,400	3,931	4,075	2,203	4,269	3,043	4,109	2,960
Sugar	273	296	362	347	473	396	470	486	276	480	341	502	400
Copra	22.0	27.0	30.9	26.1	21.8	22.8	20.5	21.6	24.0	25.0	21.0	25.0	13.0
Rice	18.0	16.0	18.0	16.1	18.7	17.8	17.0	20.3	16.2	21.5	28.0	25.0	23.5
Cocoa	...	...	...	...	0.2	0.1	0.2	0.1	0.2	0.2	0.3	0.3	0.4
Ginger	...	...	...	...	1.8	1.5	2.7	4.5	3.8	3.3	4.9	5.0	5.1
Beef	2.0	2.1	2.3	2.7	3.6	3.5	3.4	3.4	3.5	3.4	3.4	3.6	3.8
Fish[1]	...	...	4.8	9.7	12.1	14.6	14.3	13.2	13.9	13.1	12.2	10.9	13.9
Gold (in thousands of fine ounces)	69	66	49	28	30	25	31	46	39	48	60	91	85

Source: Data provided by the Fiji authorities.
[1] Does not include subsistence catch.

Table 4. Fiji: Consumer Price Index, 1975–87
(Annual average percentage change)

	Weights	1975	1976	1977	1978	1979	1980	1981	1982	1983	1984	1985	1986	1987
Food	33.3	12.4	3.2	7.2	5.6	6.7	15.3	12.8	9.3	5.9	4.6	8.3	-1.8	6.1
Beverages and tobacco	6.4	...	...	...	...	...	15.2	10.5	12.9	8.9	10.8	8.2	16.0	7.0
Housing	18.6	11.9	17.8	8.2	7.1	7.7	4.4	11.7	5.7	13.0	4.4	1.2	4.4	1.7
Heating and lighting	4.9	...	...	7.1	8.1	9.2	41.2	18.8	4.8	0.7	1.0	0.7	-9.2	3.7
Durable household goods	7.6	...	...	...	...	...	14.0	4.6	3.1	5.4	2.5	0.1	3.0	9.8
Clothing and footwear	6.3	...	...	6.3	7.8	5.3	16.3	10.5	3.9	2.8	2.8	-0.4	1.4	3.1
Transport	11.3	...	...	7.5	4.5	14.0	20.6	10.0	6.3	6.8	7.4	4.6	2.7	6.6
Services	6.7	...	...	...	...	...	6.1	12.1	5.0	4.5	7.3	1.8	1.4	6.4
Miscellaneous	4.3	...	...	2.6	3.5	10.7	15.7	7.3	7.3	6.2	7.2	2.7	6.6	12.5
Overall index	100.0	13.1	11.2	7.3	6.1	8.3	14.5	11.2	7.0	6.8	5.3	4.4	1.8	5.7
							(End-of-period percentage change)							
Memorandum item:														
Overall index	100.0	13.2	7.8	7.8	5.0	10.5	15.0	9.7	6.3	6.0	4.6	2.9	3.0	9.5

Source: Data provided by the Fiji authorities.

Table 5. Fiji: Central Government Budget, 1975–87

(In millions of Fiji dollars)

	1975	1976	1977	1978	1979	1980	1981	1982	1983	1984	1985	1986	1987
Revenue and grants	112	121	134	157	194	222	263	265	298	335	346	346	342
Tax revenue	88	104	114	133	157	180	214	210	237	273	279	276	267
Nontax revenue	22	16	18	20	31	34	41	45	51	52	57	60	64
External grants	2	1	2	4	6	8	8	10	10	10	10	10	11
Expenditure[1]	117	147	169	188	218	250	307	339	342	377	383	415	416
Current expenditure	87	108	119	140	165	185	212	248	286	324	326	331	355
Capital expenditure	30	39	50	48	53	65	95	91	56	53	57	84	61
Overall balance	–5	–26	–35	–31	–24	–28	–44	–74	–44	–42	–36	–69	–74
Financing (net)	5	26	35	31	24	28	44	74	44	42	36	69	74
External	8	10	19	–2	8	24	19	19	5	5	—	—	–15
Domestic	–3	16	16	33	16	4	25	55	39	37	36	69	89
Banking system	–6	7	2	21	4	–8	–1	19	13	–6	5	29	55
Other	9	9	14	12	12	12	26	36	26	43	31	40	34
						(In percent of GDP)							
Memorandum items:													
Revenue and grants	19.9	19.4	19.0	22.4	22.8	22.4	24.2	23.8	26.1	26.3	26.4	23.8	24.2
Tax revenue	15.6	16.7	16.1	18.9	18.4	18.2	19.7	18.9	20.8	21.3	21.3	19.0	18.8
Expenditure[1]	20.8	23.6	23.9	26.8	25.6	25.3	28.2	30.5	29.9	29.6	29.1	28.5	29.4
Current expenditure	15.5	17.3	16.8	20.0	19.4	18.7	19.5	22.3	25.0	25.4	24.9	22.7	25.1
Capital expenditure	5.3	6.3	7.1	6.8	6.2	6.6	8.7	8.2	4.9	4.2	4.2	5.8	4.3
Overall balance	–0.9	–4.2	–5.0	–4.4	–2.8	–2.8	–4.0	–6.6	–3.9	–3.3	–2.7	–4.7	–5.2

Sources: Data provided by the Fiji authorities; and Fund staff estimates.
[1] Includes net lending.

Table 6. Fiji: Central Government Revenue, 1975–87

(In millions of Fiji dollars)

	1975	1976	1977	1978	1979	1980	1981	1982	1983	1984	1985	1986	1987
Tax revenue	88	104	114	133	157	180	214	210	237	273	279	376	267
Income and profits	45	55	63	77	84	104	113	120	129	147	141	136	129
Goods and services	11	13	13	14	17	20	23	27	31	36	41	44	45
International transactions	32	36	38	43	53	53	73	59	73	85	92	91	89
Other taxes	—	—	—	-1	3	3	5	4	4	5	5	5	4
Nontax revenue	22	16	18	20	31	34	41	45	51	52	57	60	64
UN peacekeeping	...	...	...	...	...	...	6	8	13	12	13	13	13
Reserve Bank profits	...	...	...	...	...	...	9	11	8	6	6	6	6
Other	...	...	...	...	...	...	26	26	30	3	38	41	45
Total	110	120	132	153	188	214	255	255	288	325	336	336	331
						(In percent of total revenue)							
Memorandum items:													
Tax revenue	80.0	86.7	86.4	86.9	83.5	84.1	83.9	82.4	82.3	84.0	83.0	82.1	80.7
Income and profits	40.9	45.8	47.7	50.3	44.7	48.6	44.3	47.1	44.8	45.2	42.0	40.5	39.0
Goods and services	10.0	10.8	9.8	9.2	9.0	9.3	9.0	10.6	10.8	11.1	12.2	13.1	13.6
International transactions	29.1	30.0	28.8	28.1	28.2	24.8	28.6	23.1	25.3	26.2	27.4	27.1	26.9
Nontax revenue	20.0	13.3	13.6	13.1	16.5	15.9	16.1	17.6	17.7	16.0	17.0	17.9	19.3

Source: Data provided by the Fiji authorities.

Table 7. Fiji: Central Government Expenditure by Economic Classification, 1975–87

(In millions of Fiji dollars)

	1975	1976	1977	1978	1979	1980	1981	1982	1983	1984	1985	1986	1987
Current expenditure	87	108	119	140	165	185	212	248	286	324	326	331	355
Wages and salaries	38	48	59	67	77	87	116	134	159	178	169	178	188
National Provident Fund	1	2	2	3	4	5	6	7	7	8	8	8	8
Goods and services	27	33	29	35	44	52	36	39	41	46	58	49	55
Interest payments	6	7	9	11	13	14	19	26	32	37	41	45	53
Subsidies and transfers	15	18	20	24	27	27	35	42	47	55	50	51	51
Capital expenditure and net lending	30	39	50	48	53	65	95	91	56	53	57	84	61
Total	117	147	169	188	218	250	307	339	342	377	383	415	416
(In percent of total expenditure and net lending)													
Memorandum items:													
Current expenditure	74.4	73.5	70.4	74.5	75.7	74.0	69.1	73.2	83.7	85.9	85.1	79.8	85.3
Wages and salaries	32.5	32.7	34.9	35.6	35.3	34.8	37.8	39.5	46.5	47.2	44.1	42.9	45.2
Interest payments	5.1	4.8	5.3	5.9	6.0	5.6	6.2	7.7	9.4	9.8	10.7	10.8	12.7
Other	36.8	36.1	30.2	33.0	34.4	33.6	25.1	26.0	27.8	28.9	30.3	26.0	27.4
Capital expenditure and net lending	25.6	26.5	29.6	25.5	24.3	26.0	30.9	26.8	16.4	14.1	14.9	20.2	14.7

Sources: Data provided by the Fiji authorities; and Fund staff estimates.

Table 8. Fiji: Monetary Survey, 1975–87

(In millions of Fiji dollars; end of period)

	1975	1976	1977	1978	1979	1980	1981	1982	1983	1984	1985	1986	1987
Net foreign assets	122	101	112	105	109	134	120	106	108	118	131	190	195
Monetary authority	125	108	119	103	109	131	117	110	107	115	130	187	183
Commercial banks	–8	–10	–9	1	–1	1	3	–4	—	3	—	2	11
Government	5	3	2	1	1	2	—	—	1	—	1	1	1
Domestic credit	83	131	141	172	224	232	279	334	381	412	438	471	541
Government (net)	–5	15	7	24	30	22	20	39	33	29	28	47	82
Official entities	10	14	15	21	26	21	26	49	73	58	60	56	66
Private sector	78	102	119	127	168	189	233	246	275	325	350	368	393
Broad money	195	201	236	255	306	343	365	395	444	490	502	587	608
Money supply	86	89	87	103	117	105	126	130	142	142	146	179	173
Currency	27	31	34	39	45	44	49	53	59	61	62	63	65
Demand deposits	59	58	53	64	72	61	77	77	83	81	84	116	108
Quasi–money	109	112	149	152	189	238	239	265	302	348	356	408	435
Other items (net)	10	31	17	21	27	23	35	45	45	40	67	75	128
						(Annual percentage change)							
Memorandum items:													
Domestic credit	—	57.8	7.6	22.0	30.2	3.6	20.3	19.7	14.1	8.1	6.3	7.5	14.9
Public sector	–35.4	480.0	–24.1	104.5	24.4	–23.2	7.0	91.3	20.5	–17.9	1.1	17.0	43.7
Private sector	3.6	30.8	16.7	6.7	32.3	12.5	23.3	5.6	11.8	18.2	7.7	5.1	6.8
Broad money	26.7	3.1	17.4	8.1	20.0	12.1	6.4	8.2	12.4	10.4	2.4	16.9	3.6

Source: Data provided by the Fiji authorities.

Table 9. Fiji: Interest Rate Structure, 1975–87

(In percent per annum; end of period)

	1975	1976	1977	1978	1979	1980	1981	1982	1983	1984	1985	1986	1987
Reserve Bank													
Minimum lending rate	6.0	5.5	5.5	6.5	6.5	7.5	9.5	9.5	10.5	11.0	11.0	8.0	11.0
Commercial bank deposit rates													
Savings deposits	4.0	4.0	4.0	4.5	4.5	4.5	6.0	6.0	6.0	6.0	6.0	6.0	6.0
Regulated time deposits													
1–3 months	—	4.45	4.2	4.5	4.5	4.5	6.0	6.0	6.0	6.0	6.0	6.0	6.0
3–6 months	5.0	4.5	4.5	5.0	5.0	5.5	6.5	6.5	6.5	6.5	6.5	6.5	6.5
6–12 months	6.0	5.5	5.5	5.7	5.7	6.2	7.2	7.2	7.2	7.2	7.2	7.2	7.2
1–2 years	6.7	6.7	6.7	6.5	6.5	7.0	8.0	8.0	8.0	8.0	8.0	8.0	8.0
2–3 years	6.5	7.0	7.0	7.2	7.2	8.0	9.0	9.0	9.0	9.0	9.0	9.0	9.0
3 years or longer	—	—	—	—	—	8.5	10.0	10.0	10.0	10.0	10.0	10.0	10.0
Unregulated time deposits													
1–3 months	—	—	—	—	—	—	—	—	—	—	11.3	3.4	11.1
3–6 months	—	—	—	—	—	—	—	—	—	—	11.0	4.7	18.4
6–12 months	—	—	—	—	—	—	—	—	—	—	12.1	5.4	18.4
1–2 years	—	—	—	—	—	—	—	—	—	—	12.5	7.1	16.2
Commercial bank lending rates													
Maximum	10.0	10.0	10.0	10.5	10.5	12.0	13.5	13.5	13.5	13.5	13.5	13.5	24.5
Average (estimates)	8.7	8.7	9.0	9.2	9.5	9.7	11.9	12.8	12.7	12.9	13.0	12.0	13.7
Public sector securities													
Treasury bills (90-day)	4.5	4.3	4.3	5.3	5.3	5.6	6.4	6.1	6.6	7.2	7.7	6.3	11.2
3–year bonds	6.3	6.2	6.2	7.0	7.0	7.6	9.0	9.0	9.0	9.7	—	8.1	9.0
5–year bonds	6.3	6.6	6.5	7.4	7.4	8.5	9.4	9.4	9.4	11.4	10.4	9.7	9.7
10–year bonds	6.9	6.9	6.7	7.9	7.9	9.1	10.4	9.4	9.4	11.5	11.0	10.4	9.6

Source: Data provided by the Fiji authorities.

Table 10. Fiji: Balance of Payments, 1975–87

(In millions of SDRs)

	1975	1976	1977	1978	1979	1980	1981	1982	1983	1984	1985	1986	1987
Trade balance	-48.1	-75.4	-79.1	-90.6	-127.7	-107.4	-223.5	-168.9	-190.8	-156.0	-172.4	-102.9	-9.3
Exports, f.o.b.	142.2	119.9	140.9	141.2	187.8	262.0	239.4	230.8	204.1	225.6	203.8	211.7	234.2
Domestic exports	115.9	88.8	119.8	120.0	156.5	221.5	192.4	177.8	165.1	179.0	164.6	182.2	211.2
Re-exports	26.3	31.1	21.1	21.2	31.3	40.5	47.0	53.0	39.0	46.6	39.2	29.5	23.0
Imports, f.o.b.	190.3	195.3	220.0	231.8	315.5	369.4	462.9	399.7	394.9	381.6	376.2	314.7	243.5
Retained imports[1]	164.0	164.2	198.9	210.6	284.2	328.9	415.9	346.7	355.9	335.0	337.0	285.2	220.5
Re-exports	26.3	31.1	21.1	21.2	31.3	40.5	47.0	53.0	39.0	46.6	39.2	29.5	23.0
Services, net	43.9	32.4	59.0	63.6	62.2	62.3	65.3	70.7	108.7	117.7	137.8	100.8	21.4
Receipts	...	105.1	59.1	147.8	169.3	203.9	242.0	262.5	276.2	290.6	311.0	264.3	186.9
Payments	...	72.7	78.9	84.2	107.1	141.6	176.7	191.8	167.5	172.9	173.0	163.1	165.5
Private transfers, net	-4.1	-1.3	-3.4	-3.2	-6.6	-3.5	-7.5	-2.7	-1.7	-3.9	-10.3	-5.0	-14.8
Official transfers	3.7	2.9	2.5	1.6	15.0	23.4	19.3	19.5	25.0	18.1	32.5	12.6	8.0
Current account	-4.6	-41.3	-20.0	-28.6	-57.1	-25.2	-146.4	-81.4	-57.8	-24.1	-12.4	6.2	5.3
Nonmonetary capital, net	20.7	11.1	24.6	7.1	35.1	68.1	116.4	69.0	75.4	31.0	7.0	18.6	-36.7
Official	8.1	10.7	17.2	-2.3	17.1	54.4	62.9	36.4	38.2	11.0	—	-8.0	-19.6
Private	12.6	0.4	7.4	9.4	18.0	13.7	53.5	32.6	37.2	20.0	7.4	26.6	-17.1
Errors and omissions	19.5	7.0	10.3	15.1	20.9	-13.5	12.5	-3.6	-19.7	—	7.0	11.0	-23.1
Allocation of SDRs	—	—	—	—	1.9	1.9	1.9	—	—	—	—	—	—
Overall balance	35.6	-23.3	13.9	-6.4	0.8	31.3	-15.6	-16.0	-3.1	6.5	2.0	35.2	-54.7
Memorandum items:													
Current account													
(in percent of GDP)	-0.8	-6.8	-3.0	-4.3	-7.2	-2.7	-13.6	-7.5	-5.5	-2.1	-1.1	0.6	0.6
Fiji dollars per SDR (period average)	1.00	1.04	1.07	1.06	1.08	1.06	1.01	1.03	1.09	1.11	1.17	1.33	1.58

Sources: Data provided by the Fiji authorities; and Fund staff estimates.

[1] Excludes fuel sold to foreign aircraft and ships.

Table 11. Fiji: Exports by Commodity, 1975–87

(Value in millions of SDRs, volume in thousands of metric tons, unit value in SDRs per metric ton)

	1975	1976	1977	1978	1979	1980	1981	1982	1983	1984	1985	1986	1987
Sugar													
Value	94.7	65.1	87.4	78.6	108.3	163.7	130.8	121.6	103.0	99.3	95.5	100.7	117.8
Volume	254	246	324.1	287.0	428.0	442.0	407.5	410.0	342.6	380.0	410.4	324.1	429.6
Unit value	372.8	264.6	269.7	273.9	253.0	370.4	321.0	296.6	300.6	261.3	232.8	310.6	274.1
Molasses													
Value	1.2	0.9	1.8	4.3	6.9	11.3	9.5	5.0	2.9	6.1	5.6	5.9	6.7
Volume	69.0	70.9	90.4	121.3	123.0	161.0	141.0	156.8	92.9	155.1	140.0	125.6	126.6
Unit value	17.4	12.7	19.9	35.4	56.1	70.2	67.4	31.9	31.2	39.3	39.7	47.4	52.9
Coconut oil													
Value	5.1	4.4	8.3	8.4	10.8	6.1	6.4	6.0	9.8	16.7	6.5	3.2	1.9
Volume	15.8	14.4	17.5	18.0	15.0	13.0	14.0	14.9	14.8	15.5	10.6	15.4	6.6
Unit value	322.8	305.6	474.3	466.7	720.0	469.2	457.1	402.7	662.2	1,077.4	612.7	205.4	287.3
Gold[1]													
Value	8.6	6.6	6.1	4.7	6.0	11.7	11.8	15.2	15.6	18.5	18.6	29.1	32.0
Volume	68.8	66.0	48.8	25.9	29.0	25.0	28.1	45.8	39.8	51.3	93.1	84.0	85.7
Unit value	125.0	100.0	125.0	181.5	206.9	468.0	419.9	331.9	392.0	360.6	200.1	346.0	573.2
Fish products[2]													
Value	—	—	7.1	13.2	11.9	14.3	19.7	9.8	14.3	14.0	11.7	13.7	15.9
Forest products[3]													
Value	1.0	1.6	0.7	1.4	2.5	4.8	3.7	4.0	4.0	7.1	6.2	5.9	10.4
Other (value)	5.3	10.2	8.4	9.4	10.1	9.6	10.5	16.2	15.5	17.3	20.5	23.7	26.7
Domestic exports	115.9	88.8	119.8	120.0	156.5	221.5	192.4	177.8	165.1	179.0	164.6	182.2	211.2

Source: Data provided by the Fiji authorities.

[1] In thousands of fine ounces and SDRs per ounce.

[2] Domestic exports plus imported fish processed at the cannery.

[3] Comprises logs, sawn timber, veneer, and plywood.

Table 12. Fiji: Imports by Commodity Group, 1975–87

(In millions of SDRs)

	1975	1976	1977	1978	1979	1980	1981	1982	1983	1984	1985	1986	1987
Food, beverages, and tobacco	39.9	43.5	54.5	60.1	61.6	64.6	81.2	72.7	75.2	70.7	72.1	61.1	57.5
Raw materials	1.8	1.7	2.2	2.4	3.8	3.1	4.3	3.6	4.8	3.2	2.8	2.2	2.0
Mineral fuels	37.1	35.7	50.6	44.6	67.1	99.4	137.6	133.1	105.7	96.6	98.5	61.8	49.4
Oils and fats	3.4	3.2	3.9	4.4	4.8	4.8	5.8	5.1	6.3	8.5	9.0	4.4	4.9
Chemicals	16.0	13.7	18.9	21.0	25.5	28.7	37.1	34.0	35.9	40.0	33.2	31.1	28.9
Manufactured goods	38.1	39.9	47.7	54.3	69.6	80.4	88.4	76.7	84.2	82.1	86.1	80.0	56.8
Machinery and transport equipment	43.0	46.2	48.1	55.1	81.8	97.6	117.2	79.7	85.6	78.1	78.3	87.5	56.2
Other	33.9	38.5	36.6	41.1	49.7	52.6	65.1	57.4	56.4	60.3	54.0	45.9	41.4
Total imports	213.2	222.4	262.5	283.0	363.9	431.2	536.7	462.3	454.1	439.5	434.0	374.0	297.1
Less: re-exports	26.3	31.1	37.2	41.9	42.5	71.4	74.9	84.1	61.9	74.3	69.0	53.0	37.3
Retained imports	186.9	191.3	225.3	241.1	321.4	359.8	461.8	378.3	392.2	365.2	365.0	321.0	259.8

Source: Data provided by the Fiji authorities.

Table 13. Fiji: External Debt and Debt Service, 1975–87[1]

(In millions of SDRs)

	1975	1976	1977	1978	1979	1980	1981	1982	1983	1984	1985	1986	1987
External debt (end of period)	101.6	104.6	124.4	116.7	140.1	185.3	252.1	345.5	384.7	385.8	372.2	334.4	272.1
Bilateral	15.3	28.0	37.0	28.0	38.1	48.7	78.6	90.7	91.3	82.7	71.0	62.0	54.0
Multilateral	24.0	27.1	29.6	34.2	39.4	51.8	72.8	95.6	127.6	131.8	130.0	136.0	115.5
Commercial	62.3	49.5	51.4	48.0	56.1	84.8	100.7	145.7	152.3	157.8	158.0	130.0	99.5
Use of IMF credit	—	—	6.5	6.5	6.5	—	—	13.5	13.5	13.5	13.2	6.4	3.1
Debt service	20.2	23.6	18.5	18.1	16.0	32.7	35.5	55.7	50.5	57.0	73.0	73.0	77.5
Amortization	12.7	15.1	10.7	10.8	9.4	18.8	15.2	25.9	22.8	29.0	45.0	45.0	53.1
Interest	7.5	8.5	7.8	7.3	6.6	13.9	20.3	29.8	27.7	28.0	28.0	28.0	24.1
External debt (in percent of GDP)	18.0	17.4	18.8	17.6	17.8	19.9	23.3	31.9	36.9	33.9	34.9	32.2	39.3
Debt service (in percent of exports of goods and services)	10.3	14.6	8.5	6.8	4.9	7.7	8.2	12.7	11.5	11.1	14.3	15.3	18.4

Source: Data provided by the Fiji authorities.
[1]Includes private sector debt; disbursed debt only.

Table 14. Fiji: International Reserves, 1975–87

(In millions of SDRs)

	1975	1976	1977	1978	1979	1980	1981	1982	1983	1984	1985	1986	1987
Official assets	126.9	100.3	121.1	103.4	103.8	131.5	118.0	118.0	111.9	116.0	119.0	139.6	83.2
Reserve Bank	126.9	98.6	118.8	102.6	102.9	129.4	117.7	117.7	111.3	116.0	118.8	139.5	83.2
Government	—	1.7	2.3	0.8	0.9	2.1	0.3	0.3	0.6	—	0.2	0.1	—
Official liabilities[1]	—	—	6.5	6.5	6.5	—	—	12.9	13.5	13.1	12.9	5.9	4.6
Net official reserves	126.9	100.3	114.6	96.9	97.3	131.5	118.0	105.1	98.4	102.9	106.1	133.6	78.7
Commercial banks	−10.5	−14.9	−9.1	1.2	−0.6	1.4	2.9	−3.3	0.2	2.4	0.6	1.5	—
Assets	5.4	4.3	3.9	3.9	2.8	6.5	8.6	4.5	7.5	8.6	40.5	91.5	14.7
Liabilities	15.9	19.2	13.0	2.7	3.4	5.1	5.7	7.8	7.3	6.2	39.9	90.0	14.7
Net total reserves	116.4	85.4	105.5	98.1	96.7	132.9	120.9	101.8	98.6	105.3	106.7	135.0	78.7
Memorandum items:													
Official assets (in months of imports)[2]	9.3	7.3	7.3	5.9	4.4	4.8	3.4	4.1	3.8	4.2	4.2	5.9	4.5
Fiji dollars per SDR (end of period)	1.01	1.09	1.06	1.07	1.11	1.01	1.02	1.05	1.10	1.12	1.23	1.40	2.04

Source: Data provided by the Fiji authorities.
[1] Drawings under the International Monetary Fund's compensatory financing facility.
[2] Retained imports only.

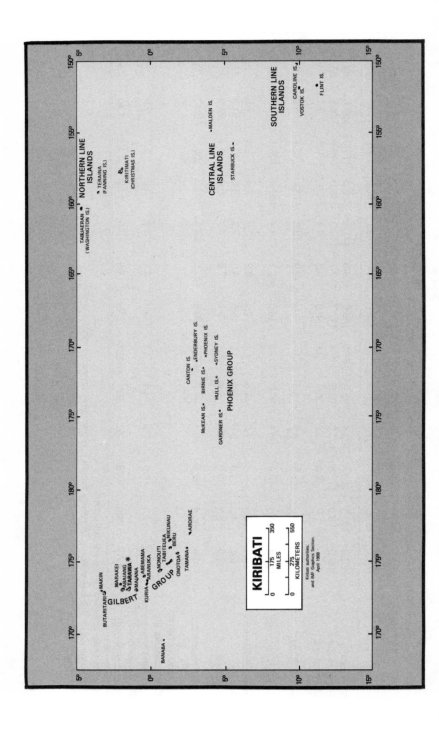

KIRIBATI

NORTHERN LINE
ISLANDS

TABUAERAN •
(WASHINGTON IS.)

TERAINA •
(FANNING IS.)

KIRITIMATI •
(CHRISTMAS IS.)

CENTRAL LINE
ISLANDS

MALDEN IS. •

STARBUCK IS. •

SOUTHERN LINE
ISLANDS

CAROLINE IS. •

VOSTOK IS. •

FLINT IS. •

CANTON IS. •

ENDERBURY IS. •

McKEAN IS. • BIRNIE IS. •

PHOENIX IS. •

HULL IS. • • SYDNEY IS.

GARDNER IS. •

PHOENIX GROUP

BUTARITARI • • MAKIN

MARAKEI •
• ABAIANG
S TARAWA ✶
• MAIANA

KURIA • • ABEMAMA
ABANUKA

• NONOUTI
TABITEUEA • • NIKUNAU

ONOTOA •   • BERU

TAMANA •

GILBERT

GROUP

ARORAE •

BANABA • •

0   175   350
|————|————|
MILES

0   275   550
|————|————|
KILOMETERS

Kiribati authorities;
and IMF Graphics Section
April 1988

3
Kiribati

The Republic of Kiribati consists of 33 islands, with a land area of 726 square kilometers, widely scattered over the Central Pacific Ocean on both sides of the equator and the international dateline. The population of 66,000 is 98 percent Micronesian. The Gilbert group, where nearly all of the population resides, is a chain of 16 islands extending for 700 kilometers in a northwesterly to southeasterly direction. The Phoenix group is 1,600 kilometers to the east and is presently uninhabited. The Line group is 3,000 kilometers to the east and only the three northern islands are inhabited. Although the land mass is very small, the 200-mile economic zone around the islands covers an area of more than 3 million square kilometers, a much larger share of the ocean than enjoyed by any other country in the region.

Except for Banaba, which is of limestone origin, all the islands are coral atolls, with shallow topsoil and a low water absorption capacity that prevents the cultivation of most crops. Although immune from cyclones, the islands see considerable variations in rainfall and suffer periodically from drought. The population density is high in relation to the scant resources; life expectancy is only 53 years; and health and education facilities are poor. There is a strong, persistent movement in search of employment from the outer islands to the national capital, Tarawa, which now contains one third of the population. In addition, 1,000 citizens are employed abroad as seamen on foreign ships and as phosphate workers on the neighboring island of Nauru, but there is little permanent emigration.

Kiribati gained independence from the United Kingdom in 1979. The President, who is Head of State and of Government, is selected from the popularly elected members of the 39-seat House of Assembly; the normal parliamentary term is four years. The British colonial presence dated back to 1892 when the Gilbert Islands were proclaimed a protectorate. These islands were joined in 1916 with the Ellice Islands to form the Gilbert and Ellice Islands Colony, which was later expanded to include other British possessions in the Central Pacific. The Ellice Islands separated and became the independent state of

Tuvalu in 1975. From 1900, the main economic activity in Kiribati was phosphate mining on Banaba, which was undertaken by the British Phosphate Commission on behalf of the governments of Australia, New Zealand, and the United Kingdom.

Independence coincided with the exhaustion of the phosphate deposits. As a result, exports fell by 80 percent and government revenue and real GDP declined by about one half. However, in anticipation of the depletion of the phosphate resources, the Government began in 1956 to accumulate a reserve fund of foreign securities, primarily from the proceeds of royalties on exports. While it was originally envisaged to use these funds to help maintain the quality of government services in the post-phosphate era, in view of Kiribati's early stage of development and the fragility of its external situation, the Government decided after independence to continue adding to the capital value of the fund. These external assets are at present equivalent to about six years of imports of goods and services.

Economic Structure

Production and Prices

Kiribati has the smallest GDP among Fund members and its standard of living, with an annual per capita GDP of SDR 275, is well below that of most countries in the Pacific region. Apart from the large quantities of tuna fish that are found around the islands, resource constraints severely limit the potential supply of exportables. The agricultural base is narrow; copra, which is produced mainly on small family plots, is the only important cash crop. Marketed output is purchased and exported solely by the Kiribati Copra Cooperative Society, which also operates a price stabilization scheme to mitigate the impact of fluctuations in world prices on growers' income. Commercial fishing is undertaken by the four-vessel fleet of the national fishing corporation. Manufacturing is nonexistent; the scale of copra and fish production is insufficient to support processing activities. There is no infrastructure for tourism; transport and communications between islands and with foreign countries are difficult and time consuming.

Prices are largely determined by the cost of imports, especially from Australia. Wages are not adjusted automatically for price changes. Virtually all paid employment is in the public sector, where the number of employees and the wage and salary bill is held down by restraints on government budgetary expenditure. Although real wages have declined substantially since independence, unemployment has been high and rising. At the same time, an acute shortage of skilled manpower exists, which can be met only to a limited extent by expatriate staff in view of the difficult living conditions, especially the lack of housing. Outside the national capital, the population continues to be wholly engaged in subsistence activities. Urban incomes, despite declining in recent years, appear to have remained substantially higher than rural incomes. However, the differential in earnings is reduced markedly when full account is taken of the large transfers to rural households both from abroad and from family members residing in the national capital.

Balance of Payments

The external trade account (including grants) moved from surplus to substantial deficit after the cessation of phosphate production. Exports of goods represent less than 10 percent of GDP and consist almost entirely of copra and fish. Copra is sent for processing either within the Pacific region or to Western Europe, depending on the availability of shipping. Frozen tuna is sent for canning to American Samoa. A small amount of fresh fish from Christmas Island is exported to Hawaii. Imports are equivalent to about 50 percent of GDP, reflecting the narrow resource base and the limited opportunities for substitution by domestic production. Food and beverages comprise about one third and mineral fuels about one sixth of the total. Consumer goods and petroleum products are supplied primarily from Fiji and Australia. Machinery and transport equipment, almost entirely financed with external development assistance, represent a further one third of the total.

Services and transfers show a net surplus equivalent to about two thirds of GDP. Service receipts include interest earnings and fees under fishing agreements with foreign countries to permit their vessels to operate in Kiribati waters. Service payments include freight and insurance, which account for about one fourth of the value of imports. Private remittances are received from residents employed abroad as seamen and as phosphate miners. Official transfers are equivalent to more than one half of GDP. The main donors are Australia, the European Community, Japan, New Zealand, and the United Kingdom, and nearly all aid is provided in the form of grants. Although the long-term

objective is to reduce dependence on foreign assistance, Kiribati rec-
ognizes that such help will be needed for a considerable period.

The external current account (including grants) normally registers
a surplus equivalent to about 20–25 percent of GDP. While the capital
account usually records a deficit, the overall balance of payments is also
in surplus. Both official and private capital flows are minor. Official
outflows occur mainly in the form of the reinvestment abroad of interest
earnings and the purchase of other assets by the public sector. External
commercial borrowing is generally avoided and debt service, mainly
related to a loan for an aircraft purchase, is only 3 percent of exports of
goods and services.

Public Sector

The public sector consists of the central government, which is
organized in nine ministries; local government, which is administered
through 19 Island Councils; and 12 nonfinancial public enterprises. The
central government budget, which consists of the current revenue and
expenditure estimates and development fund estimates, is prepared on
a calendar-year basis and presented to parliament by the Minister of
Finance in November. In recent years, parliament has not exercised its
power to change the budget, which is normally approved in early
December. Supplementary financing requests may also be approved
during the budget year. Although Kiribati emphasizes the devolution of
powers, the local councils account for no more than 3 percent of total
public expenditure. There are seven major public enterprises engaged
in air services, shipping, fishing, shipbuilding, telecommunications,
public utilities, and housing. While their investment programs are
financed by external aid channeled through the central government
budget, the corporations are expected to achieve operating surpluses.

Central government receipts and expenditure are each equivalent
to more than 80 percent of GDP. Tax receipts are relatively small, with
personal and corporate income taxes equivalent to 5 percent of GDP,
most of which is paid by the commercial bank. Indirect taxes are
equivalent to 10 percent of GDP, virtually all in the form of import
duties, which have risen substantially since the full-scale review of the
tariff structure in 1984. Nontax revenue is equivalent to one third of
GDP, of which the largest sources are interest on foreign assets and
receipts from fishing agreements. Interest earnings are used to finance
current expenditure only to the extent necessary to prevent the emer-

gence of overall budgetary deficits; the remaining amounts, if any, are reinvested. Fishing receipts are subject to considerable uncertainty and fluctuation, since most agreements are negotiated annually and are subject to renewal. Development grants are equivalent to about 30 percent of GDP, excluding technical assistance, which is a major component of total external aid.

Current expenditure is equivalent to more than 50 percent of GDP. A detailed economic and functional classification of expenditure is not available. Budget estimates for individual ministries suggest that wages and salaries account for at least 40 percent of the total. The local cost component of development spending is included in current expenditure, and the amounts involved are minor. Development spending, which is financed almost entirely out of external aid, is concentrated in fishing, transport and communications, and social infrastructure, including water and sewerage services. Government expenditure policy is the main instrument to influence growth, price stability, and the balance of payments, given Kiribati's small export sector; limitations on taxation, monetary, and exchange rate policies; and the dominance of the public sector in the economy.

Financial Sector

The financial sector comprises a commercial bank, a development bank, and the National Provident Fund. The Bank of Kiribati, which is 51 percent owned by an Australian banking group and 49 percent owned by the Government, is expected to remain as the only licensed commercial bank and foreign exchange dealer at least until 1991. The Kiribati Development Bank, which opened in mid-1987 with assistance from the Asian Development Bank, is authorized to make long-term loans to private enterprises engaged in agriculture, fisheries, industry, and services. The Development Bank took over the assets of the National Loans Board, which had been inactive for several years, because of the absence of allocations of budgetary funds. The National Provident Fund, established in 1977, operates a compulsory superannuation scheme to which employers and employees must each contribute 6 percent of wages and salaries; its assets are largely invested abroad.

There is no central monetary institution. The Australian dollar is legal tender and the sole circulating medium of exchange; exchange controls are not used. The scope for monetary policy is severely circumscribed. The amount of currency in circulation is difficult to estimate. Since the Australian dollar is used as the domestic currency, monetary growth is ultimately linked to balance of payments surpluses. With the limited demand for money for transaction purposes, much of the growth in liquidity represents financial savings in the form of time deposits; few alternative instruments for these funds are available. Internationally competitive interest rates are paid on large time deposits to encourage their placement with the domestic banking system rather than foreign financial institutions. At present, little use is made of domestic savings to finance investment and growth. The Government makes no recourse to domestic borrowing; opportunities for profitable lending to the public enterprises and the private sector are extremely small. Consequently, the commercial bank's foreign assets are equivalent to more than 95 percent of deposit liabilities.

Developments in the 1970s

The sparsity of official statistics makes a detailed assessment of developments in the 1970s difficult. However, the Kiribati economy certainly prospered during this period because of relatively high phosphate prices. Assisted by buoyant receipts from mining company taxation and export duties, the overall budgetary position also registered large surpluses. While several pay raises were granted to public employees, particularly during the second half of the decade, the Government tried to contain the growth of current expenditure in order to avoid disruption during the transition to the post-phosphate era. As a result, persistent foreign trade, current account, and overall external surpluses were recorded. Substantial amounts of capital were paid into the phosphate reserve fund and all investment income accruing to the fund was automatically reinvested.

Economic planning focused primarily on policies to develop alternative sources of income. With respect to employment creation, the only notable success was the seamen's training school. Efforts to promote agricultural, manufacturing, and tourism activities were not successful. No development occurred in the financial system. The public investment program was small, and economic and social infrastructure remained rudimentary. At the time of independence, prospects for economic growth appeared bleak, with little likelihood of quickly reducing dependence on external assistance.

Developments in the 1980s

Preliminary national accounts data suggest that real GDP growth has been negligible during this decade and, on a per capita basis, GDP remains far below that in the days of phosphate mining. Central government expenditure data and import statistics confirm the absence of any firm upward trend in activity. Annual fluctuations in copra and fish output are considerable, mainly owing to climatic changes. The fragility of the economic base was demonstrated in 1987, when unfavorable weather diminished copra production by one half and the fish catch was only one fourth of its potential with the existing fleet.

A major aim of fiscal policy has been to develop infrastructure and productive resources that would lay the foundations for future growth. Investment by the central government and public enterprises has averaged 30 percent of GDP since independence, although the impact on economic growth has been limited by the long gestation period of major projects and the high capital-output ratio, because of the small and widely dispersed population. Only projects that could be financed out of external concessional assistance have been undertaken. The pursuit of a more expansive investment program, for which local resources might have been made available, has been precluded by the lack of absorptive capacity of the economy.

Kiribati has exercised marked restraint on current budgetary spending so that public services could be curtailed to a level sustainable in the medium term. To avoid overall budgetary deficits, current expenditure was reduced from 65 percent of GDP in 1980 to 52 percent in 1987. A major part of this adjustment was accomplished through substantial cuts in the real wage and salary bill of the public sector. Wage increases were much lower than the rise in the cost of living. Established posts were abolished on several occasions and recruitment freezes were imposed for lengthy periods.

The Government has been successful in strengthening the finances of the public enterprise sector. Budgetary subsidies, which reached 10 percent of GDP during 1980–82, chiefly because of losses incurred by the national airline on international routes, were reduced to about 2 percent of GDP by 1987. The curtailment of regional services enabled the elimination of payments to the airline. Payments to the shipyard and telecommunications enterprises were limited primarily to assistance with starting costs. More flexible pricing policies were implemented and, in several enterprises, management took decisive steps to contain operating costs.

Public expenditure restraint was crucial for the achievement of a viable external payments position, particularly since domestic budgetary revenue declined in relation to GDP for several years after independence. Little scope existed to increase domestic taxes to compensate for the loss of phosphate-related revenues. Tax revenue was sluggish because of the low growth of household earnings, corporate income, and dutiable imports; nontax revenue was generally stagnant. To prevent an undue decline in the availability of services, the authorities during 1980–85 utilized the cash budgetary support offered by the United Kingdom under the terms of the financial agreement negotiated at independence. The Government also used all the interest earnings on external assets as a source of budgetary revenue in this period. Beginning in 1986, when the revenue position strengthened following the negotiation of a one-year fishing agreement with the U.S.S.R., it was decided not to request further cash budgetary support from the United Kingdom and to draw down only part of the interest earnings on external assets, thereby permitting the remainder of these receipts to be reinvested abroad. However, tight control over current expenditure was continued.

Monetary developments have not conflicted with external objectives. The rate of growth of domestic liquidity was modest during 1980–83 when interest rates were held to a maximum of 8 percent annually. Since this was often well below the rates available abroad on Australian dollar-denominated funds, most financial savings were held at foreign financial institutions. Following the decision to offer competitive yields on large time deposits, which caused rates to be increased up to 12.5 percent, strong deposit growth occurred during 1984–85. With the completion of the shift in portfolios from foreign to domestic assets, the growth of liquidity then moderated. The commercial bank reinvested virtually all of these funds abroad, although the Government sought to encourage bank lending to promote private sector activity. The ratio of advances to deposits, which had reached a peak equivalent to 50 percent in 1982 as a result of loans to public enterprises, fell to 7 percent in 1984 after the airline used the proceeds of an aircraft sale to repay its borrowing. Thereafter, domestic lending comprised only small amounts for working capital for fishermen and retail traders.

The current account, including official transfers, registered deficits in 1980–82, even though Kiribati, with its small export sector and large and stable flows of official transfers, appeared less vulnerable to the deterioration in the terms of trade and the world recession than other Pacific island economies. The trade deficit widened markedly because of low copra export prices, the high volume of imports of capital equipment including aircraft, and the increased cost of petroleum products. In 1983–84, a combination of factors contributed to a strengthening of the trade account and the achievement of current account surpluses. Exports of copra were unusually high because of favorable weather and strong foreign demand. Imports declined because of fiscal restraint and lower fuel imports following the sale of aircraft, and higher services receipts reflected the negotiation of several fishing agreements.

The external current account remained strong in subsequent years, although the surplus declined in relation to GDP, partly because exports reverted to the equivalent of less than one fifth of imports, in view of lower prices and the poor fish catch. The impact on the trade balance was mitigated by the decline in the cost of imports, reflecting cheaper petroleum prices, lower aid-related imports, and weak consumer demand. The balance on services and transfers continued to register surpluses with continued inflows in the form of interest earnings, fishing royalties, seamen's remittances, and concessional aid. The overall balance of payments, which had been in deficit during 1980–81, registered surpluses thereafter, and external assets accumulated steadily. Expenditure from the phosphate reserve fund was limited to the repurchase of Fanning and Washington Islands from an Australian trading company that had operated plantations there for many years.

Table 1. Kiribati: Gross Domestic Product
by Sectoral Origin, 1979–86
(In thousands of Australian dollars at current prices)

	1979	1980	1981	1982	1983	1984	1985	1986
Agriculture	4,026	1,528	3,012	2,846	3,340	5,977	4,151	3,728
Copra	3,385	855	2,242	1,946	2,264	4,852	2,904	2,328
Fishing	2,008	2,327	2,842	3,296	4,293	4,931	4,878	4,800
Commercial	873	1,106	1,348	1,568	2,487	2,689	2,325	2,200
Manufacturing	304	321	496	494	508	627	594	600
Electricity and water	541	328	398	456	661	715	824	900
Construction	934	992	1,121	1,126	616	842	1,053	1,500
Trade and hotels	2,353	3,212	3,290	4,478	3,455	3,538	3,586	3,600
Transport and communications	2,137	3,871	3,702	6,032	4,766	3,072	3,940	4,500
Finance and insurance	193	144	637	682	595	747	1,020	1,100
Ownership of dwellings	502	636	628	152	754	536	824	850
Government administration	6,382	7,322	6,819	6,678	7,727	7,462	7,974	8,100
Community services	449	456	491	527	543	603	733	750
Less: bank service charges	−114	−111	−572	−643	−484	−796	−1,205	−1,200
GDP at factor cost	34,745	21,025	22,866	26,424	26,774	28,253	28,372	29,228
Plus: indirect taxes	4,085	3,925	3,985	3,938	3,682	3,916	4,200	4,500
Less: subsidies	−1,786	−2,491	−3,859	−4,260	−3,657	−2,504	−2,164	−1,800
GDP at market prices	37,044	24,460	22,992	26,103	26,799	29,665	30,407	31,928
Monetary GDP	34,762	20,033	20,044	22,741	23,067	25,449	25,708	26,978
Nonmonetary GDP	2,282	2,427	2,948	3,362	3,732	4,217	4,699	4,950
Agriculture	641	673	771	900	1,077	1,125	1,246	1,400
Fishing	1,135	1,221	1,495	1,728	1,805	2,242	2,553	2,600
Other	506	533	682	734	850	850	900	950
Memorandum items:								
GDP at 1980 prices[1]	43,099	22,460	21,348	22,973	22,188	23,303	22,857	22,518
Change in real GDP (in percent)	...	−47.8	−5.0	7.6	−3.4	5.0	−1.9	−1.5
				(In metric tons)				
Copra output	8,937	7,527	11,270	9,889	6,947	13,389	8,483	5,911
Gilbert Islands	6,791	6,071	9,502	8,081	6,362	11,403	5,334	4,411
Line Islands	2,146	1,456	1,768	1,808	585	1,986	3,149	1,500
Fish catch	...	...	628	492	1,638	2,058	718	1,358

Sources: Data provided by the Kiribati authorities; and Fund staff estimates.
[1] Deflated by the Tarawa retail price index.

Table 2. Kiribati: Consumer Price Index, 1979–86
(Annual average percentage change)

	Weights[1]	1979	1980	1981	1982	1983	1984	1985	1986
Food	50.0	10.1	15.7	6.8	3.7	3.5	4.6	4.2	7.3
Beverages and tobacco	14.0	13.2	20.4	0.6	10.4	14.5	5.1	3.5	8.0
Clothing and footwear	8.0	−1.0	14.3	8.7	4.7	3.8	8.9	14.0	1.6
Transport	8.0	6.7	15.2	24.7	8.9	7.4	1.2	11.3	10.3
Household operations	7.5	7.3	21.3	14.0	9.6	11.4	10.4	−2.5	6.3
Miscellaneous	12.5	12.5	5.6	3.3	5.1	4.4	6.0	2.6	7.6
Overall index	100.0	8.9	16.1	7.7	5.5	6.3	5.4	4.5	6.6
		(End-of-period; percentage change)							
Memorandum item: Overall index	100.0	9.5	17.8	4.7	6.3	7.4	3.2	0.7	7.8

Source: Data provided by the Kiribati authorities.
[1] Tarawa retail price index, fourth quarter 1975 = 100.

Table 3. Kiribati: Central Government Budget, 1979–86

(In thousands of Australian dollars)

	1979	1980	1981	1982	1983	1984	1985	1986
Revenue and grants	22,648	22,669	22,232	22,542	24,411	24,465	25,332	27,238
Tax revenue	13,115	6,159	4,417	4,465	4,605	4,536	4,947	5,698
Nontax revenue	4,433	8,610	9,498	8,277	8,606	9,455	9,800	10,540
External grants	5,100	7,900	8,317	9,800	11,200	10,474	10,585	11,000
Current[1]	—	2,000	2,017	3,500	3,500	1,774	1,485	—
Development[2]	5,100	5,900	6,300	6,300	7,700	8,700	9,100	11,000
Total expenditure	18,511	20,450	22,553	22,191	23,622	24,295	25,907	27,632
Current expenditure	13,411	14,550	16,253	15,891	15,922	15,595	16,807	16,632
Development expenditure	5,100	5,900	6,300	6,300	7,700	8,700	9,100	11,000
Overall balance	4,137	2,219	–321	351	789	170	–575	–394
				(In percent of GDP)				
Memorandum items:								
Revenue and grants	61.1	100.9	96.7	86.4	91.1	82.5	83.3	85.3
Tax revenue	35.4	27.4	19.2	17.1	17.2	15.3	16.3	17.8
Nontax revenue	12.0	38.3	41.3	31.7	32.1	31.9	32.2	33.0
External grants	13.8	35.2	36.2	37.5	41.8	35.3	34.8	34.5
Total expenditure	50.0	91.1	98.1	85.0	88.1	81.9	85.2	86.5
Current expenditure	36.2	64.8	70.7	60.9	59.4	52.6	55.3	52.1
Capital expenditure	13.8	26.3	27.4	24.1	28.7	29.3	29.9	34.5
Overall balance	11.2	9.9	–1.4	1.3	2.9	0.6	–1.9	–1.3

Sources: Data provided by the Kiribati authorities; and Fund staff estimates.

[1]Budgetary grant from the United Kingdom.

[2]Development budgets of the central government and public enterprises, which are derived from the balance of payments statistics after excluding technical assistance costs.

Table 4. Kiribati: Central Government Revenue, 1979–86

(In thousands of Australian dollars)

	1979	1980	1981	1982	1983	1984	1985	1986
Tax revenue	13,115	6,159	4,417	4,465	4,605	4,536	4,947	5,698
Income and profits	1,309	1,020	919	1,020	1,278	1,054	1,195	1,559
Companies	45	111	126	273	211	100	164	400
Individuals	1,264	909	793	747	1,067	954	1,031	1,159
Indirect taxation	11,806	5,139	3,498	3,445	3,327	3,482	3,752	4,139
Import duties	3,315	3,380	3,483	3,428	3,299	3,472	3,702	4,052
Phosphate tax	8,354	1,669	—	—	—	—	—	—
Other	137	90	15	17	28	10	50	87
Nontax revenue	4,433	8,610	9,498	8,277	8,606	9,455	9,800	10,540
Reserve fund income[1]	—	4,250	5,751	4,750	5,500	5,500	5,182	5,200
Meteorology[2]	191	267	275	316	223	625	233	104
Fishing royalties	614	616	1,255	—	983	1,936	3,006	3,767
Bank of Kiribati	—	—	—	—	—	—	25	150
Rent	144	246	201	1,047	1	—	17	56
Philatelic sales	457	489	590	—	—	2	1	—
Aircraft landing fees	47	6	30	108	104	1	10	64
School fees	90	90	104	183	171	103	103	105
Telecommunications	112	136	151	426	265	243	200	—
Interest	266	801	455	66	145	133	329	296
Shipyard sales	107	147	191	73	57	37	10	—
Fish sales	36	121	33	221	510	34	140	47
Public works charges	254	370	307	—	—	360	—	19
Other fees and charges	2,115	1,071	155	1,087	647	482	385	730
Total	17,548	14,769	13,915	12,742	13,211	13,991	14,747	16,238

Sources: Data provided by the Kiribati authorities; and Fund staff estimates.

[1] Amounts drawn. The amounts earned are shown in the balance of payments.

[2] Payments by the Japanese space agency for the use of Christmas Island facilities to obtain meteorological information.

Table 5. Kiribati: Central Government Current Expenditure, 1979–86

(In thousands of Australian dollars)

	1979	1980	1981	1982	1983	1984	1985	1986
General services	2,879	3,039	3,359	3,245	3,708	3,653	4,323	4,090
Office of the President	125	477	358	479	486	538	588	636
Judiciary	112	130	162	161	189	173	218	243
Public Service Commission	17	27	19	14	16	10	12	11
Parliament	131	232	186	174	217	237	276	311
Attorney General	28	28	37	32	48	43	36	51
Audit	45	52	60	66	86	91	89	90
Pensions	544	523	403	449	278	491	511	312
Home Affairs	1,346	929	1,444	1,380	1,723	1,489	1,551	1,594
Finance	531	641	690	490	665	581	1,042	842
Public order and safety	749	1,094	763	896	1,311	1,220	1,393	1,311
Education	2,607	3,031	3,077	2,949	2,647	2,673	2,993	3,022
Health	1,153	1,482	1,735	1,807	1,735	1,647	1,690	1,966
Economic services	6,023	5,904	7,319	6,994	6,521	6,402	6,408	6,243
Natural resources	686	740	608	834	907	1,221	1,347	2,087
Trade and industry	1,774	167	1,341	215	508	539	457	541
Communications[1]	3,464	4,916	4,618	2,986	2,862	2,236	1,707	1,299
Works and energy	—	—	—	2,277	1,513	1,603	1,523	1,306
Line and Phoenix Islands	99	81	752	682	731	803	1,374	1,010
Total	13,411	14,550	16,253	15,891	15,922	15,595	16,807	16,632

Sources: Data provided by the Kiribati authorities; and Fund staff estimates.

[1]Includes expenditure on works and energy during 1979–81.

Table 6. Kiribati: Commercial Bank Balance Sheet, 1979–86[1]

(In millions of Australian dollars; end of period)

	1979	1980	1981	1982	1983	1984	1985	1986
Net foreign assets[2]	7.8	8.3	5.8	4.4	7.9	19.4	28.0	28.5
Domestic credit	0.4	1.0	3.7	4.3	3.6	0.8	1.0	1.7
Public enterprises	—	0.4	3.0	3.6	2.9	0.5	0.4	0.3
Air Tungaru	—	0.4	2.0	2.7	2.3	—	—	—
Kiribati Shipping Corporation	—	—	1.0	0.9	0.6	0.4	0.3	0.3
Te Mautari Limited[3]	—	—	—	—	—	0.1	0.1	—
Private sector	0.4	0.6	0.7	0.7	0.7	0.3	0.6	1.4
Deposits	8.0	9.1	9.3	8.5	11.3	19.5	28.2	29.2
Demand	2.5	3.0	4.2	3.4	4.5	3.6	2.6	3.4
Savings	2.5	2.8	2.3	2.7	2.7	3.1	3.6	4.1
Time	3.0	3.3	2.8	2.4	4.1	12.8	22.0	21.7
Other items, net	0.2	0.2	0.2	0.2	0.2	0.7	0.8	1.0
Memorandum item:								
Time deposits (as percent of total deposits)	37.5	36.3	30.1	28.2	36.3	65.6	78.0	74.3

Sources: Data provided by the Kiribati authorities; and Fund staff estimates.

[1] Bank of Kiribati Limited is the country's only commercial bank.

[2] The change in net foreign assets corresponds to the overall balance of payments surplus or deficit (after allowance for statistical discrepancies caused by differences in the timing of the recording of certain transactions).

[3] The national fishing corporation.

Table 7. Kiribati: Interest Rate Structure, June 1987
(In percent per annum; end of period)

Commercial bank deposit rates	
Savings deposits[1]	5.00
Term deposits under $A 50,000	
3 months	6.00
6 months	7.00
12 months	8.00
Term deposits over $A 50,000	
7 days	13.75
14 days	13.75
1 month	14.28
2 months	14.22
3 months	14.09
6 months	14.15
Commercial bank lending rates	
Secured loans	12.00
Unsecured loans	13.00

Source: Data provided by the Kiribati authorities.

[1] Island accounts, with a minimum deposit of $A 100 and no restrictions on withdrawal, were introduced at an interest rate of 6.5 percent with effect from April 1987.

Table 8. Kiribati: Balance of Payments, 1979–86

(In thousands of SDRs)

	1979	1980	1981	1982	1983	1984	1985	1986
Trade balance	5,448	-13,715	-18,766	-18,815	-13,430	-7,028	-10,811	-11,057
Exports, f.o.b.	19,068	2,276	3,487	2,168	3,376	10,718	4,214	1,419
Imports, f.o.b.	-13,620	-15,991	-22,252	-20,983	-16,806	-17,746	-15,025	-12,476
Services, net	433	-1,707	1,219	-230	1,266	1,888	4,060	3,374
Receipts	6,143	6,610	10,187	7,879	8,611	10,383	10,134	9,893
Reserve fund interest	4,066	3,721	5,605	4,377	4,643	4,720	3,577	3,431
Payments	-5,710	-8,317	-8,967	-8,109	-7,345	-8,495	-6,074	-6,519
Private transfers, net	1,211	1,226	1,657	2,304	2,111	1,888	1,657	1,830
Official transfers[1]	7,960	13,220	13,743	13,546	15,196	13,558	11,181	10,580
Current account	15,052	-976	-2,146	-3,196	5,142	10,306	6,087	4,726
Capital account[2]	-6,749	-2,101	-292	553	-1,435	-1,287	-621	-4,403
Overall balance[3]	8,303	-3,077	-2,439	-2,643	3,707	9,018	5,466	323
Memorandum items:								
Current account (in percent of GDP)	47.0	-5.0	-9.6	-13.3	22.7	38.2	29.6	25.6
Australian dollars per SDR (period average)	1.16	1.14	1.03	1.09	1.18	1.17	1.45	1.75

Sources: Data provided by the Kiribati authorities; and Fund staff estimates.

[1] Including aid-in-kind and technical assistance.

[2] Outflows consist primarily of the reinvestment of interest earnings of the reserve fund, investment abroad by the National Provident Fund, and repayments of the commercial borrowing for the purchase of an aircraft. Inflows comprise small amounts of concessionary loans, mainly from the Asian Development Bank. Few private capital transactions have been identified.

[3] Corresponds to the change in net foreign assets of the Bank of Kiribati (apart from differences in timing of the recording of transactions).

Table 9. Kiribati: Exports by Commodity, 1979–86

(Value in thousands of SDRs, volume in metric tons,
unit value in SDRs per metric ton)

	1979	1980	1981	1982	1983	1984	1985	1986
Fish								
Value	131	164	683	475	1,269	1,472	706	1,006
Volume	65	112	743	579	1,858	2,298	1,034	1,523
Unit Value	2,010	1,462	920	820	683	641	683	661
Copra								
Value	3,187	1,901	2,571	1,340	1,822	5,996	3,256	262
Volume	7,250	6,960	11,957	8,795	6,764	11,333	10,377	5,900
Unit Value	440	273	215	152	269	529	314	44
Shark fins								
Value	22	17	15	28	14	39	17	13
Volume	--	1	1	2	1	3	1	1
Unit Value	--	16,635	14,621	13,823	14,351	13,158	14,379	10,484
Phosphate[1]								
Value	15,533	--	--	--	--	--	--	--
Volume	445,700	--	--	--	--	--	--	--
Unit Value	35	--	--	--	--	--	--	--
Other (Value)	22	20	22	18	18	18	28	22
Domestic exports	18,895	2,101	3,292	1,860	3,123	7,526	4,007	1,303
Re-exports[2]	173	175	195	309	253	3,192	207	116
Total (Value)	19,068	2,276	3,487	2,168	3,376	10,718	4,214	1,419

Sources: Data provided by the Kiribati authorities; and Fund staff estimates.
[1]Phosphate mining was halted in 1979.
[2]Including an aircraft in 1984.

Table 10. Kiribati: Imports by Commodity Group, 1979–86

(In thousands of SDRs)

	1979	1980	1981	1982	1983	1984	1985	1986
Food and live animals	4,063	4,759	4,835	4,804	4,616	4,841	4,123	3,243
Beverages and tobacco	1,302	1,141	1,082	1,082	1,010	967	716	707
Raw materials	227	265	394	346	444	261	135	193
Mineral fuels	1,954	2,192	3,578	3,171	1,934	2,365	2,348	1,280
Oils and fats	16	19	22	28	12	33	20	13
Chemicals	745	791	846	845	676	967	749	651
Manufactured goods	1,609	2,277	2,426	2,620	2,923	1,803	1,412	2,508
Machinery and transport equipment	2,372	2,914	7,519	5,783	3,864	5,280	4,386	2,545
Miscellaneous manufactured articles	1,253	1,429	1,352	2,171	1,238	1,143	978	1,244
Other	79	204	198	133	89	86	158	92
Total	13,620	15,991	22,252	20,983	16,806	17,746	15,025	12,476

Source: Data provided by the Kiribati authorities.

Table 11. Kiribati: External Grants and Concessionary Loans, 1979–86

(In millions of SDRs)

	1979	1980	1981	1982	1983	1984	1985	1986
Australia	2.1	2.1	2.4	2.2	1.9	2.0	1.7	1.7
Sewerage project	0.9	0.9	1.0	1.7	0.6	—	—	—
Water project	—	—	—	—	0.8	1.0	0.8	1.0
Other aid	1.2	1.2	1.4	0.6	0.5	1.0	0.9	0.7
New Zealand	0.1	0.1	0.2	0.3	0.3	0.4	0.7	1.2
Japan	0.1	0.4	1.5	2.1	2.0	1.9	2.8	3.1
Fishing vessels	—	—	1.2	1.3	1.1	1.3	2.4	—
Cold storage	—	—	—	0.4	0.7	0.5	—	—
Causeway	—	—	—	—	—	—	—	2.9
Other aid	0.1	0.4	0.3	0.4	0.3	0.1	0.4	0.2
United Kingdom	4.2	10.1	8.2	7.7	8.4	5.8	4.1	3.1
Budgetary grant	—	1.8	1.9	3.2	3.0	1.5	1.0	—
Project aid	2.4	5.3	3.7	1.7	3.0	1.7	1.0	1.4
Technical assistance	1.8	3.0	2.5	2.9	2.4	2.6	2.1	1.7
Asian Development Bank	0.3	—	—	0.2	0.2	0.4	0.4	0.4
Loans	0.3	—	—	—	—	—	0.2	0.2
Technical assistance	—	—	—	0.2	0.2	0.4	0.2	0.2
European Community	1.2	0.3	0.9	0.2	1.7	1.9	0.7	0.3
Bilateral program	—	0.3	0.4	0.2	0.8	0.9	0.3	0.2
Regional program	—	—	—	—	—	1.0	1.4	0.1
STABEX	1.2	—	0.5	—	0.8	—	—	—
Other[1]	0.3	0.3	0.6	0.8	0.7	1.4	1.0	1.0
Total	8.2	13.2	13.7	13.5	15.2	13.8	11.4	10.8

Sources: Data provided by the Kiribati authorities; and Fund staff estimates.

[1] The bilateral assistance of Canada, China, and the Federal Republic of Germany; the activities of UN agencies; and the programs of private organizations.

Table 12. Kiribati: External Assets, 1979–86

(In millions of SDRs; end of period)

	1979	1980	1981	1982	1983	1984	1985	1986
Phosphate reserve fund	57.1	65.8	62.2	70.9	73.8	76.2	82.2	97.2
Government bank accounts[1]	8.0	12.2	6.4	5.4	5.3	3.2	3.5	2.8
National Provident Fund[1]	1.7	3.2	2.9	4.1	5.3	6.1	5.3	6.3
Bank of Kiribati investments[2]	6.5	7.7	5.6	3.9	6.7	16.4	17.4	16.4
Total assets	73.3	89.0	77.1	84.4	91.1	101.9	108.5	122.7
Memorandum items:								
External debt	0.3	0.3	0.3	1.8	1.6	1.7	1.7	1.7
(In percent of GDP)	1.0	1.5	1.5	7.5	7.0	6.6	8.0	9.3
Debt service	—	—	—	0.2	0.3	0.3	0.3	0.4
(In percent of goods and services)	—	—	—	1.5	2.5	1.5	2.0	3.1
Australian dollars per SDR (end of period)	1.19	1.08	1.03	1.12	1.16	1.18	1.61	1.84

Sources: Data provided by the Kiribati authorities; and Fund staff estimates.

[1]Excluding deposits with the Bank of Kiribati.

[2]These assets are shown in Australian dollars in the commercial bank balance sheet.

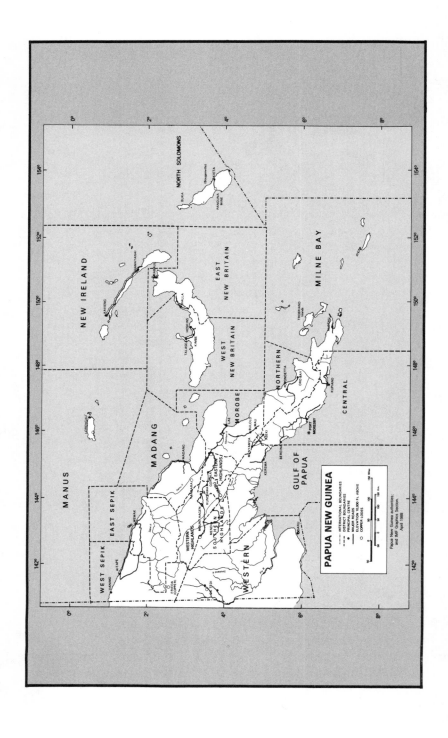

PAPUA NEW GUINEA

INTERNATIONAL BOUNDARIES
DISTRICT BOUNDARIES
PRINCIPAL CENTRE
MAJOR ROADS
ELEVATION 10,000 Ft. ABOVE
COPPER LODES

Papua New Guinea authorities;
and IMF Graphics Section.
April 1988

NORTH SOLOMONS

Buka

Bougainville

PANGUNA MINE

NEW IRELAND

Kavieng

NAMATANAI

TALASEA
HOSKINS
KIMBE

EAST NEW BRITAIN

WEST NEW BRITAIN

MILNE BAY

Trobriand Islands

Misima

NORTHERN

POPONDETTA
ORO BAY

KOKODA

CENTRAL

PORT MORESBY

MANUS

LORENGAU

MADANG

MOROBE

Madang

LAE

KAINANTU
GOROKA
EASTERN HIGHLANDS

KUNDIAWA
MOUNT HAGEN

WESTERN HIGHLANDS

MENDI
SOUTHERN HIGHLANDS

WABAG

WEST SEPIK

EAST SEPIK

VANIMO

AITAPE

WEWAK

BULOLO
WAU

MENYAMYA
KEREMA

BEREINA

KEREMA

GULF OF PAPUA

WESTERN

OK TEDI (COPPER)

DARU

Sepik R.

Fly R.

MIles
Km.

142°   144°   146°   148°   150°   152°   154°

0°   2°   4°   6°   8°

4

Papua New Guinea

Papua New Guinea comprises the eastern half of the island of New Guinea and several hundred islands to the east and north. The land area is 463,000 square kilometers and the population of 3.6 million is largely Melanesian. Resources include plentiful arable land, extensive forests, rich mineral deposits, and hydroelectric potential. However, much of the terrain is mountainous, which makes travel and communications difficult. The population density is only eight persons per square kilometer and substantial areas of the interior remain unexplored. There are some 700 local languages, and allegiances are closely tied to villages. While social obligations differ among kinship groups, most land is communally owned and members assist others in need. For many inhabitants, contact with the modern world is recent and access to health, education, and other social facilities remains limited. Life expectancy is 52 years and poverty is more pronounced than in other Pacific island countries.

In 1828, the Netherlands took possession of the western half of New Guinea, which is now the Indonesian province of Irian Jaya. In 1884, Germany assumed a protectorate over the northern part and the United Kingdom over the southern part of eastern New Guinea. In 1905, Australia took over responsibility for British New Guinea, which was renamed Papua, and in 1914, following the outbreak of war, acquired German New Guinea. After World War II, the two territories were combined to form the Territory of Papua and New Guinea and Australia's administrative mandate under trusteeship was reaffirmed by the United Nations. Papua New Guinea became independent in 1975. The National Parliament, which consists of 109 representatives, is democratically elected every five years. The Prime Minister is selected from among its members and appoints a cabinet. Legislation passed in 1976 established elected provincial governments, which assuaged the movements for self government in several regions and for secession on the island of Bougainville. Nevertheless, political consensus has been difficult to achieve and this periodically impedes economic policy formulation.

Despite the country's ample resource endowment, economic growth after independence did not keep pace with population growth. Few businesses were owned by local citizens and there was a serious shortage of educated nationals to take over the jobs previously performed by expatriates. Successive governments followed generally cautious economic policies, aimed at providing a stable environment conducive to growth, while maintaining sustainable budgetary and external positions. However, structural obstacles to development include adverse topography that fragments domestic markets, limited domestic savings, a high wage structure, shortages of skilled workers, and uncertainty over land rights. Papua New Guinea liberalized policies on land sales and transfers in 1980, but procedures for the leasing of land remain cumbersome. While Australia continues to provide large external grants, the amount has gradually declined in real terms. Annual per capita GDP is about SDR 650.

Economic Structure

Production and Prices

Agriculture is the source of livelihood for about four fifths of the population and accounts for about one third of GDP. The size of the plantation sector has diminished over the past decade because of low investment and difficulties associated with land tenure. Coffee, cocoa, coconut products, and palm oil are the main agricultural exports. A marketing board and stabilization fund exists for each of these crops to lessen the impact of fluctuations in world prices on rural incomes. This is accomplished by building reserves with levies when export prices are high and by making payments when export prices are low. Minor export crops include tea and rubber. The main products for domestic consumption are rice, taro, other root crops, poultry, and pork. Marketing is made difficult by the high cost of transport to urban areas, and the irregularity of and variation in supplies. In addition, rising incomes in urban areas have contributed to growing preferences for imported goods. Production of logs and wood products has grown over the past decade. The fish catch has been small since world tuna prices slumped in the early 1980s.

Mineral resources play a large role in the economy, accounting for two thirds of total exports. The bulk of production originates in two of the world's largest copper and gold mines, in each of which foreign investors have equity of 80 percent and the Government holds 20 percent. The Bougainville mine commenced production in 1972, and the Ok Tedi mine in 1985. However, as enclave operations far removed from major population centers, the projects have limited impact outside their immediate areas. Small-scale alluvial gold production, which dates back to the late nineteenth century, accounts for the remainder of mining output. The development of a number of major new gold mines is projected for the mid-1990s. Recent exploration suggests that Papua New Guinea could also become an important producer of oil and natural gas.

For most of the period since independence, the economy has not been able to generate employment at a rate sufficient to absorb the growing labor force, including that drawn from traditional village societies. Although firm data are not available, there appears to have been a worsening of unemployment in recent years in the capital, Port Moresby, and other urban areas, especially among young people. The manufacturing sector contributes less than 10 percent of GDP. High wages, lack of managerial and technical skills, and inadequate infrastructure have hampered investment. The exchange and trade system remains largely free of restrictions, with the exception of a few items that are subject to import bans or quotas. The public sector is the most important service activity, providing about one fourth of all formal sector employment.

Consumer prices are influenced by the cost of imports, which come mainly from Australia. Wages are determined largely by regulation rather than by market forces and traditionally have been partially or fully indexed for price changes, a system that has wide social acceptance and is considered helpful to the maintenance of industrial harmony. The key institution in the labor market is the Minimum Wages Board, which is composed of representatives of employers, employees, the Government, and the community at large. The Board oversees the process of wage determination every three years and also establishes minimum urban and rural nominal wages. This wage determination covers about one half of all private sector employees and exercises a strong influence on wages of other employees, including those in the public sector.

Balance of Payments

The external sector is large relative to GDP. Exports, virtually all in the form of semiprocessed mineral and agricultural goods, are equivalent to more than 40 percent of GDP, a much greater ratio than in most other Pacific island countries. The trade balance normally shows a small surplus. However, imports fluctuate considerably in value and composition, reflecting mainly the status of mining projects. A high proportion of other imports consist of food, beverages, and consumer goods. The main destinations for exports are Japan and the Federal Republic of Germany and other Western European countries. The main sources of imports are Australia, which supplies 40 percent of the total, Japan, Singapore, and the United States. The services and transfers account is in substantial deficit, because of payments for freight and insurance, and dividends and interest. The overall balance has generally been in surplus.

Cautious policies are pursued with respect to external debt, reserves, and the exchange rate. External debt was equivalent to about 70 percent of GDP in 1987. About one third of the total represents private borrowing, the bulk of which is guaranteed by the foreign partners in mining operations. Debt service was 20 percent of current account receipts in 1987. Gross official international reserves average the equivalent of about 5–6 months' imports. The exchange rate is fixed to a weighted basket of currencies of Papua New Guinea's major trading partners. Since 1983, the rate has been depreciated against the basket several times in order to strengthen the balance of payments.

Public Sector

The public sector consists of the central government, 19 provincial administrations, and about 40 nonfinancial public enterprises. Central government budgetary receipts were equivalent to about 30 percent of GDP in 1987. Domestic revenue represented 23 percent of GDP. The share of direct taxes in total taxation—at two thirds—is large, compared with most other Pacific island countries. Other main sources of taxation are excise and import duties. Revenue from the mineral sector in the form of income tax, dividend withholding tax, and dividends on government equity participation is only 5 percent of the total. The rate of profitability of the Bougainville mine is small, while the taxable profits of the Ok Tedi mine are held down by accelerated depreciation allowances. Recent tax reform included lower personal income tax rates, through the widening of tax bands and the reduction in the maximum marginal rate from 50 to 48 percent; a simplification of the tariff structure, with a maximum rate of duty for most goods of 50 percent; and the introduction of capital gains tax of 15 percent on the sale of most assets, except for family homes.

External grants, virtually all of which are provided by Australia, were equivalent to 7 percent of GDP in 1987. Their share declined from more than half of the total budgetary receipts prior to independence to less than one fifth within the context of a series of five-year financial agreements. For 1976–81, the nominal increase in grants was set at 6 percent annually, which was expected to result in a slight fall in real terms. For 1981–86, the agreement provided for annual reductions of 5 percent in real terms. In light of the severity of the world recession, the agreement was renegotiated in 1983. The rate of reduction was set for Australian fiscal years (July 1–June 30) at 1 percent in 1983/84, 2 percent in 1984/85, and 3 percent in 1985/86. For 1986–91, annual declines of 5 percent at constant prices were agreed for direct budgetary support but, including project aid, the fall in total assistance would be limited to 3 percent annually.

Current expenditure was equivalent to 28 percent of GDP in 1987. Departmental expenses were 40 percent of the total; the public sector wage bill is large in relation to GDP. Transfers to the provinces represented 30 percent of the total, mainly to finance primary and secondary education, health care, and the provision of local infrastructure. Development expenditure was 5 percent of GDP in 1987, with priority assigned to agriculture, transport, and education. Opportunities to orient government spending to better serve development objectives are evolving only slowly as progress is made toward extending national skills; restraining the public sector wage and salary bill; and improving the efficiency of public administration, especially in project planning and implementation.

Fiscal policy is formulated within a medium-term framework, at the center of which is a rolling five-year public investment plan based on the expected availability of resources and macroeconomic objectives. In the shorter-term context, the plan establishes priorities and a level of expenditure for the coming year, which is estimated to be sustainable over the medium term. Projects have to meet specific criteria with regard to their eligibility for concessional financing from abroad and their effect on employment, the balance of payments, and future revenue generation. Whereas immediately after independence, distributional and welfare objectives were of overriding importance, the focus has gradually shifted more toward growth. Under the present strategy, the order of spending priorities is economic services, infrastructure, social services, law and order, and general administration.

Budgetary support for the public enterprises is relatively small, although external grants and government assistance help to finance their investment programs. Guidelines for their operations include a market-oriented pricing policy and minimum rates of profitability for investment projects. Each enterprise must annually submit five-year corporate plans, which should be deemed consistent with overall development objectives, for government approval. As part of its efforts to streamline public sector operations and improve efficiency, Papua New Guinea has adopted a general policy of privatization. It is also considering the reorganization of departmental functions into commercial statutory authorities.

Financial Sector

The financial system consists of a central bank (The Bank of Papua New Guinea), which was established in 1973; six commercial banks, most of which are subsidiaries of foreign banks and provide an extensive branch network throughout the country; the Agriculture Bank of Papua New Guinea, which was transformed from the Development Bank in 1985 with the requirement that 80 percent of its loans should be in agriculture; the Investment Corporation of Papua New Guinea, which was established in 1972 to promote local ownership of business enterprises; savings and loans societies; and finance and insurance companies. The Australian dollar was the domestic currency prior to independence. The national currency, the kina, was introduced in April 1975 and the Australian dollar ceased to be legal tender in December of that year. Exchange control procedures were applied uniformly to transactions with residents of all foreign countries, including Australia, in January 1976.

A main objective of the monetary authorities is to maintain financial stability by neutralizing the impact of temporary fluctuations in liquidity emanating from the external sector, while maintaining credit expansion at a sustainable medium-term rate. For many years, target rates for the growth in broad money were established for this purpose. This approach was discontinued in 1983 because of the limited control that the authorities could exercise over monetary growth. The main instrument for influencing commercial bank liquidity is the liquid asset requirement that specifies the minimum commercial bank holdings of currency, central bank deposits, treasury bills, short-term government securities, and other prescribed assets as a percentage of deposit liabilities. Quantitative ceilings on the permissible growth in bank lending and guidelines on the allocation of bank lending by sector are also issued. Bank interest rates have been largely market determined in recent years, although controls were applied in 1986.

Developments in the 1970s

Real GDP growth averaged 4 percent annually during the first half of the 1970s, despite the adverse impact of the oil price increases. The main impetus to growth was the commencement of operations at the Bougainville mine. Agricultural output also expanded steadily, including diversification into palm oil, in response to favorable world markets. Rising incomes spread rapidly from the export sector to the rest of the economy. During 1972–75, real urban minimum wages doubled as a result of decisions by the newly formed Minimum Wages Board. These decisions were based primarily on the concept of family needs as well as the general economic prospects. Although inflationary pressures intensified as a result of the favorable export performance and rising Australian grant assistance, the economy accommodated large increases in import demand without creating external payments difficulties.

The worldwide economic slowdown during 1975–76 was reflected in weakening demand for copper, and attendant implications for fiscal revenue and the balance of payments. Higher prices for essential imports contributed to domestic inflationary pressures. To restrain domestic demand, budgetary policy was tightened mainly by expenditure restraint; urban minimum wages were frozen for a 15-month period from January 1976; and more pronounced efforts were made to enforce existing price controls. The measures succeeded in restoring financial stability. From mid-1976, prices for Papua New Guinea's exports turned sharply higher. In view of the improved balance of payments prospects, the kina was appreciated by 5 percent in July 1976 to moderate the impact of rising import prices on domestic prices.

The rate of growth remained modest, with real GDP increasing by only 1–2 percent annually during the second half of the decade. Developments in the plantation sector, including management difficulties and land tenure problems after independence, depressed agricultural output. Declining ore grades at the Bougainville mine constrained the growth of mineral production. However, higher world market prices resulted in buoyant export receipts, while import growth was subdued. As a result, the external current account was generally in surplus and the overall balance of payments remained satisfactory. External commercial borrowing was limited, and gross official reserves increased from five months of imports in 1976 to eight months in 1979.

The average annual rate of inflation during the second half of the 1970s was several percentage points lower than the average for Papua New Guinea's major trading partners. This favorable outcome was attributable partly to the agreement reached with the managements of the commodity price stabilization funds to sterilize part of the higher agricultural export earnings. Reserves were largely placed in accounts at the central bank, rather than in commercial bank deposits, which would have added considerably to liquidity in this period. Full indexation was reintroduced for most employees under the three-year wage agreement for the period 1977–79. With the abatement of inflation, the rate of wage increases moderated. In view of the sound external position, the kina was revalued on several occasions to further hold down price rises. Price controls were eased to permit adjustments that were broadly in line with market developments.

Fiscal and monetary policies were fully consistent with the maintenance of financial stability and a sound external position. In view of reduced Australian budgetary support, domestic revenue was increased in relation to GDP, mainly through higher mining taxation, and tight controls were implemented to limit expenditure growth. The budget deficit was limited to an average of 2 percent of GDP during 1976–79, and nonbank borrowing largely provided the required financing. Balance of payments surpluses were the source of rapid liquidity expansion. The agreement by which most of the reserves of the commodity boards were held in the form of interest-bearing deposits at the central bank offset much of the potential for credit creation. This practice constrained the growth in commercial bank liquidity and facilitated monetary management.

Developments in the 1980s

The further round of oil price increases and the global recession had a severe impact on Papua New Guinea during 1980–82, with deteriorating terms of trade and stagnant output combining to produce large reductions in real incomes. Wage adjustments continued to be based primarily on providing compensation for price increases, without regard to the adverse impact on national income of the change in the terms of trade. Faced with growing fiscal and external imbalances, the Government borrowed abroad and external debt rose sharply. In light of the weak external position, demand management policies were gradually reoriented to promote adjustment. Economic conditions improved considerably during 1983–84, principally because of higher export prices. With the more favorable terms of trade, incomes recovered and the overall balance of payments strengthened. The rate of economic growth rose substantially in 1985–87, led by increased mining output. In addition, progress was made in medium-term efforts to restrain public spending and limit fiscal deficits. The Government also refrained from further foreign commercial borrowing.

Domestic and External Imbalances in 1980–82

During 1980–82, real GDP fell slightly. Agricultural production declined mainly in response to lower export prices, although the effects of the downturn on producer incomes were partially alleviated by the operations of the commodity stabilization boards. Gold and copper production declined, reflecting lower ore grades from the Bougainville mine. The fall in output would have been much more pronounced except for high expenditure at the Ok Tedi mine, as a result of which domestic investment rose from 25 percent of GDP in 1980 to 32 percent in 1982. The rate of inflation rose sharply, mainly because of higher import prices. Despite the poor economic climate, under the Minimum Wages Board determination for the period 1980–83, wages were fully adjusted for increases in the consumer price index up to 8 percent per annum, with partial indexation for increases up to 14 percent.

The external current account recorded deficits of 11 percent of GDP in 1980 and over 20 percent in both 1981 and 1982. Apart from the increased costs of petroleum products and other imports, capital equipment imports for the mining sector were substantial. Increased freight and insurance, as well as dividends and interest payments, contributed to the deficit on the services account. Private capital inflows financed part of the investment in the mining sector, but the Government borrowed extensively from external commercial sources. External debt increased from 24 percent of GDP in 1980 to 54 percent in 1982, while official reserves declined from seven months of imports to four months of imports over the same period. The debt service ratio increased from 7 percent in 1980 to 17 percent in 1982.

The overall budget deficit rose from 1 percent of GDP in 1980 to 6 percent in 1981. Total receipts remained relatively stable at 33 percent of GDP. However, total expenditure increased from 35 percent of GDP in 1980 to 39 percent in 1981, reflecting the growth in wages and salaries, debt service on external commercial borrowing, and increased public investment. As the balance of payments problem became increasingly severe, fiscal policy was tightened to contain imports. Expenditure cuts were made in the 1982 budget, although because of the decline in revenue from the mining sector, the deficit remained at 6 percent of GDP.

After a sharp increase in credit during 1980, a marked tightening of credit conditions occurred in 1981–82. The balance of payments deficit reduced bank liquidity, while administered interest rates were increased to levels that were high by international standards. Steps were also taken to improve the flexibility of monetary policy, including the introduction of an auction system for treasury bills. However, by late 1982 the Government alleviated some of the adverse consequences of the restrictive monetary conditions, because of a concern that additional restraint would exacerbate the already sluggish state of the economy and that more of the adjustment burden would therefore need to be borne by fiscal and other policies.

Adjustment and Recovery in 1983–87

During 1983–87, real GDP grew at an annual average rate of about 4 percent. The operations of the Ok Tedi mine contributed substantially to growth, although its export revenue and government tax payments were below expectations. Disagreements in 1984–85 between the Government and the other shareholders about the pace of copper and gold production and the timing of additional investments caused interruptions in output and cost overruns. After a new agreement was negotiated in 1986, operations proceeded smoothly. Modest growth was achieved in the agricultural sector, with the procurement prices of the commodity boards gradually adjusted upward in view of rising export prices. Domestic investment fell from 32 percent of GDP in 1983 to 22 percent in 1985–87 because of lower spending in the mining sector and the squeeze on public expenditure.

In response to the Government's increased emphasis on employment creation, rigidity in real wages was reduced from 1983. The
Minimum Wages Board determination in that year provided for full
indexation only for the first 5 percent of inflation, with no compensation
for higher inflation. A broadly similar system was incorporated into the
1986 determination, under which wages were fully indexed for the first
5 percent of inflation, with no adjustment for larger increases up to
10 percent and compensation for only half of any inflation between 10
and 15 percent. The Board also established a new youth minimum wage
of half of the adult minimum; it applies to all new young entrants into the
labor market. Although the decline in real wages under these arrangements has so far been relatively modest, because the rate of inflation
exceeded the threshold level only in 1983, the rigid link between wages
and prices has been broken.

Fiscal policy was employed with great success as the chief instrument of external adjustment. The Government reduced budgetary
expenditure by 3 percentage points of GDP in 1983–84, which cut the
deficit to 1 percent of GDP. It streamlined administrative functions and
retrenched 6 percent of the public sector work force. Unintended
shortfalls in development spending, associated with difficulties in project implementation, also aided the adjustment effort. Against the
background of the improved fiscal and external balance, budgetary
policy shifted toward supporting growth. Some of the services that had
been cut during the recession were reinstated in 1985. However, later
in that year, a reassessment was made of the assumptions underlying
the budget, including copper and gold prices and the exchange value of
the Australian dollar. Additional expenditure cuts were imposed to
limit the overall deficit to 2 percent of GDP in 1985. Consistent with the
re-establishment of the cautious external borrowing policy, expenditure was restrained to hold the overall deficit at about the 1986–87
level. By holding down the growth in purchases of goods and services,
wages and salaries, and transfers to the provinces and public enterprises, total spending was steadily reduced from 36 percent of GDP in
1983 to 31 percent of GDP in 1987.

Monetary conditions eased abruptly from mid-1983 as the balance
of payments improved, but private sector credit demand was slow to
respond to the upturn in economic activity. The authorities de-
controlled virtually all bank lending and deposit rates in late 1983 and
maintained an accommodative monetary stance throughout 1984 that

was guided primarily by a desire to support the expansion. When credit rose rapidly in 1985, action to tighten bank liquidity was taken through the withdrawal of access to the discount facility and interest rates increased sharply. In the face of continued strong credit demand during 1986, interest rates remained positive in real terms on most bank deposits and loans. For most of 1987, the emphasis was placed on frequent changes in the liquid assets ratio to ensure adequate bank liquidity, while slowing the rate of growth of private sector credit.

The external current account deficit was reduced to 16 percent of GDP in 1983, 13 percent in 1984, and 9 percent in 1985. As a result of the export recovery and the fall in imports by the mining sector, the trade account moved back into surplus. The deficit on services and transfers was broadly unchanged. The kina was depreciated in line with the 10 percent devaluation of the Australian dollar in March 1983 and by 5 percent against the basket of currencies in November 1985. Financing of the current account deficit still required considerable private and official external borrowing. Outstanding external debt rose to 91 percent of GDP and the debt service ratio reached 30 percent in 1985. More restrictive demand management policies held the external current deficit to 5 percent of GDP in 1986 and 7 percent in 1987 and permitted a halt in external commercial borrowing. Assisted by the conversion into equity of substantial foreign loans for the Ok Tedi mining operation, outstanding external debt was reduced considerably in relation to GDP.

Table 1. Papua New Guinea: Gross Domestic Product by Expenditure, 1978–87

(In millions of kina at current prices)

	1978	1979	1980	1981	1982	1983	1984	1985	1986	1987
Consumption	1,141.8	1,258.3	1,462.5	1,558.6	1,586.0	1,716.3	1,848.7	2,016.4	2,127.9	2,292.1
Private sector	788.5	890.6	1,051.3	1,104.2	1,117.9	1,245.0	1,343.6	1,479.1	1,576.1	1,693.3
Central government	353.3	367.7	411.2	454.4	468.1	471.3	505.1	537.3	551.8	598.8
Gross investment	296.3	383.3	430.7	458.1	562.3	626.2	605.2	500.7	541.0	644.6
Fixed investment	268.5	326.2	394.3	450.7	576.7	632.4	533.7	466.9	572.5	610.5
Change in stocks	27.8	57.1	36.4	7.4	-14.4	-6.2	71.5	33.8	-31.5	34.1
Statistical discrepancy	23.6	-8.6	-11.9	9.2	14.5	-5.4	-5.2	5.2	-13.3	-12.7
Domestic demand	1,461.7	1,633.0	1,881.3	2,025.9	2,162.8	2,337.9	2,448.7	2,522.3	2,655.6	2,924.0
External balance[1]	-48.4	-1.8	-173.2	-344.7	-413.9	-363.5	-314.4	-238.8	-188.2	-149.6
Exports	579.1	742.5	737.6	642.9	644.3	766.1	893.2	1,004.2	1,098.8	1,214.5
Imports	627.5	744.3	910.8	987.6	1,058.2	1,129.6	1,207.6	1,243.0	1,287.0	1,364.1
GDP at market prices	1,413.3	1,629.4	1,708.1	1,681.2	1,749.1	1,973.7	2,134.4	2,283.5	2,467.5	2,774.4
Market	1,201.0	1,403.1	1,445.8	1,395.0	1,448.5	1,650.2	1,802.2	1,947.9	2,115.4	2,386.7
Nonmarket	212.3	226.3	262.3	286.2	300.5	323.4	332.2	335.6	352.1	387.7
Memorandum items:										
Investment (in percent of GDP)	21.0	23.5	25.4	25.9	32.2	31.7	28.4	21.9	21.9	22.0
Change in real GDP (in percent)	6.2	1.8	-2.5	1.4	-0.2	2.0	-1.3	4.8	5.0	5.8

Sources: Data provided by the Papua New Guinea authorities; and Fund staff estimates.
[1] Goods and nonfactor services.

Table 2. Papua New Guinea: Output of Main Commodities, 1978–87

(In thousands of metric tons)

	1978	1979	1980	1981	1982	1983	1984	1985	1986	1987
Coffee	47.7	47.4	54.2	47.2	41.1	52.5	44.9	44.0	44.9	60.9
Smallholders	33.4	33.2	36.9	33.0	28.8	39.4	32.6	28.6	30.8	42.6
Plantations	14.3	14.2	17.3	14.2	12.3	13.1	12.3	15.4	14.1	18.3
Cocoa	31.3	27.6	27.5	31.9	26.6	26.3	33.0	28.9	33.0	33.9
Smallholders	16.0	15.0	14.2	18.5	16.0	18.4	23.5	20.1	23.7	23.1
Plantations	15.3	12.6	13.3	13.4	10.6	7.9	9.5	8.8	9.3	10.8
Copra	140.4	145.4	140.3	139.9	138.4	137.5	155.0	142.7	158.5	144.5
Smallholders	68.7	71.3	71.7	73.3	82.5	82.5	95.4	89.4	98.2	92.9
Plantations	71.7	74.1	68.6	66.6	55.9	55.0	59.6	53.3	60.3	51.6
Rubber	4.0	4.2	4.2	4.5	2.3	2.7	3.9	5.3	5.1	5.3
Smallholders	0.5	0.6	0.6	0.4	0.2	0.1	0.2	1.6	1.8	2.0
Plantations	3.5	3.6	3.6	4.1	2.1	2.6	3.7	3.7	3.3	3.3
Tea	7.0	7.0	7.5	7.0	6.5	7.2	6.5	7.8	6.5	7.0
Smallholders	0.5	0.4	0.5	0.5	0.4	—	—	0.2	—	—
Plantations	6.5	6.6	7.0	6.5	6.1	7.2	6.5	7.6	6.5	7.0
Palm oil	...	...	...	...	102.4	106.9	141.4	140.4	127.6	125.0
Smallholders	...	...	...	...	46.0	46.3	66.7	58.7	66.5	62.4
Plantations	...	...	...	...	56.4	60.6	74.7	81.7	61.1	62.6
Copper metal-in-concentrates	198.6	170.8	146.8	165.4	170.0	181.1	163.3	168.6	192.2	214.5
Gold (in metric tons)	23.4	19.7	14.0	16.8	17.5	19.1	19.4	32.1	36.5	36.4

Source: Data provided by the Papua New Guinea authorities.

Table 3. Papua New Guinea: Consumer Price Index, 1978–87

(Annual average percentage change)

	Weights	1978	1979	1980	1981	1982	1983	1984	1985	1986	1987
Food	40.9	4.1	4.5	16.8	7.9	4.9	4.4	7.2	3.9	2.5	2.3
Beverages and tobacco	20.0	4.9	6.7	9.3	10.1	5.0	21.0	9.3	–0.9	2.2	5.6
Clothing and footwear	6.2	7.9	4.1	6.6	2.7	5.0	3.0	6.8	6.3	3.7	2.7
Rent, fuel, and power	7.2	6.6	19.5	15.9	6.0	4.2	2.4	–0.7	1.5	–0.6	1.2
Household equipment and operations	5.3	7.3	5.3	7.8	6.9	3.1	4.9	7.5	5.8	4.3	1.1
Transport and communications	13.0	9.7	6.6	8.4	10.2	9.5	7.3	9.1	8.7	22.2	4.9
Miscellaneous	7.4	7.0	–3.0	4.3	6.6	7.4	4.1	9.4	6.4	5.9	2.9
Overall index	100.0	5.8	5.8	12.1	8.1	5.5	7.9	7.5	3.7	5.5	3.2
					(End-of-period percentage change)						
Memorandum item: Overall index		4.2	7.9	11.7	5.6	6.9	8.5	4.4	4.3	5.3	3.0

Source: Data provided by the Papua New Guinea authorities.

Table 4. Papua New Guinea: Central Government Budget, 1978–87

(In millions of kina)

	1978	1979	1980	1981	1982	1983	1984	1985	1986	1987
Revenue and grants[1]	434.5	460.5	574.3	558.0	559.7	628.9	719.5	713.4	763.2	824.8
Tax revenue	221.2	235.3	327.7	321.4	313.6	337.0	412.8	416.1	442.7	500.5
Nontax revenue	41.4	49.0	71.1	52.6	59.4	78.7	74.7	81.2	115.8	140.0
External grants	171.9	176.2	175.5	184.0	186.7	213.2	232.0	216.1	204.7	184.3
Total expenditure	456.1	504.4	597.8	658.8	667.1	713.1	742.4	767.1	837.2	858.3
Current expenditure	408.3	421.8	478.2	536.8	539.7	602.2	647.4	709.0	727.6	761.6
Capital expenditure	47.8	82.6	119.6	122.0	127.4	110.9	95.0	58.1	109.5	96.7
Overall balance	−21.6	−43.9	−23.5	−100.8	−107.4	−84.2	−22.9	−53.7	−74.0	−33.5
External financing (net)	2.5	26.9	47.4	83.7	75.7	111.0	43.0	2.0	56.2	61.7
Concessionary loans	...	...	...	...	19.8	48.0	52.0	4.0	44.0	105.6
Commercial loans	...	...	...	...	53.8	62.0	−15.0	−5.0	12.2	−43.9
Domestic financing (net)	19.1	17.0	−23.9	17.1	31.7	−26.8	−20.1	51.7	18.3	−28.2
Banking system	9.8	21.7	−20.0	28.1	30.6	−34.0	−23.0	40.0	17.5	−30.1
Other domestic	−9.3	−4.7	−3.9	−11.0	1.1	7.2	2.9	11.7	0.8	1.9
(In percent of GDP)										
Memorandum items:										
Revenue and grants	30.8	28.2	33.6	33.2	32.0	31.9	33.7	31.3	31.0	29.7
Tax revenue	15.7	14.4	19.2	19.1	17.9	17.1	19.3	18.3	18.0	18.0
Nontax revenue	2.9	3.0	4.2	3.1	3.4	4.0	3.5	3.6	4.7	5.0
External grants	12.2	10.8	10.3	10.9	10.7	10.8	10.9	9.5	8.3	6.6
Total expenditure	32.3	30.9	35.0	39.2	38.1	36.1	34.8	33.7	34.0	30.9
Current expenditure	28.9	25.8	28.0	31.9	30.9	31.2	30.3	31.1	29.6	27.5
Capital expenditure	3.4	5.1	7.0	7.3	7.3	4.9	4.5	2.6	4.4	4.6
Overall balance	−1.5	−2.7	−1.4	−6.0	−6.1	−4.3	−1.1	−2.4	−3.0	−1.2

Sources: Data provided by the Papua New Guinea authorities; and Fund staff estimates.
[1]Includes income tax, dividend withholding tax, and dividends on the government equity from mining operations that are paid into the Mineral Resources Stabilization Fund.

Table 5. Papua New Guinea: Central Government Revenue, 1978–87

(In millions of kina)

	1978	1979	1980	1981	1982	1983	1984	1985	1986	1987
Tax revenue	221.2	235.3	327.7	321.4	313.6	337.0	412.8	416.1	442.7	500.5
Income and profits	136.0	135.3	214.6	201.3	176.4	183.4	231.0	225.9	227.0	258.5
Companies	62.7	63.9	120.0	95.3	61.7	57.3	88.0	84.8	70.8	96.7
Mining sector	13.5	23.1	73.4	51.7	19.5	13.0	39.3	15.2	18.8	31.0
Other	49.2	40.8	47.5	43.6	42.2	44.3	48.7	69.6	52.0	65.7
Individuals	67.1	61.6	75.9	94.8	108.7	118.6	132.2	133.0	145.0	146.8
Dividend withholding	6.2	9.8	17.8	11.2	6.0	7.5	10.8	8.1	11.2	15.0
Mining sector	2.7	6.0	12.7	6.4	1.4	3.7	5.2	2.1	4.6	5.9
Other	3.5	3.8	5.1	4.8	4.6	3.7	5.6	6.0	6.6	9.1
Excise duties	36.3	41.0	46.1	47.2	49.8	51.5	58.5	61.8	65.2	68.2
International transactions	47.8	56.3	64.5	68.2	82.1	93.3	112.3	117.0	137.0	161.2
Import duties	41.7	48.0	55.1	63.7	77.6	88.4	99.5	103.9	122.7	144.0
Export duties	6.1	8.3	9.4	4.5	4.5	4.9	12.8	13.1	14.3	17.2
Other	2.0	2.7	2.5	4.7	5.3	8.8	11.0	11.4	13.5	12.7
Nontax revenue	41.4	49.0	71.1	52.6	59.4	78.7	74.7	81.2	115.8	140.0
Revenue from investment	7.5	17.8	39.7	15.7	13.6	26.1	37.6	30.0	61.2	65.1
Mining sector[1]	4.9	10.3	22.6	13.1	2.3	5.7	7.6	3.1	6.9	8.4
Nonmining sector	2.6	7.5	17.1	2.6	11.3	20.4	30.0	26.9	54.3	56.7
Other	33.9	31.2	31.4	36.9	45.8	52.6	37.1	51.2	54.6	74.9
Total	262.6	284.3	398.8	374.0	373.0	415.7	487.5	497.3	558.5	640.5
Mining sector	21.1	39.4	108.7	71.2	23.2	22.5	52.1	20.4	30.3	45.2
Other	241.5	244.9	290.1	302.8	349.8	393.2	435.4	476.9	528.2	595.3

Sources: Data provided by the Papua New Guinea authorities; and Fund staff estimates.
[1] Excludes royalties to provincial governments and local authorities (less than 1 percent).

Table 6. Papua New Guinea: Central Government Expenditure, 1978–87

(In millions of kina)

	1978	1979	1980	1981	1982	1983	1984	1985	1986	1987
Departmental	214.6	216.4	283.2	302.2	291.4	273.0	303.6	332.9	341.0	373.6
Grants to provincial governments	102.7	125.5	140.6	150.0	159.1	199.3	210.4	225.0	220.9	233.5
Other grants	32.3	35.3	37.2	48.2	38.6	41.9	44.7	52.1	51.0	46.2
Interest payments	21.0	27.5	26.3	52.1	61.0	67.6	72.9	70.9	83.5	77.6
Maintenance works	28.0	31.6	34.9	30.9	34.5	41.9	35.0	39.6	42.1	37.8
Capital works	40.7	33.3	56.4	55.9	44.9	44.8	48.2	37.1	59.7	56.5
Net lending and investment	6.4	9.6	12.7	13.8	32.5	39.3	21.2	2.9	32.0	24.6
Other	10.4	11.0	6.5	5.7	5.1	5.3	4.4	6.6	7.5	8.5
Total	456.1	504.4	597.8	658.8	667.1	713.1	742.4	767.1	837.2	858.3

Source: Data provided by the Papua New Guinea authorities.

Table 7. Papua New Guinea: Monetary Survey, 1978–87

(In millions of kina; end of period)

	1978	1979	1980	1981	1982	1983	1984	1985	1986	1987
Net foreign assets	265.0	353.9	281.8	221.8	205.0	320.3	353.6	397.2	413.9	406.8
Monetary authority	276.3	355.1	277.8	235.2	217.3	338.0	389.2	435.4	443.1	444.1
Commercial banks	-11.3	-1.2	4.0	-13.4	-12.3	-17.8	-35.6	-38.2	-29.1	-37.3
Domestic credit	207.8	264.0	312.0	365.0	425.8	417.6	504.7	617.1	711.6	744.0
Government, net	13.3	35.0	8.1	43.4	71.2	5.2	13.6	21.0	30.6	9.8
Monetary authority	-5.9	6.2	-59.3	-26.8	15.4	-46.1	-71.4	-39.5	-73.6	-80.8
Commercial banks	19.2	28.9	67.4	70.2	55.8	50.9	89.5	60.5	104.2	90.6
Private sector	194.5	229.0	303.9	321.6	354.6	412.5	501.1	596.1	681.1	734.2
Broad money (M3)[1]	307.9	362.9	382.7	412.8	434.5	498.8	590.8	642.9	745.9	808.3
Money supply	174.1	193.5	199.2	193.2	187.6	204.2	249.3	243.4	254.5	276.8
Quasi–money	133.8	169.4	183.5	219.6	246.9	294.7	341.5	399.4	491.4	531.4
Deposits of stabilization funds	105.6	147.8	156.1	137.2	130.4	125.6	154.8	160.6	165.5	110.6
Deposits of Bougainville Copper Ltd.	35.6	61.0	14.3	4.6	2.9	25.2	3.3	10.6	17.5	24.1
Total liquidity	449.0	571.7	553.1	554.6	567.8	649.6	749.0	814.0	928.8	943.0
Other items, net	-23.8	-46.2	-40.7	-32.2	-63.0	-88.1	-109.3	-200.4	-196.7	-207.8
					(Annual percentage change)					
Memorandum items:										
Domestic credit	47.2	27.0	18.2	17.0	16.7	-1.9	20.9	22.3	15.3	4.6
Broad money	5.4	17.9	5.5	7.9	5.3	14.8	18.4	8.8	16.0	8.4

Sources: Data provided by the Papua New Guinea authorities; and Fund staff estimates.

[1] Total liquidity less deposits of stabilization funds and of Bougainville Copper Ltd.

Table 8. Papua New Guinea: Interest Rate Structure, 1978–87

(In percent per annum; end of period)

	1978	1979	1980	1981	1982	1983	1984	1985	1986	1987
Commercial bank deposit rates										
Passbook savings	3.8	3.8	5.8	8.0	6.5	6.0	6.0	3.0–6.0	3.0–7.0	3.0–7.0
Term deposits under K 50,000										
3–6 months	4.5	4.8	6.8–6.9	10.0	8.0	6.0–7.8	6.0–8.5	8.3–11.0	7.0–8.8	8.0–9.3
6–12 months	5.5	5.5	7.5	10.6–11.0	8.5–8.8	6.5–8.0	6.5–8.0	8.3–12.0	7.0–9.0	8.3–9.5
Commercial bank over-draft minimum rate	9.3	9.3	9.0	14.5	12.5	10.3	11.0	13.0	11.0	12.3
Bank of Papua New Guinea										
Discount rate	—	—	—	—	—	9.8	8.8	—[1]	11.1	10.0
Treasury bills (182 days)	6.0	6.0	8.6	14.8	11.7	9.0	9.5	12.3	9.4	9.5
Inscribed stock (2 years)	—	—	—	11.5	12.5	—	9.8	12.5	12.5	—

Source: Data provided by the Papua New Guinea authorities.

[1]The discount facility was suspended from November 1985 to February 1986.

Table 9. Papua New Guinea: Balance of Payments, 1978–87

(In millions of SDRs)

	1978	1979	1980	1981	1982	1983	1984	1985	1986	1987
Trade balance	66	176	–26	–217	–226	–135	–34	43	106	101
Exports, f.o.b.	601	783	758	714	698	787	902	903	896	921
Imports, f.o.b.	–535	–607	–784	–931	–924	–922	–936	–860	–790	–820
Services, net	–191	–239	–312	–357	–335	–358	–427	–364	–310	–347
Receipts	58	71	80	112	140	125	113	118	140	120
Payments	–249	–310	–392	–469	–475	–483	–540	–482	–450	–467
Transfers, net	133	122	125	131	125	151	160	127	114	77
Official	203	196	205	238	237	241	254	215	182	158
Private	–70	–74	–80	–107	–112	–90	–94	–88	–67	–81
Current account	8	59	–213	–443	–436	–342	–301	–194	–90	–169
Nonmonetary capital, net	–29	29	78	358	437	439	276	180	110	130
Official	–6	29	50	98	92	143	16	52	26	39
Private	–23	12	34	249	346	294	240	125	92	83
Commercial banks	—	–12	–6	21	–1	2	20	3	–8	8
Errors and omissions	–23	–7	60	33	–23	–9	54	27	–20	32
Allocation of SDRs	—	3	3	3	—	—	—	—	—	—
IMF Trust Fund loan	8	—	11	—	—	—	—	—	—	—
Overall balance	–36	84	–61	–49	–24	88	28	13	—	–7
Memorandum items:										
Current account (in percent of GDP)	0.5	3.3	–10.9	–20.9	–20.4	–15.5	–12.9	–8.6	–4.6	–7.0
Kina per SDR (period average)	0.89	0.92	0.87	0.79	0.81	0.89	0.92	1.02	1.14	1.17

Sources: Data provided by the Papua New Guinea authorities; and Fund staff estimates.

Table 10. Papua New Guinea: Exports by Commodity, 1978–87

(Value in millions of SDRs, volume in thousands of metric tons, unit value in SDRs per metric ton)

	1978	1979	1980	1981	1982	1983	1984	1985	1986	1987
Copper										
Value	138.2	200.1	159.6	169.8	150.8	180.6	147.9	161.7	136.7	223.6
Volume	193.1	172.0	142.2	164.0	173.2	181.1	163.3	168.6	178.7	211.5
Unit value	715.6	1,163.5	1,122.4	1,035.4	870.7	997.2	906.1	959.3	764.7	1,056.8
Gold										
Value	117.0	177.3	198.2	201.0	211.1	225.3	200.0	314.0	351.4	360.0
Volume[1]	23.4	20.3	14.5	17.6	19.1	19.1	19.4	32.1	36.5	34.5
Unit value[1]	5,009.5	8,756.2	13,666.2	11,422.0	11,067.3	11,827.2	10,287.5	9,782.5	9,626.4	10,434.0
Coffee										
Value	120.9	136.0	136.1	93.6	95.5	106.2	120.8	115.7	182.6	110.3
Volume	45.8	49.6	51.0	47.1	41.1	52.5	49.4	40.6	53.2	64.3
Unit value	2,622.6	2,753.0	2,668.6	1,987.3	2,324.0	2,021.5	2,444.3	2,850.7	3,433.2	1,715.1
Cocoa										
Value	71.0	65.2	51.6	43.0	39.1	46.4	73.1	61.6	49.4	48.2
Volume	27.1	27.1	28.8	27.8	28.7	26.3	34.1	30.9	30.9	34.7
Unit value	2,619.9	2,388.2	1,876.4	1,547.0	1,361.7	1,764.6	2,145.7	1,992.3	1,598.9	1,389.1
Copra										
Value	25.9	47.4	28.2	24.6	15.8	26.9	53.6	32.9	8.8	13.0
Volume	97.1	105.3	91.7	101.9	74.4	78.7	93.5	103.5	91.9	85.5
Unit value	280.9	450.1	307.5	244.4	212.6	341.7	572.9	317.9	95.3	152.4
Coconut oil										
Value	14.0	25.4	17.0	15.8	14.9	22.5	43.1	23.3	9.1	12.3
Volume	27.6	34.4	33.6	34.8	37.6	36.2	40.7	41.4	40.7	40.1
Unit value	481.1	738.4	505.9	453.0	395.2	620.9	1,057.7	563.9	223.8	305.8
Fish (tuna)										
Value	12.1	27.3	28.3	25.2	1.7	0.3	0.6	5.0	—	—
Volume	45.8	27.3	33.1	29.8	2.7	0.5	0.9	11.7	—	—
Unit value	593.1	964.7	855.2	846.4	649.0	547.0	705.3	429.4	—	—
Palm oil										
Value	12.1	15.7	15.4	17.9	26.6	26.6	82.7	60.6	24.8	28.8
Volume	33.5	30.9	37.3	44.0	76.7	77.9	129.9	123.8	122.3	123.4
Unit value	441.6	455.0	402.1	407.0	346.7	341.8	636.5	489.3	202.7	233.3
Timber products										
Value	27.8	39.0	52.5	55.4	75.7	61.3	89.1	66.3	65.5	92.3
Silver										
Value	6.3	13.1	11.7	9.0	9.2	12.6	8.7	6.9	6.0	9.0
Other (value)	55.3	36.6	58.9	58.5	57.6	78.6	81.6	55.2	61.7	51.5
Total (value)	600.6	783.1	757.5	713.8	698.0	787.3	901.2	903.2	896.0	949.0

Source: Data provided by the Papua New Guinea authorities.
[1] Volume in thousands of kilograms; unit value per kilogram.

Table 11. Papua New Guinea: Imports by Commodity Group, 1978–86

(In millions of SDRs)

	1978	1979	1980	1981	1982	1983	1984	1985	1986
Food and live animals	104.2	118.2	152.5	171.9	170.3	152.2	167.8	150.8	152.5
Beverages and tobacco	7.0	7.9	10.0	10.6	10.3	9.4	11.1	9.4	7.4
Raw materials	1.6	1.8	2.4	4.5	4.4	5.6	6.7	6.3	6.4
Mineral fuels	92.0	104.4	135.1	199.0	179.4	188.8	169.5	151.4	88.3
Oils and fats	1.6	1.8	2.2	2.4	2.7	2.9	4.2	3.3	3.3
Chemicals	28.4	32.2	41.9	56.9	48.3	72.9	74.1	64.1	75.5
Manufactured goods	71.7	81.3	105.0	132.4	146.0	147.5	151.1	132.6	137.9
Machinery and transport equipment	161.6	183.3	236.4	271.3	282.9	263.3	264.0	258.4	270.9
Miscellaneous manufactured articles	41.2	46.7	60.6	68.9	66.2	68.9	74.6	73.0	67.3
Other	25.7	28.8	37.8	12.9	12.5	10.5	12.9	10.7	11.5
Total	535.0	607.0	783.9	930.8	923.0	922.0	936.0	860.0	821.0

Sources: Data provided by the Papua New Guinea authorities; and Fund staff estimates.

Table 12. Papua New Guinea: External Debt and Debt Service, 1978–87

(In millions of SDRs)

	1978	1979	1980	1981	1982	1983	1984	1985	1986	1987
External debt (end of period)	423	380	467	791	1,159	1,669	1,918	1,895	1,656	1,456
Public sector	295	309	401	551	653	886	1,010	966	989	894
Bilateral	85	75	75	75	64	38	82	106	145	130
Multilateral	95	106	153	177	204	300	341	346	335	359
IMF	23	18	24	65	65	65	35	26	12	8
Commercial	114	128	173	255	340	547	587	514	508	406
Private sector	57	71	66	240	506	783	908	929	667	562
Debt service	105	79	75	130	196	263	366	368	294	224
Amortization	79	55	50	68	102	150	220	239	174	122
Interest	26	24	25	62	94	113	146	129	120	102
Memorandum items:										
External debt (in percent of GDP)	26.5	21.4	23.9	37.3	54.0	73.8	78.8	91.4	76.4	68.3
Debt service (in percent of current receipts)	12.2	7.5	7.2	11.5	17.1	22.2	28.4	29.9	21.3	19.8

Sources: Data provided by the Papua New Guinea authorities; and Fund staff estimates.

Table 13. Papua New Guinea: International Reserves, 1978–87

(In millions of SDRs; end of period)

	1978	1979	1980	1981	1982	1983	1984	1985	1986	1987
Official assets	285	356	358	366	331	431	456	414	403	393
Gold	7	8	12	14	13	12	12	10	10	9
SDRs	—	1	—	33	31	17	5	6	3	3
Reserve position in IMF	—	2	4	—	—	5	5	5	5	7
Foreign exchange	278	345	342	319	287	397	434	393	385	374
Official liabilities	16	11	6	50	45	65	35	27	13	9
Net official reserves	269	345	352	316	286	366	421	387	390	384
Memorandum items:										
Official assets (in months of imports)	6.6	8.0	7.1	5.6	4.3	5.6	5.9	5.3	5.6	6.0
Commercial banks' net foreign assets	–13	–1	5	–17	–15	–19	–39	–34	–25	–31
Kina per SDR (end of period)	0.90	0.91	0.82	0.79	0.83	0.92	0.92	1.11	1.18	1.25

Source: Data provided by the Papua New Guinea authorities.

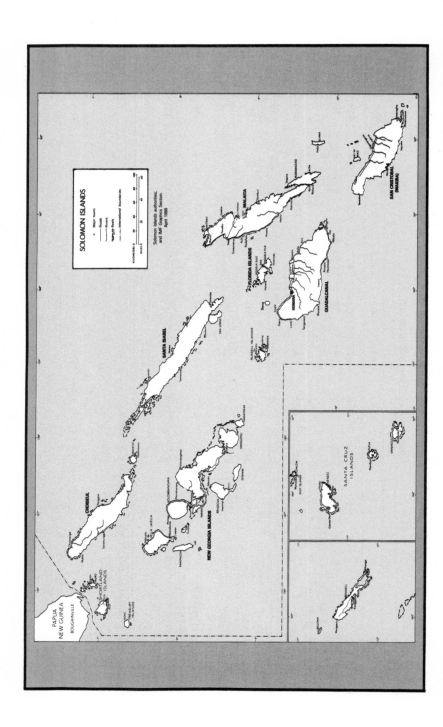

SOLOMON ISLANDS

Major towns
Roads
Rivers
Reefs
International boundaries

KILOMETRES 0 20 40 60 80 100
MILES 0   20   40   60

Solomon Islands authorities;
and IMF Graphics Section
April 1988

PAPUA
NEW GUINEA
BOUGAINVILLE

SHORTLAND
ISLANDS
TREASURY ISLANDS

CHOISEUL

SANTA ISABEL

NEW GEORGIA ISLANDS

RUSSELL ISLANDS

FLORIDA ISLANDS

MALAITA

GUADALCANAL
HONIARA

SAN CRISTOBAL
(MAKIRA)

SANTA CRUZ
ISLANDS

REEF ISLANDS

VANIKORO

5

Solomon Islands

Solomon Islands is a scattered archipelago with a land area of 28,000 square kilometers that stretches across 1,500 kilometers of the South Pacific Ocean. The six main islands, which range up to 200 kilometers in length and 50 kilometers in width, account for 80 percent of the total area. Most of the islands are characterized by precipitous mountain ranges covered with dense tropical forest and intersected by deep and narrow valleys. Rivers are generally narrow and unnavigable, and the coasts are surrounded by extensive coral reefs and lagoons. Rainfall is heavy, and cyclones periodically cause considerable damage to settlements and crops.

The population of 300,000 is increasing by more than 3 percent per year, one of the fastest rates in the region. About 93 percent of the residents are Melanesian and most of the remainder are other Pacific islanders. Nearly all live in small and widely dispersed rural settlements along the coasts; the national capital, Honiara, accounts for about 10 percent of the total population and is the only urban center. Since a large proportion of the country is too rugged to support more than a small population, the overall density is relatively low. Although the area suitable for mechanized agriculture is limited, the shortage of arable land is not a serious problem. Village life, the extended family system, and the custom of sharing income among relatives exercise a pervasive influence on economic activity. While there are several large agricultural plantations jointly owned by the Government and foreign investors, 87 percent of land is communally owned. Investment in agriculture is impeded by the land tenure system and unresolved claims over land.

Solomon Islands, which had been a British protectorate since 1893, became independent in 1978. A unicameral legislative assembly is popularly elected every four years. From among its 38 members, a Prime Minister is chosen who, in turn, appoints a Cabinet; the British sovereign is the Head of State. In the absence of strong party allegiances, the governments since independence have been essentially coalitions. Political consensus has been difficult to achieve and sustain, and this has hampered the cohesive and timely implementation of economic policies, including the ability to carry out longer-term planning and project formulation. Moreover, the authorities have begun devolving power to the provinces, a process that is proving to be slow and expensive.

Annual per capita GDP, which was SDR 380 in 1987, has grown more rapidly than in other Pacific island countries over the past two decades, albeit from a low base. Economic performance was highly favorable in the 1970s, when a large and diversified export sector grew with the assistance of considerable private investment. Experience was more in line with the regional norm during the 1980s, when economic policy was primarily focused on adjustment to a less favorable external environment. Although the expansion of the export sector lost momentum, balance of payments financing difficulties were generally avoided.

Economic Structure

Production and Prices

Primary production accounts for about 70 percent of GDP, including large-scale joint ventures with foreign enterprises for export-oriented production of copra, timber, fish, palm oil, and cocoa. Copra is the major source of income for smallholders. Producer prices of copra are set by the Commodity Export Marketing Board to mitigate the effects of fluctuations in export prices on growers' income and ensure the maintenance of production incentives, as well as the financial viability of the support operations. Industry is based on the processing of primary commodities, including a fish cannery and sawmills, but represents only 5 percent of GDP. Major elements of the services sector are the government administration; marine transportation, which is a vital communications link throughout the country; and the trading sector.

The economy is highly open and prices, which are essentially market determined, are strongly influenced by the cost of imported goods. Wages in the formal sector are determined through collective bargaining, generally on the basis of annual negotiations; disputes are subject to arbitration. Relatively large wage settlements in the public and private sectors reflect the scarcity of skilled labor and effective trade union representation. Wage awards generally have compensated for price increases associated with higher import prices, despite the loss of national income that occurs when the terms of trade deteriorate. There are indications that wage rigidities impeded adjustment and the creation of employment opportunities. Recently, government policy has encouraged agreements that limit general wage increases to a maximum of two thirds of the increase in consumer prices, but some groups have obtained considerably larger increases.

Balance of Payments

The foreign trade account is in approximate balance. Exports are equivalent to about 55 percent of GDP on average, the highest ratio among Pacific island countries, and are about the same magnitude as imports. Unprocessed primary products still represent a high proportion of exports. Among the main categories of imports, food and beverages represent only 20 percent of the total, reflecting plentiful local food supplies. The share of finished consumer goods is also relatively modest. By contrast, machinery and transport equipment, financed mainly with external aid, account for one third of the total, and petroleum products for about one fourth. The direction of the country's trade has shifted since independence away from the traditional links with the United Kingdom and Australia and toward Japan and other Asian regional markets.

There is a net deficit on services and transfers. The deficit on services is equivalent to about 25 percent of GDP. Services receipts are modest; tourist potential, in particular, remains to be exploited. Payments for services include freight, which represents about one fifth of the cost of imports; charter payments associated with the fishing industry; and dividends to foreign partners in joint ventures. Private transfers are small; inward remittances are limited primarily to church donations. Most concessional aid is received in the form of grants, which are equivalent to about 15 percent of GDP. Since the mid-1970s, aid dependence on the United Kingdom has been reduced and major donors now include Australia, Japan, New Zealand, and the European Community. In 1986 and 1987, Solomon Islands received substantial disbursements of grants from the Community, averaging about 8 percent of GDP, in connection with a shortfall in commodity export earnings.

The overall balance of payments normally registers a surplus. External commercial loans are mainly limited to private sector borrowing for export-oriented agricultural projects and a line of credit that the Government may draw on to ensure that gross reserves remain adequate. Although external debt is over 70 percent of GDP, it contains a large concessional element in the form of loans from multilateral financial institutions and the debt service ratio remains below 10 percent of current receipts. Gross official international reserves are normally equivalent to 5–6 months of imports of goods. The exchange rate is determined in relation to a basket of the currencies of Solomon Islands' four main trading partners and managed flexibly with adjustments geared primarily to underlying trends in export profitability. The Central Bank is authorized to change the rate by up to 2 percent per month with respect to the basket; larger variations need government approval.

Public Sector

The public sector consists of the central government, 8 provincial governments, and 17 public enterprises. There are no consolidated public sector accounts. Provincial activities, including public works, education, health, and economic services, are financed mainly through transfers from the central government, reflecting the commitment to the constitutional mandate for devolution. The tax on wages and salaries, business license fees, rents from public housing, and charges for public services are the main provincial sources of revenue, which finance about one third of local current expenditure. The public enterprises provide basic social and economic services, including electricity generation, telecommunication services, port services, and housing. Their investment programs are financed primarily from budgetary transfers.

The central government budget is prepared on a calendar year basis. The revenue estimates tend to be based on conservative assumptions about the outlook for the domestic economy and external transactions. Current expenditure projections in recent years have made only modest allowance for wage and other cost increases. Expenditure overruns and programs adopted outside the regular budget cycle have sometimes required the submission of supplementary budgets. On the other hand, appropriations in the capital budget have usually been in excess of the amounts actually utilized. Noncash development grants, which are excluded from the budget, are difficult to monitor.

Domestic budgetary revenue was equivalent to about 23 percent of GDP during 1981–87. The main sources of revenue are import and export duties, which account for more than half of the total, and income taxes on corporations and individuals. Indirect taxes are small, and nontax revenue is limited to property income, central bank profits, and fees and charges. External cash grants recorded in the budget averaged about 5 percent of GDP. Cash budgetary support from the United Kingdom, which financed about half of current expenditure in the 1970s, was terminated in 1980 in accordance with the agreement negotiated at independence. Grant receipts were sharply higher in 1986–87 owing to the large inflow of STABEX funds.

Total budgetary expenditure was equivalent to about 35 percent of GDP during 1981–87, with current expenditure of about 25 percent of GDP. Development expenditure, which averaged about 10 percent of GDP while fluctuating considerably from year to year, was directed toward the improvement of infrastructure, the exploitation of natural resources, and the expansion of education and health services. External loans, chiefly on concessional terms, financed about three fourths of the overall budget deficits, which averaged 7 percent of GDP. Nonbank domestic sources met most of the remaining financing needs.

Financial Sector

The banking system comprises the Central Bank of Solomon Islands, which was established in 1983, and four commercial banks. The Central Bank succeeded the Solomon Islands Monetary Authority (SIMA), which had been created in 1976 as an initial step in establishing a national monetary policy. The SIMA enjoyed most central banking powers, including the sole right of currency issue, control and supervision of banks and other financial institutions, and management of the government accounts and foreign exchange reserves. The policy instruments available to the monetary authority to influence credit developments included reserve and liquidity requirements, limits on its own lending to commercial banks, and the ability to influence the switching of the deposits of various public institutions from the commercial banks. The Solomon Islands dollar was introduced in October 1977 to replace the Australian currency, which had traditionally circulated as domestic currency and was withdrawn during a one-year conversion period. The four commercial banks, which are all branches or subsidiaries of foreign banks, are the principal institutions for mobilizing financial savings. In order to encourage the spread of banking facilities to the rural population and to promote domestic lending, the Government in 1980 acquired a 49 percent share holding in one of the existing banks.

There are three other financial institutions. The National Provident Fund, which was created in 1976, mobilizes compulsory savings and provides social security benefits for all persons in paid employment. Rates of contribution are 5 percent of earnings for employees and 7.5 percent of earnings for employers; most of its surpluses are invested in government securities. The Government Shareholding Agency, which was established in 1977, acquires equity in major commercial undertakings, including plantations, fishing, sea and air transport, and hotels, using resources that come primarily from the budget. The agency was converted into the Investment Corporation of the Solomon Islands in 1988, with broader powers to borrow in domestic and external capital markets. The Development Bank, which opened in 1978, promotes economic development and concentrates its lending in rural areas, processing, and industrial activities.

Developments in the 1970s

Economic performance in the 1970s was impressive. Real GDP increased by 7–8 percent annually, reflecting the expansion of export production and high public and private investment. Growth was achieved with reasonable price stability. At the beginning of the decade, timber emerged as an important export, and fishing was transformed from a subsistence occupation to a major commercial activity following the establishment of a joint venture between a Japanese company and the Government. During the second half of the decade, the palm oil industry was established as another joint venture and grew rapidly. Large-scale rice production was also undertaken with the assistance of foreign capital and technology in order to replace imports. However, the venture was eventually abandoned owing to insufficient profitability.

The strong expansion of exports and sustained nonmonetary capital inflows, mostly on account of foreign direct investment, permitted vigorous growth in imports, and also contributed to persistent overall balance of payments surpluses. The foreign trade balance improved and the larger net deficit on services, reflecting rising freight and dividends, was more than offset by higher official grants. The external current account recorded surpluses averaging 6 percent of GDP during 1976–79. Gross official reserves rose steadily, which was welcomed by the authorities as a contributory factor to postindependence confidence and as a safeguard against the economy's vulnerability to fluctuations in export earnings and external aid. Reflecting the strength of the external position and hoping to mitigate the effects of rising import costs on domestic prices, the Government appreciated the exchange rate by 5 percent against the Australian dollar in early 1979, breaking the fixed parity that had existed since the introduction of domestic currency.

The central government budget remained in approximate balance during the latter part of the decade. Revenue from export and import duties was buoyant because of the expansion of international trade, and income tax receipts also rose sharply. Prior to independence, the United Kingdom helped to finance a substantial rise in current expenditure, including the high administrative costs associated with the country's political evolution. After independence, external grants grew strongly, as a wide range of donors helped to finance an expansion of public investment. Solomon Islands emphasized the need to ease the development constraints arising from the difficult terrain, seeking to improve roads and interisland shipping and communications. The Government also played a key role in inducing and coordinating major investments in the private sector, especially through equity participation.

After independence, monetary policy was guided primarily by the concern to prevent monetary conditions from restraining growth, while preserving financial stability. The external surplus was the principal factor allowing annual additions to the domestic money stock. This source injected considerable liquidity, particularly during the second half of the decade. The Government took few steps to use instruments of credit control that could moderate this expansionary influence; reserve requirements were not introduced when the central monetary authority acquired the foreign assets of the commercial banks in 1978. The local currency received by the banks in return for these funds added greatly to their liquidity. However, in view of the Government's small financing needs and limited private sector demand, the authorities considered it unlikely that external pressures would emerge if bank lending decisions were allowed to determine the pace of domestic credit expansion.

Developments in the 1980s

Solomon Islands achieved only modest output growth during 1980–87, despite the continued development of marine and forestry resources and a rising investment rate. Less favorable world economic conditions had a greater impact on Solomon Islands than other Pacific island countries, because of the size of its export sector and the damage to tree crops caused by a severe cyclone in 1986. The rate of real GDP growth averaged only about 2 percent during 1980–87, and real national income fell after adjustment for the decline in the terms of trade. In response to the deterioration in the balance of payments, the Government adjusted financial and structural policies to mobilize public sector resources, contain private sector credit demand, limit imports, and increase the profitability of the export sector. The programs were supported by two stand-by arrangements with the Fund in the early 1980s. Financial stability was restored in 1983–84. Although subsequent shocks, including low export prices and the cyclone, hampered efforts to strengthen economic growth, an upsurge in external grants provided temporary relief to the balance of payments and the budget in 1986–87.

External Imbalances During 1980–83

During 1980–81, the terms of trade declined sharply and the external current account deficit reached 18 percent of GDP. Export prices of copra, timber, and palm oil fell dramatically, and the increase in petroleum prices further worsened the trade balance. The deficit on services rose because of higher freight payments, and external grants fell following the agreed-upon reduction in British financial assistance after independence. In addition, uncertainty about economic growth and external stability triggered a surge in private capital outflows. External borrowing and a drawdown in official reserves financed the overall balance of payments deficit.

Central government finances deteriorated because of adverse external developments, including lower grants, and strong public pressure for increased expenditure, which followed the transfer of functions from the colonial to national authorities. The overall budget deficit widened to 7 percent of GDP in 1981. To accommodate the borrowing needs of the Government, initial issues were made of five-year development bonds and treasury bills that were taken up by the commercial banks and the National Provident Fund. Following a pronounced growth in domestic credit, reserve requirements were imposed on commercial banks for the first time in 1981 at 5 percent of deposit liabilities.

The Government felt that additional measures were needed to strengthen the external position. An economic program was developed in 1981 that aimed at expanding exports, restraining less essential imports, mobilizing public sector domestic resources, and sustaining investment in order to restore growth with external stability. The measures included action to increase government revenue, including a 20 percent rise in non-oil import duties; efforts to contain current expenditure, including wages and salaries; the use of external commercial borrowing to expand investment; and a currency depreciation of 6 percent.

The circumstances and adjustments that were necessary to secure the required improvement in the external accounts and to restore public confidence in the economy were not forthcoming. A modest recovery in export production failed to offset the decline in export prices. The value of the Solomon Islands dollar did not depreciate because of the rise in domestic inflation. Strong growth in current expenditure reflected pressures for an increased range of services after independence and increased wages. Despite substantial cuts in public investment that were made in order to limit the budget deficit, government credit from the domestic banking system rose rapidly.

In the face of a continued fall in the terms of trade, the value of the Solomon Islands dollar was depreciated further by 10 percent on a trade-weighted basis in mid-1982. To strengthen the fiscal position, the Government increased import duties and improved tax administration. While capital outflows were halted and the overall balance of payments reverted to surplus, the external current account recorded a deficit of 7 percent of GDP in 1982. The fiscal position did not improve because lower economic activity held down revenue, and inadequate expenditure controls thwarted attempts to contain current spending. The overall budget deficit was held at 7 percent of GDP only because of limited investment capacity, despite the plentiful availability of external concessional assistance.

Although the fiscal and external positions were weak, Solomon Islands redirected policies in early 1983 to promote economic recovery through private investment in the export sector, supported by increased public expenditure on infrastructure. It introduced measures for public resource mobilization and current expenditure restraint, and raised bank deposit rates to encourage private savings. The Government introduced a liquid assets requirement of 15 percent of deposit liabilities to replace the 5 percent reserve requirement. The value of the Solomon Islands dollar was further depreciated on a trade-weighted basis to help shift resources toward the traded goods sector.

Export Recovery in Late 1983 and 1984

External economic conditions turned strongly and unexpectedly in favor of Solomon Islands after mid-1983. International prices of copra and palm oil began to rise because of shortfalls in other producing countries, and warm ocean temperatures led to an increase in the fish catch. With expansionary financial policies, imports rose considerably and the current account deficit was 9 percent of GDP in 1983. However, the Government achieved the objectives of reduced inflation and renewed real economic growth. In this situation, the further rise in the overall budget deficit to 8 percent of GDP was permitted, although its financing required considerable recourse to the domestic banking system.

The balance of payments strengthened as a result of the one-third improvement in the terms of trade during 1984, mainly because of the continued rise in export prices. With higher export volume, the trade balance became positive. Despite an increased deficit on services owing to higher profit remittances, the external current account recorded a surplus of 3 percent of GDP. The stronger external position enabled commercial debt to be reduced, while official international reserves increased. The depreciation of the Solomon Islands dollar was discontinued.

The overall budget deficit fell markedly to 3 percent of GDP in 1984, principally because of cutbacks in current expenditure. Monetary policy continued to be guided by the traditional aim of avoiding constraints on real growth. Consequently, little attempt was made to offset the strong monetary growth that emanated from the higher export earnings. Although government borrowing was small, private sector demand led to rapid domestic credit expansion. Given the acceleration in the rate of inflation, the Government adopted a more restrictive monetary stance from late 1984. To tighten commercial bank liquidity, the copra board was required to transfer resources from the commercial banks to the Central Bank and a rise in the liquid assets ratio to 25 percent of deposit liabilities was announced. However, while nominal bank interest rates increased during the year, most deposit rates and some lending rates became negative in real terms.

Domestic Financial Strains in 1985–87

The rate of growth of real GDP slowed in 1985 and became negative in 1986 mainly as a result of adverse developments in the export sector. In 1985, export prices fell steeply, with the increase in world supply of vegetable oils contributing to a one-third decline in the terms of trade. Imports remained high because of strong domestic demand. The external current account deficit rose to 12 percent of GDP, and the overall balance of payments moved into deficit. In mid-1986, a cyclone caused heavy loss of life and extensive damage to export crops of copra, palm oil, and cocoa, as well as to economic and social infrastructure. Imports declined, despite the boost from reconstruction needs, because of lower incomes and reduced petroleum prices. Additional aid was received, including the early disbursements of large compensatory grants for export shortfalls from the European Community. The external current account deficit was reduced to 9 percent of GDP, and the overall balance of payments reverted to surplus.

Real GDP and exports fell again in 1987 because of the continued depressive effect of the cyclone and temporary factors that curtailed fish and timber exports. Following the earlier downturn in export prices, exchange rate flexibility had been reintroduced. The depreciation of the Solomon Islands dollar on a trade-weighted basis, by about 30 percent in real effective terms between mid-1985 and end-1987, helped to contain the deterioration in the external position and mitigate the impact on export profitability of low commodity prices. The continued high level of grants, including additional receipts from the European Community equivalent to almost one fifth of exports of goods and services, cushioned the balance of payments. The external current account deficit was reduced to 3 percent of GDP and, with external commercial borrowing to help finance investment, the overall balance of payments remained in surplus.

Despite the rise in external grants, fiscal imbalances increased during 1985–87. The overall budget deficit widened to 9 percent of GDP in 1985, when there was a pronounced rise in current expenditure, because of wage increases, transfers to local government to promote decentralization, and subsidies to public enterprises. The deficit remained high in 1986. Although revenue increased as a result of higher rates of import duties, the fall in export incomes depressed collections of income tax. The Government provided relief to the fishing industry in the form of lower export taxes and reduced rates of import duties on imported fuel and other materials. Capital expenditure rose by three fourths as a result of spending on fishing vessels, road building, airport expansion, and cyclone reconstruction. The budget deficit increased again to 12 percent of GDP in 1987, despite considerable revenue growth and a further rise in external grants. Wage payments and transfers to public enterprises exceeded budget estimates. Capital expenditure, partly financed from abroad, continued to surge largely because of investments in fishing vessels and a cannery.

The main aim of monetary policy was to reduce the pressure on domestic prices and the underlying balance of payments, while providing adequate credit for development. With the large decline in net foreign assets, the rate of growth of broad money was small in 1985. However, the growth of domestic credit was high because of the Government's financing needs and private sector demand. In 1986, the availability of external finance enabled the Government to repay domestic bank borrowing and limit the increase in domestic credit; the rate of growth of broad money remained moderate. In 1987, the growth of broad money accelerated because of the rise in net foreign assets stemming from the grant inflows. While the Government continued to repay the banking system, private sector credit demand strengthened. In view of the acceleration in inflation, the liquidity ratio was increased to 27.5 percent of deposit liabilities and the Central Bank closed the facility through which banks had automatic access to central bank funding. Tighter monetary conditions were designed to help strengthen the balance of payments, when external grants declined from the unusually high levels of 1986–87.

Table 1. Solomon Islands: Gross Domestic Product by Sectoral Origin, 1980–87

(In millions of Solomon Island dollars at 1984 prices)

	1980	1981	1982	1983	1984	1985	1986	1987
Agriculture	65.4	72.2	72.6	73.1	81.0	82.2	71.3	69.3
Monetary	37.4	43.4	43.1	42.6	49.6	49.8	38.3	35.7
Nonmonetary	28.0	28.8	29.5	30.5	31.4	32.4	33.0	33.6
Forestry and sawmilling	12.0	12.3	13.7	14.0	13.9	13.5	15.6	11.3
Fishing	9.3	9.6	9.1	12.7	12.9	11.2	15.3	13.3
Gold mining	0.2	0.3	0.2	0.3	0.5	0.5	0.7	0.4
Manufacturing	7.1	6.4	6.6	6.6	6.0	6.8	7.1	7.1
Electricity and water	1.3	1.4	1.5	1.6	1.7	1.9	2.0	2.1
Construction	7.8	10.0	7.0	8.1	7.4	9.6	10.5	9.6
Monetary	5.6	7.7	4.6	5.7	4.9	7.0	7.4	6.5
Nonmonetary	2.2	2.3	2.4	2.4	2.5	2.6	3.1	3.1
Wholesale and retail trade	17.2	18.5	19.1	17.6	21.1	22.1	21.5	21.4
Transport and communications	8.4	8.7	8.7	9.3	10.3	10.9	10.7	11.0
Finance and services	36.7	37.4	37.9	40.3	41.3	44.9	47.9	48.6
GDP at factor cost	165.4	176.9	176.4	183.6	196.2	203.5	202.5	193.1
Memorandum items:								
GDP at current market prices (in millions of Solomon Island dollars)	109.7	128.0	143.7	162.3	221.0	234.1	247.2	283.0
Change in real GDP (in percent)	-5.5	7.0	-0.3	4.1	6.8	3.8	-0.5	-4.6

Sources: Data provided by the Solomon Islands authorities; and Fund staff estimates.

Table 2. Solomon Islands: Output of Main Commodities, 1975–87

(In thousands of metric tons)

	1975	1976	1977	1978	1979	1980	1981	1982	1983	1984	1985	1986	1987
Fish	7.5	15.5	12.1	17.5	23.9	22.9	25.5	20.6	34.7	35.9	31.1	44.2	31.8
Copra	26.5	23.8	29.2	27.5	33.6	29.2	33.7	32.2	28.4	42.6	41.9	31.1	27.1
Smallholders	14.0	13.4	18.1	17.7	23.2	20.4	23.7	22.5	19.5	31.8	32.2	22.1	18.8
Plantations	12.5	10.4	11.1	9.8	10.4	8.8	10.0	9.7	8.9	10.8	9.7	9.0	8.3
Timber[1]	228.6	264.1	259.0	274.2	298.8	298.8	364.5	388.3	394.8	422.9	378.0	431.5	321.0
Palm oil	...	7.0	10.9	13.0	14.2	18.1	19.2	19.7	19.7	19.7	20.0	14.6	12.0
Cocoa	0.2	0.1	0.2	0.2	0.3	0.3	0.6	0.7	1.2	1.7	1.7	2.0	2.7
Rice	1.2	3.8	6.3	7.7	10.2	14.3	13.9	10.5	9.5	7.1	5.7	2.4	0.2

Source: Data provided by the Solomon Islands authorities.

[1]In thousands of cubic meters.

Table 3. Solomon Islands: Consumer Price Index, 1980–87

(Annual average percentage change)

	Weights[1]	1980	1981	1982	1983	1984	1985	1986	1987
Food	51.0	15.0	19.6	12.9	6.5	15.0	6.4	11.4	7.9
Beverages and tobacco	10.0	11.5	21.2	16.1	2.1	9.3	8.8	37.9	30.0
Clothing and footwear	4.9	4.3	6.8	11.8	8.0	9.0	17.9	5.4	5.8
Transport	6.6	13.3	18.8	14.3	9.0	10.7	13.9	22.6	11.5
Housing	12.5	9.4	9.1	12.7	6.7	0.3	3.4	8.4	3.0
Miscellaneous	15.0	9.5	9.3	10.7	8.8	10.1	23.3	8.3	11.1
Overall index	100.0	12.6	16.4	13.0	6.2	11.0	9.5	13.5	11.1
				(End-of-period percentage change)					
Memorandum item:									
Overall index	100.0	15.9	14.6	9.7	5.8	12.3	8.6	17.2	6.3

Source: Data provided by the Solomon Islands authorities.
[1] Honiara retail price index, fourth quarter 1984 = 100. Data for 1980–84 are based on the index, fourth quarter 1977 = 100.

Table 4. Solomon Islands: Central Government Budget, 1975–87

(In millions of Solomon Islands dollars)

	1975	1976	1977	1978	1979	1980	1981	1982	1983	1984	1985	1986	1987
Revenue and grants	13.0	16.8	19.5	27.2	32.3	36.9	37.2	39.3	40.4	52.4	54.3	86.1	99.6
Tax revenue	5.5	6.3	8.5	10.8	16.6	18.4	24.7	29.3	28.9	43.7	47.5	52.1	63.6
Nontax revenue	1.3	2.0	2.6	2.8	4.3	5.0	5.2	4.5	5.5	4.0	4.7	5.0	5.8
External grants	6.2	8.5	8.4	13.6	11.4	13.5	7.3	5.5	6.0	4.7	2.1	29.0	30.2
Total expenditure	13.0	16.8	20.4	27.4	35.3	40.5	46.5	49.7	53.8	58.9	75.1	98.2	133.7
Current expenditure	9.5	10.9	14.1	16.7	20.1	24.4	30.9	34.5	39.2	46.1	57.6	66.5	77.1
Capital expenditure and net lending	3.5	5.9	6.3	10.7	15.2	16.1	15.6	15.2	14.6	12.8	17.5	31.7	56.6
Overall balance	—	—	-0.9	-0.2	-3.0	-3.6	-9.3	-10.4	-13.4	-6.5	-20.8	-12.1	-34.1
Financing (net)	—	—	0.9	0.2	3.0	3.6	9.3	10.4	13.4	6.5	20.8	12.1	34.1
External	0.2	—	0.2	0.6	2.4	3.1	3.3	5.4	7.7	4.6	6.8	18.3	35.1
Domestic	-0.2	—	0.7	-0.4	0.6	0.5	6.0	5.0	5.7	1.9	14.0	-6.2	-1.0
								(In percent of GDP)					
Memorandum items:													
Revenue and grants	29.1	31.7	29.6	35.7	31.4	33.6	29.1	27.4	24.9	23.7	23.2	33.4	35.2
Tax revenue	12.3	11.9	12.9	14.2	16.2	16.8	19.3	20.4	17.8	19.8	20.3	21.1	22.5
Nontax revenue	2.9	3.8	3.9	3.7	4.2	4.6	4.1	3.1	3.4	1.8	2.0	2.0	2.0
External grants	13.9	16.0	12.8	17.8	11.1	12.3	5.7	3.8	3.7	2.1	0.9	10.3	10.7
Total expenditure	29.1	31.7	31.0	35.9	34.4	36.9	36.3	34.6	33.1	26.7	32.1	39.7	47.2
Current expenditure	21.2	20.6	21.4	21.9	19.6	22.2	24.1	24.0	24.1	20.9	24.6	26.9	27.2
Capital expenditure	7.8	11.1	9.6	14.0	14.8	14.7	12.2	10.6	9.0	5.8	7.5	12.8	20.0
Overall deficit													
Including grants	—	—	-1.4	-0.2	-2.9	-3.3	-7.3	-7.2	-8.3	-2.9	-8.9	-6.4	-12.0
Excluding grants	-13.9	-16.0	-14.1	-18.0	-14.0	-15.6	-13.0	-11.1	-12.0	-5.1	-9.8	-16.6	-22.7

Sources: Data provided by the Solomon Islands authorities; and Fund staff estimates.

Table 5. Solomon Islands: Central Government Revenue, 1980–87

(In millions of Solomon Islands dollars)

	1980	1981	1982	1983	1984	1985	1986	1987
Tax revenue	18.4	24.7	29.3	28.9	43.7	47.5	52.1	63.6
Income and profits	7.4	9.6	10.8	10.6	14.2	17.1	17.7	22.7
Companies	4.3	4.9	4.2	4.6	5.8	6.8	5.7	5.8
Individuals	3.1	4.7	6.6	6.0	8.4	10.3	12.0	16.9
Goods and services	0.9	1.2	1.3	1.2	1.1	2.1	1.7	1.8
Excise duties	0.2	0.3	0.2	0.3	0.2	0.4	0.4	0.4
Business licenses and other[1]	0.7	0.9	1.1	0.9	0.9	1.7	1.3	1.4
International transactions	10.1	13.9	17.2	17.1	28.4	28.3	32.7	39.2
Import duties	5.6	9.3	13.1	12.5	17.3	20.3	25.8	31.4
Export duties[2]	4.4	4.5	4.1	4.6	11.1	7.9	6.9	7.8
Nontax revenue	5.0	5.2	4.5	5.5	4.1	4.7	5.0	5.8
Property income	2.8	3.1	1.9	3.4	1.7	0.9	2.7	3.7
Fees and charges	1.6	1.9	1.8	1.9	1.7	2.5	2.0	2.0
Sale of fixed assets	0.5	0.1	0.2	0.2	0.4	0.7	—	—
Other[3]	0.1	0.1	0.6	—	0.2	0.6	0.3	0.1
Total	23.4	29.9	33.8	34.4	47.7	52.2	57.1	69.4

Source: Data provided by the Solomon Islands authorities.

[1] Including stamp duties.

[2] Including receipts from the levy on log exports earmarked for reforestation.

[3] Including surpluses of departmental enterprises and financial public enterprises.

Table 6. Solomon Islands: Central Government Expenditure by Economic Classification, 1980–87

(In millions of Solomon Islands dollars)

	1980	1981	1982	1983	1984	1985	1986	1987
Current expenditure	24.4	30.9	34.5	39.2	46.1	57.6	66.5	77.1
Expenditure on goods and services	18.4	22.1	24.5	28.1	32.7	36.3	43.4	49.9
Wages and salaries	10.8	13.1	15.6	18.0	21.4	26.0	30.8	34.9
Other purchases	7.6	9.0	8.9	10.1	11.3	10.3	12.6	15.0
Interest payments	0.2	0.6	0.8	1.0	2.1	3.3	4.3	7.5
Subsidies and current transfers	5.8	8.1	9.2	10.1	11.3	18.0	18.8	19.7
Subsidies to public enterprises	1.7	2.3	2.5	2.8	3.0	3.7	5.9	5.8
Transfers to local governments	2.8	4.2	5.3	5.5	6.9	9.4	8.4	8.0
Transfers to households	0.8	1.2	1.0	1.4	0.6	3.4	3.3	4.4
Transfers abroad	0.4	0.3	0.4	0.4	0.8	1.5	1.1	1.5
Capital expenditure	11.8	11.0	12.0	10.7	10.1	17.1	30.4	48.6
Acquisition of fixed capital assets	10.5	9.8	10.2	9.4	9.2	16.2	29.6	47.2
Capital transfers	1.3	1.2	1.8	1.3	0.9	0.9	0.7	1.4
Nonfinancial public enterprises	0.5	0.5	0.7	0.7	0.5	0.9	0.5	1.4
Net lending	4.3	4.6	3.2	3.9	2.7	0.4	1.3	8.0
To local governments	0.5	0.4	-0.4	0.4	0.5	—	—	—
To nonfinancial public enterprises	1.2	1.3	1.2	0.8	0.7	—	1.4	7.8
To financial institutions	3.5	3.0	2.4	2.3	0.2	0.4	-0.1	0.2
Other	-0.9	—	—	0.4	1.3	—	—	—
Total	40.5	46.5	49.7	53.8	58.9	75.1	98.2	133.7

Source: Data provided by the Solomon Islands authorities.

Table 7. Solomon Islands: Monetary Survey, 1980–87

(In millions of Solomon Islands dollars; end of period)

	1980	1981	1982	1983	1984	1985	1986	1987
Net foreign assets	23.3	12.6	19.3	26.8	41.5	24.7	40.8	65.2
Domestic credit	19.2	27.2	29.2	25.4	38.5	62.3	63.4	73.1
Government, net	-3.3	-1.0	3.7	-0.9	2.3	12.7	9.6	6.5
Private sector[1]	19.6	25.3	22.0	20.9	35.1	48.5	52.0	58.1
Other financial institutions	2.8	2.9	3.5	5.4	1.1	1.1	1.8	8.5
Other items (net)	-3.5	-7.6	-8.7	-4.3	-15.4	-20.6	-31.5	-40.7
Broad money	39.0	32.2	39.8	47.9	64.6	66.3	72.7	97.6
Money supply	15.2	14.2	15.8	18.4	28.3	28.3	30.4	37.2
Quasi-money	23.9	18.0	24.0	29.5	36.3	38.0	42.3	60.4
				(Annual percentage change)				
Memorandum items:								
Domestic credit	14.5	41.7	7.2	-13.0	51.6	61.8	1.8	15.3
Private credit	16.2	29.4	-13.0	-5.0	67.9	38.1	7.2	11.7
Broad money	-8.7	-17.5	23.5	20.4	34.9	2.6	9.7	34.3

Source: Data provided by the Solomon Islands authorities.
[1] Including nonfinancial public enterprises.

Table 8. Solomon Islands: Interest Rate Structure, 1980–87

(In percent per annum; end of period)

	1980	1981	1982	1983	1984	1985	1986	1987
Commercial bank deposit rates								
90-day deposits	5.25–6.0	6.25–6.75	7.0	8.5	7.5	10.0	11.0	10.5
12-month deposits	...	7.25	8.25	9.25	8.0	11.75	12.5	11.0
Commercial bank lending rates								
Minimum overdraft rate	9.5	9.0	11.0	12.0	12.0	12.5	16.0	15.0
Average lending rates	...	...	12.5–13.0	12.9–13.8	13.5–14.5	15.9	16.0–19.6	16.0–19.6
Treasury bills	...	7.0	7.0	9.0	9.0	10.0	12.0	11.0
Development bonds	...	10.0	11.0	11.0	11.0	12.0	13.0	13.0

Source: Data provided by the Solomon Islands authorities.

Table 9. Solomon Islands: Balance of Payments, 1975–87

(In millions of SDRs)

	1975	1976	1977	1978	1979	1980	1981	1982	1983	1984	1985	1986	1987
Trade balance	-10.8	-1.2	3.6	-0.3	7.8	-0.2	-8.3	-0.8	0.5	25.3	0.8	-0.8	-2.6
Exports	12.7	21.1	28.1	28.0	53.0	56.7	56.1	52.8	58.0	89.4	69.1	56.2	49.6
Imports, f.o.b.	-23.5	-22.3	-24.5	-28.3	-45.2	-56.9	-64.4	-53.6	-57.5	-64.1	-68.3	-57.0	-52.1
Services, net	-7.7	-8.6	-9.8	-12.4	-15.2	-24.0	-24.3	-14.9	-23.4	-32.5	-29.8	-35.9	-35.4
Receipts	2.0	2.6	2.8	4.2	4.5	9.0	11.0	16.5	15.6	17.2	17.4	18.0	20.4
Payments	-9.7	-11.2	-12.6	-16.6	-19.7	-33.0	-35.3	-31.4	-39.0	-49.7	-47.2	-53.9	-55.8
Freight and insurance	-4.7	-4.4	-4.9	-5.7	-8.9	-11.4	-12.9	-10.7	-11.5	-12.8	-13.7	-11.7	-11.9
Other	-5.0	-6.8	-7.7	-10.9	-10.7	-21.6	-22.4	-20.7	-27.5	-36.9	-33.5	-42.2	-43.9
Private transfers, net	1.5	1.5	1.4	1.6	1.8	0.6	-4.9	-4.1	-2.4	-1.7	-1.3	2.1	2.3
Official transfers	6.6	9.8	9.7	13.7	13.6	14.7	14.8	10.7	13.9	14.2	11.6	23.6	32.2
Current account	-10.4	1.5	4.9	2.6	8.0	-8.9	-22.7	-9.1	-11.4	5.3	-18.7	-11.0	-3.5
Nonmonetary capital, net	6.5	4.2	3.8	3.7	4.5	2.4	5.7	11.7	5.9	7.4	7.7	9.9	11.3
Official	—	—	—	—	1.8	3.1	3.3	4.7	2.5	4.2	5.6	4.8	5.0
Private	6.5	4.2	3.8	3.7	2.7	-0.7	2.4	7.0	3.4	3.2	2.1	5.1	6.3
Allocation of SDRs	—	—	—	—	0.2	0.2	0.2	—	—	—	—	—	—
Errors and omissions	5.0	-4.1	-2.8	5.9	-6.5	0.7	8.2	2.8	10.9	-5.0	-3.5	2.6	-2.2
Overall balance	1.1	1.6	5.9	12.2	6.1	-5.5	-8.6	5.4	5.4	7.7	-14.5	1.8	5.6
Memorandum items:													
Terms of trade (1980=100)	50.5	73.9	98.3	80.7	116.7	100.0	80.7	78.8	70.5	93.6	82.1	62.9	73.3
Export unit value	42.1	59.4	76.9	69.3	98.9	100.0	89.1	90.5	80.1	107.7	93.9	64.7	77.6
Import unit value	83.2	80.4	78.2	85.8	84.8	100.0	110.4	114.9	113.1	115.1	114.4	102.8	105.9
Current account (in percent of GDP)													
Including grants	-21.6	2.7	7.8	3.7	8.7	-8.7	-18.2	-6.9	-8.6	3.1	-12.0	-9.1	-3.1
Excluding grants	-35.2	-14.7	-7.6	-15.8	-6.1	-23.2	-30.0	-14.9	-19.1	-5.3	-19.4	-28.6	-32.6
Solomon Islands dollars per SDR (period average)	0.93	0.94	1.05	1.09	1.12	1.08	1.02	1.07	1.23	1.30	1.50	2.03	2.59

Sources: Data provided by the Solomon Islands authorities; and Fund staff estimates.

Table 10. Solomon Islands: Exports by Commodity, 1975–87

(Value in millions of SDRs, volume in thousands of metric tons, unit value in SDRs per metric ton)

	1975	1976	1977	1978	1979	1980	1981	1982	1983	1984	1985	1986	1987
Copra													
Value	5.0	3.8	7.6	9.3	15.1	9.7	7.8	7.5	6.8	24.6	15.6	2.9	4.0
Volume	27.5	23.0	26.9	32.1	34.4	31.7	31.8	33.9	25.5	42.0	43.6	32.4	17.9
Unit value	183	167	282	291	440	307	247	222	267	587	359	89	142
Palm oil													
Value	—	1.2	2.7	4.3	5.9	6.2	6.9	6.4	6.3	11.7	8.3	2.7	2.7
Volume	—	3.5	6.2	10.3	12.8	15.6	16.9	18.6	20.0	21.5	18.6	14.5	11.6
Unit value	—	346	440	412	461	394	409	343	318	545	444	189	231
Fish, fresh and frozen													
Value	1.4	6.3	6.1	4.6	13.0	18.3	18.6	9.2	19.8	19.2	18.4	23.0	16.6
Volume	3.6	12.1	9.8	10.3	23.4	21.6	23.7	15.3	30.8	33.2	27.2	39.6	26.5
Unit value	376	522	616	441	556	848	783	604	645	578	678	580	627
Fish, canned													
Value	1.3	1.3	1.4	1.4	1.7	2.4	2.5	2.7	2.9	2.4	2.4	2.3	2.7
Volume	0.9	0.7	0.7	0.7	0.8	0.8	0.8	0.9	1.1	0.7	0.9	1.0	1.2
Unit value	1,438	1,886	2,155	2,170	2,239	3,167	3,335	2,914	2,544	3,186	2,661	2,350	2,250
Logs													
Value	3.3	6.4	7.3	6.3	13.2	13.8	14.4	19.9	15.3	22.0	15.8	16.6	13.6
Volume[1]	208	241	238	246	258	258	315	333	337	392	330	433	262
Unit value[2]	16	27	31	25	51	53	46	60	45	56	48	38	52
Sawn timber													
Value	0.1	0.2	0.2	0.3	1.0	1.0	1.3	1.4	1.0	1.0	0.7	0.9	0.8
Volume[1]	1.0	2.0	2.0	3.0	9.0	7.0	7.0	7.0	7.0	7.0	3.7	5.8	3.4
Unit value[2]	113	116	95	98	116	143	187	195	138	144	180	152	239
Cocoa													
Value	0.1	0.2	0.5	0.5	0.6	0.6	0.9	0.8	1.8	2.6	3.3	3.2	3.7
Volume	0.2	0.1	0.2	0.2	0.3	0.3	0.6	0.6	1.2	1.4	1.8	2.0	2.9
Unit value	755	1,703	3,203	2,270	2,025	1,616	1,492	1,340	1,489	1,840	1,848	1,591	1,266
Other (value)	1.8	1.7	2.3	1.3	2.5	4.7	3.7	4.8	4.0	5.9	4.6	4.6	5.5
Total (value)	12.7	21.1	28.1	28.0	53.0	56.7	56.1	52.8	58.0	89.4	69.1	56.2	49.6

Source: Data provided by the Solomon Islands authorities.
[1] In thousands of cubic meters.
[2] In SDRs per cubic meters.

Table 11. Solomon Islands: Imports by Commodity Group, 1975–87

(In millions of SDRs)

	1975	1976	1977	1978	1979	1980	1981	1982	1983	1984	1985	1986	1987
Food and live animals	3.4	3.7	3.9	4.6	5.7	6.1	6.8	7.9	6.7	10.1	10.4	8.8	7.8
Beverages and tobacco	0.9	1.1	1.2	1.3	1.7	1.7	2.3	2.0	2.2	2.9	2.6	2.5	1.6
Raw materials	0.1	0.1	0.2	0.2	0.2	0.4	0.6	0.5	0.7	0.9	0.6	0.5	0.3
Mineral fuels	2.3	2.9	3.4	3.2	5.8	9.1	14.8	13.4	14.5	14.6	13.9	10.0	7.7
Oils and fats	0.3	0.2	0.3	0.2	0.5	0.4	0.3	0.5	0.6	0.6	1.2	0.5	0.3
Chemicals	1.9	1.7	1.9	2.5	2.9	2.9	3.7	3.5	3.4	3.9	4.1	3.0	3.5
Manufactured goods	5.5	4.1	4.3	5.3	7.9	9.4	11.8	8.5	10.3	10.4	10.8	9.9	10.7
Machinery and transport equipment	7.0	6.6	6.6	7.8	16.9	22.3	18.8	12.3	15.0	15.4	18.0	16.2	15.2
Miscellaneous manufactured articles	1.9	1.8	2.4	2.8	3.3	4.4	4.9	4.7	3.9	5.2	6.5	5.1	4.8
Other	0.2	0.2	0.3	0.3	0.2	0.2	0.3	0.3	0.2	0.2	0.2	0.5	0.2
Total	23.5	22.3	24.5	28.3	45.2	56.9	64.4	53.6	57.5	64.1	68.3	57.0	52.2

Source: Data provided by the Solomon Islands authorities.

Table 12. Solomon Islands: External Debt and Debt Service, 1980–87

(In millions of SDRs)

	1980	1981	1982	1983	1984	1985	1986	1987
External debt								
(end of period)	21.4	25.3	37.1	61.7	60.0	74.5	74.1	80.8
Public sector	5.9	12.5	23.2	42.2	35.7	48.0	46.9	55.1
Use of Fund credit	—	0.8	2.4	3.4	3.2	2.8	2.8	1.6
Eurocurrency loan	—	4.3	9.1	19.1	10.2	13.7	4.1	—
Private sector	15.5	12.8	13.9	19.5	24.3	26.5	27.2	25.7
Debt service	3.5	2.9	5.0	6.0	7.6	6.8	5.8	7.2
Amortization	2.7	1.4	1.9	1.6	2.1	3.5	1.7	4.0
Public sector	—	—	—	0.2	0.3	1.6	0.2	0.4
Private sector	2.7	1.4	1.9	1.3	1.9	1.9	1.5	3.6
Interest	0.8	1.5	3.1	4.4	5.5	3.3	4.1	3.2
Public sector	—	0.8	2.3	2.4	3.6	1.8	2.3	1.3
Private sector	0.8	0.7	0.8	2.0	1.9	1.5	1.8	1.9
Memorandum items:								
External debt								
(in percent of GDP)	24.0	23.1	27.7	46.6	35.5	47.8	61.2	73.9
Public sector	6.6	11.4	17.3	31.9	21.1	30.8	38.7	50.4
Private sector	17.4	11.7	10.4	14.7	14.4	17.0	22.5	23.5
Debt service (in percent of exports								
of goods and services)	5.3	4.3	7.2	8.1	7.1	7.9	7.9	6.5[1]
Public debt service	—	1.2	3.3	3.7	3.5	3.9	3.4	2.4
Private debt service	5.3	3.1	3.9	4.4	3.6	4.0	4.5	4.1[1]

Sources: Data provided by the Solomon Islands authorities; and Fund staff estimates.
[1]Excluding repayments associated with a conversion of private debt to equity (SDR 2.7 million).

Table 13. Solomon Islands: International Reserves, 1980–87

(In millions of SDRs; end of period)

	1980	1981	1982	1983	1984	1985	1986	1987
Official assets	22.6	18.6	33.7	43.0	44.7	32.6	24.3	25.9
Central Bank	19.7	18.2	33.4	42.9	44.6	32.2	24.0	25.8
Government[1]	2.9	0.4	0.3	0.1	0.1	0.4	0.2	0.1
Official liabilities	—	4.9	15.0	21.3	15.2	17.5	7.0	2.9
Eurocurrency loan	—	4.1	11.6	16.3	10.2	13.7	4.1	—
Use of Fund credit	—	0.8	2.4	3.4	3.2	2.8	2.8	1.6
Other	—	—	1.0	1.6	1.8	1.0	0.1	0.9
Net official reserves	22.6	13.7	18.7	21.8	29.5	15.1	17.2	23.0
Net commercial bank reserves[2]	0.6	0.2	−0.3	1.0	0.9	0.8	0.5	0.3
Net total reserves	23.2	13.8	18.4	22.8	30.4	15.9	17.7	23.3
Memorandum items:								
Official assets (in months of imports)	4.8	3.4	7.5	9.0	8.4	5.7	5.1	6.0
Solomon Islands dollars per SDR (end of period)	1.02	1.03	1.15	1.28	1.32	1.77	2.43	2.80

Source: Data provided by the Solomon Islands authorities.
[1] Comprises only deposits with the Crown Agents.
[2] Excludes nonresident deposits and capital account of head offices abroad.

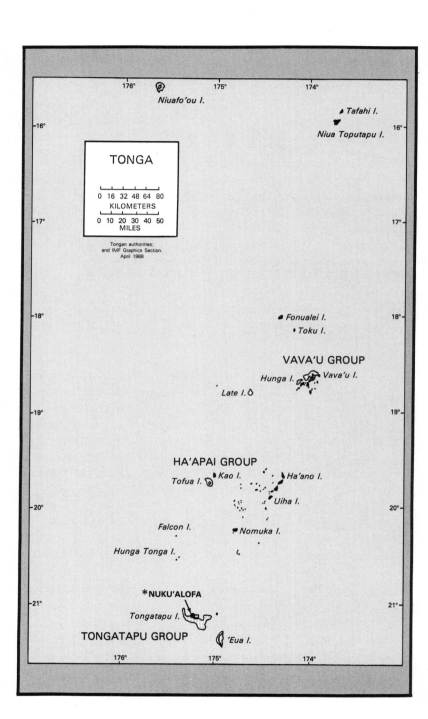

176°   175°   174°

Niuafo'ou I.

●Tafahi I.

-16°   16°-

Niua Toputapu I.

TONGA

0 16 32 48 64 80
KILOMETERS

0 10 20 30 40 50
MILES

Tongan authorities;
and IMF Graphics Section.
April 1988

-17°   17°-

-18°   ● Fonualei I.   18°-

● Toku I.

VAVA'U GROUP

Hunga I.   Vava'u I.

Late I. ◇

-19°   19°-

HA'APAI GROUP

Tofua I.   ● Kao I.   ● Ha'ano I.

● Uiha I.

-20°   20°-

Falcon I.   ● Nomuka I.

Hunga Tonga I.

*NUKU'ALOFA

-21°   21°-

Tongatapu I.

TONGATAPU GROUP   'Eua I.

176°   175°   174°

6

Tonga

The Kingdom of Tonga consists of 172 volcanic and coral islands, of which 36 are inhabited, with a total land area of 750 square kilometers. Most of the land is fertile and subject to intensive cultivation; the islands are vulnerable to cyclones. Almost one fourth of the inhabitants live in the capital, Nuku'alofa. The population, which is almost entirely of Polynesian origin, has declined in recent years to 95,000, despite a high birth rate, because of large-scale emigration. Among other Pacific island countries, only Western Samoa has experienced a comparable degree of emigration. At present, at least 30,000 Tongans live abroad, mainly in Australia, New Zealand, and the United States, and send substantial remittances to relatives at home. The family-oriented and closely knit traditional nature of Tongan society, with its inherent sharing of income, alleviates poverty and social problems associated with the lack of employment opportunities. Life expectancy is 64 years and health and education indicators are in line with or above the regional average. Annual per capita GDP is about SDR 650.

The Kingdom, which was unified during the second half of the nineteenth century, remained relatively isolated until becoming a British protectorate in 1900. The United Kingdom managed external relations, but its involvement in domestic affairs was limited. Although not formally independent until 1970, Tonga maintained a greater degree of independence than most Pacific territories while under foreign rule. The Legislative Assembly, which is elected every three years, consists of 9 nobles chosen from among the 33 peers who are the traditional owners of most land; 9 elected representatives; and 12 Ministers of the Crown. While the constitutional monarchy is based on the British model, the King exercises wide influence and other members of the royal family hold key positions in the Government.

All land is ultimately owned by the Crown, although in practice ownership is divided among the nobles, several chiefs, and the Government. In exchange for annual payments in cash or goods, every male adult is entitled to the allocation of several acres of land for his family use, which may be transferred to male offspring and certain other relatives but cannot be sold. Leasing has been permitted under certain conditions since 1976, partly because resources are no longer adequate to permit allocations to all eligible males. However, the small size of holdings and relatively short period of leases allowed by legislation discourage investment in land improvement.

Economic Structure

Production and Prices

Agriculture dominates the economy, accounting for about 40 percent of GDP; virtually all production originates on small-scale landholdings. Production has become more diversified in recent years. Partial rehabilitation of banana cultivation, assisted by external aid, and the development of vanilla beans, mainly for export, has allowed Tonga to reduce its dependence on coconuts. Root crops, fruits, and vegetables are produced primarily for the domestic market. Tonga has achieved self-sufficiency with respect to pork and poultry. The small manufacturing sector, which accounts for 9 percent of GDP, includes coconut oil and desiccated coconut plants and businesses located in the industrial processing zone near the capital. Fiscal and other incentives are provided for new businesses; equal treatment is accorded to foreign-owned concerns. A large part of GDP is generated in the services sector, reflecting the importance of government expenditure. Development of tourism has been inhibited by limited airline service and a shortage of accommodations.

Imported goods have a weight of 60 percent in the consumer price index and changes in the cost of imports from New Zealand, which is the source of most consumer goods, is the major determinant of the rate of inflation. Given the fixed link between the value of the Tongan pa'anga and the Australian dollar and the volatility of the exchange rate between the Australian and New Zealand dollars, the rate of price increase in Tonga fluctuates markedly. Public sector wage rates are adjusted periodically to compensate for price changes. These rates constitute an effective ceiling for the private sector, where a high degree of flexibility in wage determination has helped to create jobs. However, although no figures are available, unemployment and shortages of skilled labor are matters of concern.

Balance of Payments

Large foreign trade deficits characterize the balance of payments. Exports are equivalent to only 10 percent of GDP, consisting of a small range of goods because of the narrow productive base. Primary products represent about three fourths of the total, mainly coconut products, bananas, and vanilla. Industrial goods account for the other fourth and include knitwear and other labor-intensive goods. Imports are equivalent to almost 60 percent of GDP, reflecting the open nature of the economy. Food and other consumer goods constitute about one half of these imports, with items generally purchased from the proceeds of remittances. Imports of machinery, transport equipment, and industrial materials, which average about one third of the total, are closely tied to disbursements of external assistance. The share of petroleum products is about 10 percent of total imports.

The surplus on services and transfers customarily exceeds the trade deficit, so that the external current account is in surplus. The main sources of service receipts are tourism and shipping, the latter a result of the lease of a vessel to the Pacific Forum Line, which operates cargo services with Australia and New Zealand. These receipts are substantially offset by freight payments, which constitute about 18 percent of the average landed cost of imported goods. Dependence on private and official transfers has increased steadily over the past 20 years. Remittances are equivalent to about 30 percent of GDP. External grant assistance, mainly from Australia, the European Community, Japan, and New Zealand, is equivalent to 20 percent of GDP.

Capital inflows are primarily in the form of official loans obtained on highly concessional terms. Among bilateral donors, the Federal Republic of Germany has traditionally provided assistance in this form and such aid is also received from multilateral donors. Official external commercial borrowing is usually avoided and private capital flows are negligible. Consequently, external debt service is below 4 percent of current receipts. Gross official international reserves are normally equivalent to about five months of imports. The Government considers that a relatively high level of reserves is desirable in view of the fluctuations that characterize export receipts, the country's dependence on private and official transfers, and its distance from major commercial centers and transportation routes.

Public Sector

The public sector comprises the central government, which is organized through eight ministries, the island councils, and about 25 nonfinancial enterprises, many of which are relatively small departmental undertakings. The Treasury Department in the Ministry of Finance oversees the formulation of the central government budget, which comprises the current revenue and expenditure estimates and the development estimates. The fiscal year is July 1–June 30, with the budget normally approved by the Legislative Assembly in late June. Most public enterprises operate profitably, including the Electric Power Board, which generates and distributes electricity, and the Telecommunications Commission, which is responsible for domestic telegraph and telephone services. Budgetary support is required only for the domestic airline and occasionally for the Commodities Board, which purchases the main crops, conducts the price stabilization scheme, operates the coconut processing plants, and exports most agricultural goods. Consolidated public sector accounts are not available; financial data are not published on local government activities.

Fiscal policy is the most important instrument of economic policy. Over the years, the overall budget, including external grants, has been maintained in approximate balance, in order to protect the external position. Total receipts have averaged about 46 percent of GDP over the past five years. Tax revenue has been equivalent to about 19 percent of GDP, with foreign trade taxes representing four fifths of the total, and personal and corporate income tax most of the remainder. Receipts from taxes on goods and services were small until the introduction in fiscal year 1986/87 of a 5 percent retail sales tax, with exemptions limited to a small number of food items. Nontax revenue has been equivalent to about 8 percent of GDP, including the surpluses of departmental enterprises. External grants, which fluctuate widely from year to year, have been equivalent to about 19 percent of GDP.

Current expenditure has averaged about 26 percent of GDP over the past five years. About one third of this has been attributable to public administration, reflecting the role of the Government as a major employer. Personnel costs include pensions for retired civil servants equivalent to two thirds of their final salary, which are financed out of current revenue. Social and community services, focused on education and health to relieve the shortages of skilled labor and to improve living conditions, have accounted for another one third of expenditure.

Economic services have represented the final one third, mainly to support production in agriculture and industry. Development expenditure has been equivalent to about 20 percent of GDP. In keeping with the objective of improving infrastructure, spending is channeled into hurricane protection, marine projects including ports and fishing harbors, airports, and interisland telecommunications.

Financial Sector

The financial sector consists of the Bank of Tonga, a commercial bank that is owned jointly by the Government (40 percent) and three foreign commercial banks (20 percent each), and the Tonga Development ment Bank, a long-term lending institution that is owned jointly by the Government (90 percent) and the Bank of Tonga (10 percent). Legislation to establish the country's first central bank was approved by parliament in late 1988. At present, monetary authority functions are shared between the Ministry of Finance; the Board of Currency Commissioners and the Board of Coinage Commissioners, which are responsible for the issuance of notes and coins respectively; and the Bank of Tonga. Offshore banking legislation was enacted in 1984, but the amount of business is small. There is no national pension fund scheme, although a contribution plan for public employees is under consideration.

The Bank of Tonga was established in 1974 to offer a full range of commercial banking services and to undertake certain central banking functions that were assigned by the Government. The latter include holding the government accounts, managing most of the country's foreign exchange reserves, acting as the sole agent of the Government for administering the foreign exchange control legislation, and establishing its own liquidity and reserve ratios. The Development Bank was established in 1977 with a mandate to encourage economic and social advancement, mainly through the identification and promotion of new projects, the extension of loans to the private sector and public enterprises, and equity participation. Its activities are financed primarily by external concessional assistance.

Developments in the 1970s

At the time of independence, the economic structure of Tonga was barely developed; the monetized sector consisted mainly of coconut and banana production and relatively small government operations, financed in part by British assistance. During the 1970s, in the context of a pronounced widening of contacts with the rest of the world and greater external aid, the foundations for development were laid through the diversification of the economy and the expansion of the public investment program. The balance of payments was sound, and overall surpluses were normally achieved. The larger external trade deficit, which resulted from a combination of stagnant exports and increased imports, was more than offset by higher tourist receipts, emigrants' remittances, and external aid. Official international reserves rose to the equivalent of six months of imports.

The rate of real GDP growth averaged 3–4 percent annually. Despite the priority given to agriculture because of its importance in exports and employment, the growth in output was modest. Attempts to rehabilitate the coconut sector fell short of expectations because of the uncertain profitability of replanting. The banana sector declined in the face of disease, shipping problems, and poor fruit quality. Although the Government offered fiscal incentives, the range of manufacturing activity remained small. The narrow productive base constrained the growth of budgetary revenue, but fiscal balance was preserved. The growth of current expenditure was restricted to less than the rise in GDP, while capital expenditure was financed solely with external aid.

Developments in the 1980s

Tonga's economic performance in the 1980s has been satisfactory, with real GDP growth averaging 3 percent annually. A cyclone in 1982 caused loss of life and damaged coconut and banana trees and buildings on the main island. Although agricultural production was depressed for a time, the adverse impact on growth was eased by the expansion in construction activity associated with the repair of cyclone damage, financed by official external aid and private insurance receipts. Agriculture subsequently recovered, partly because of the favorable response of copra production to increased domestic prices, and lent impetus to increased activity in the industrial and services sectors. During fiscal year 1987/88, real GDP declined by about 2 percent. Agricultural output was depressed by drought. Copra procurement was reduced sharply, interrupting production at the coconut processing plants, with adverse implications for overall industrial output.

While the expansion of domestic demand has not been excessive in recent years, the economy has experienced several periods of high rates of inflation. The availability of domestic supplies has had some influence on price developments, particularly in periods of food short-ages, but the fluctuations have been mainly attributable to changes in the cost of imports from New Zealand. In periods when the pa'anga has depreciated against the New Zealand dollar, the rate of price increase has accelerated in Tonga. Although Tonga's retail trade is open to competition, the small size of the market and customary links make it difficult for new entrants to challenge the position of market leaders. In these circumstances, the benefits that may be achieved by diversifying the sources of imported supplies cannot be realized quickly.

Conservative guidelines were observed in the formulation of fiscal policy during the early 1980s. In order to maintain the ratio of domestic revenue to GDP, the Government increased import duties on several occasions, notably on tobacco, liquor, and petroleum products; raised postal service rates; and strengthened customs administration. By contrast, the growth in income tax revenue was sluggish, mainly because of concessions granted to encourage productive activities and personal savings. These measures included a lower corporate profit tax rate for export-oriented industries, higher personal income tax deduc-tions, and education allowances. Current expenditure was stable in relation to GDP. Ministries were broadly successful in remaining within the approved budgets for most categories of spending. The main public enterprises did not require budgetary subsidies. Their capital expenditure was mostly financed through the central government bud-get with concessional external assistance. Increased central govern-ment development outlays were financed essentially with concessional assistance. The Government acquired a sizable net creditor position with the domestic banking system.

The central government budget moved into deficit during the mid-1980s, mainly because of rapid expenditure growth, but a surplus was recorded in fiscal year 1987/88, primarily because of expenditure restraint. Receipts remained stable in relation to GDP, despite a reduction in direct taxation aimed at promoting savings and invest-ment. The maximum rate of income tax was reduced from 40 percent to 10 percent for individuals and 20–25 percent for most companies. To compensate for the revenue loss, a broadly based retail sales tax was introduced. Between fiscal years 1984/85 and 1986/87, current expenditure rose steadily in relation to GDP because demands for supplementary allocations were reportedly approved in most spending categories. Subsidies were paid to the Commodities Board to help maintain copra procurement prices in the face of declining world prices and to the domestic airline. Development expenditure was unusually high in fiscal year 1984/85, when an aircraft was purchased for the domestic airline and in fiscal year 1986/87, when telecommunications equipment was obtained. In each of these years, the overall deficit reached 4 percent of GDP. For the latter project, Tonga undertook external commercial borrowing, which represented a break from the past. This enabled the Government to retain its net creditor position with the domestic banking system. In fiscal year 1987/88, a budget surplus of 2 percent of GDP was achieved, mainly as a result of restraint in current spending, and lower investment. In recognition of the importance of limiting extrabudgetary spending, legislation was introduced setting a ceiling on such spending of 5 percent of appropriations.

Monetary growth has been closely linked with balance of payments developments and the Government has seen little need to counteract the impact of external factors. Target rates of monetary expansion have not been established; the evolution of official international reserves has been taken as the indicator pointing to the appropriateness of monetary policy. After the 1982 cyclone, the Ministry of Finance issued guidelines requiring the Bank of Tonga to limit lending when foreign exchange reserves declined to below the equivalent of four months' imports and to completely cease new lending if reserves declined to below three months of imports. In view of the strength of the external position and the moderate demand for credit, these guidelines were only operational for a short period. The Bank of Tonga has not otherwise been subject to liquidity requirements or controls over its lending operations. For many years, most of its funds have been invested abroad, owing to the limited opportunities for domestic lending.

Interest rates have not been employed as a tool of economic management. Bank lending rates have been subject to a 10 percent ceiling that was established in legislation passed 50 years ago. Bank deposit rates have been commensurately low, with savings and time deposit rates set between 5 and 6.5 percent since 1981. With unchanged nominal rates, bank deposit and lending rates in real terms have varied considerably and often been negative. In these circumstances, narrow money has continued to account for over 40 percent of total liquidity. The absence of any pronounced shift to savings and time deposits, even though alternative financial savings instruments were not available, has primarily reflected the low interest rates paid on these deposits. The differential with rates in Australia and New Zealand, that has existed for the past several years, has further discouraged domestic lending.

The balance of payments has been financed in recent years without difficulty. The external current account recorded surpluses averaging about 5 percent of GDP between fiscal years 1982/83 and 1986/87, although a deficit was recorded in fiscal year 1987/88, partly because the drought reduced exports and stimulated imports. Export performance has generally been disappointing, with little growth in output of traditional agricultural products. Among the limited range of manufactured exports, persistent growth has been registered only for knitwear, which has benefited from the special access to the Australian and New Zealand markets available to Pacific island producers. However, buoyant remittances and official grant assistance have financed a large and increasing share of imports. Official capital movements have normally registered a small inflow, reflecting concessional loan assistance. The exchange value of the pa'anga depreciated between 1985 and 1987 against the SDR, as a result of its link with the Australian dollar. In contrast to the experience of neighboring countries, the real effective exchange rate did not depreciate because of the high rate of inflation in Tonga stemming from the cost of imports from New Zealand. In fiscal year 1987/88, the exchange rate of the pa'anga appreciated in line with the appreciation of the Australian dollar. Despite the deterioration in the current account, the overall external payments position was in approximate balance and official international reserves were maintained at about five months of imports.

Table 1. Tonga: Gross Domestic Product by Sectoral Origin, Fiscal Years 1982/83–1987/88[1]

(In millions of pa'anga at 1981/82 prices)

	1982/83	1983/84	1984/85	1985/86	1986/87	1987/88
Agriculture	21.8	22.2	24.2	25.0	25.9	23.1
Mining and quarrying	0.4	0.4	0.4	0.4	0.4	0.4
Manufacturing	4.8	5.0	5.3	6.1	6.3	6.6
Electricity and water	0.4	0.4	0.5	0.6	0.6	0.6
Construction	3.5	4.1	4.4	3.3	3.4	3.7
Wholesale and retail trade	5.7	5.7	6.3	6.7	6.9	7.2
Transport and communications	3.5	3.3	3.4	3.5	3.6	3.7
Finance and real estate	2.4	2.1	2.6	2.6	2.7	2.8
Community and social services	9.9	10.7	10.8	11.6	12.0	12.6
GDP at factor cost	52.4	53.9	57.9	59.8	61.9	60.7
Indirect taxes less subsidies	9.0	8.9	8.5	8.7	9.0	8.7
GDP at market prices	61.4	62.8	66.4	68.5	70.9	69.4
Monetary	45.6	47.3	50.0	51.9	53.7	52.6
Nonmonetary	15.8	15.5	16.4	16.6	17.2	16.8
Memorandum items:						
Change in real GDP (in percent)	1.2	2.4	5.6	3.0	3.5	–2.0
GDP at current market prices (in millions of pa'anga)	66.9	74.5	80.0	98.9	110.1	119.8

Sources: Data provided by the Tongan authorities; and Fund staff estimates.
[1]Fiscal year July 1–June 30.

Table 2. Tonga: Consumer Price Index, Fiscal Years 1982/83–1987/88[1]

(Annual average percentage change)

	Weights	1982/83	1983/84	1984/85	1985/86	1986/87	1987/88
Food	55.1	9.2	8.9	-5.8	37.7	6.0	14.4
Beverages and tobacco	8.5	6.8	24.5	5.6	22.4	5.5	14.3
Clothing and footwear	6.2	7.5	19.5	12.2	23.7	16.5	-1.1
Housing operations	3.8	10.7	7.9	7.6	21.8	15.1	1.1
Household items	12.4	8.4	3.5	9.0	26.7	3.4	6.1
Transport	6.1	2.6	6.2	13.1	12.0	5.6	-5.7
Miscellaneous	8.0	5.5	10.9	24.2	31.1	18.0	19.4
Overall index	100.0	8.0	9.4	1.7	31.2	7.5	11.2
			(End-of-period percentage change)				
Memorandum item:							
Overall index	100.0	3.9	4.3	11.4	28.1	2.2	15.3

Source: Data provided by the Tongan authorities.
[1]Base period first quarter 1976=100.

Table 3. Tonga: Central Government Budget, Fiscal Years 1982/83–1987/88
(In millions of pa'anga)

	1982/83	1983/84	1984/85	1985/86	1986/87	1987/88
Revenue and grants	30.9	33.9	38.0	42.1	50.8	56.1
Tax revenue	12.0	12.4	15.8	18.6	21.1	24.8
Nontax revenue	5.8	5.2	6.2	7.8	8.4	11.1
External grants	13.1	16.2	15.9	15.8	21.3	20.2
Expenditure and net lending	30.4	33.0	41.3	42.9	55.1	54.0
Current expenditure	15.8	16.7	19.9	25.6	29.7	32.3
Development expenditure	14.2	15.4	20.4	17.1	24.9	20.3
Net lending	0.4	0.9	1.1	0.2	0.5	1.3
Overall balance	0.5	0.8	-3.3	-0.8	-4.3	2.1
Financing (net)	-0.5	-0.8	3.3	0.8	4.3	-2.1
External	0.2	0.7	1.4	0.1	7.0	1.0
Domestic banking system	-0.5	-1.8	1.7	0.7	-3.3	-3.1
Other domestic	-0.2	0.3	0.2	—	0.6	—
			(In percent of GDP)			
Memorandum items:						
Revenue and grants	46.2	45.5	47.5	42.6	46.2	46.8
Tax revenue	17.9	16.7	19.8	18.8	19.2	20.7
Nontax revenue	8.7	7.0	7.8	7.9	7.7	9.3
External grants	19.6	21.8	19.9	15.9	19.3	16.9
Total expenditure	45.4	44.3	51.7	43.4	50.0	45.0
Current expenditure	23.6	22.5	24.8	25.9	27.0	27.0
Development expenditure	21.2	20.7	25.5	17.3	22.6	17.0
Net lending	0.6	1.2	1.3	0.2	0.4	1.1
Overall balance	0.8	1.1	-4.2	-0.9	-3.9	1.8

Sources: Data provided by the Tongan authorities; and Fund staff estimates.

Table 4. Tonga: Central Government Revenue, Fiscal Years 1982/83–1987/88

(In millions of pa'anga)

	1982/83	1983/84	1984/85	1985/86	1986/87	1987/88
Tax revenue	12.0	12.4	15.8	18.6	21.1	24.8
Income and poll tax	2.4	2.4	2.4	2.8	2.7	3.6
Goods and services	0.3	0.3	0.4	0.4	2.6	3.0
Sales tax	0.1	0.1	0.1	0.2	2.3	2.8
License fees	0.2	0.2	0.2	0.2	0.3	0.2
International transactions	9.3	9.7	13.0	15.3	15.7	18.0
Import duties	4.9	5.1	6.4	6.9	7.6	9.0
Wharfage on goods	0.4	0.4	0.5	0.5	0.6	0.6
Ports and services tax	4.0	4.1	6.1	7.8	7.5	8.4
Airport tax	0.1	0.1	0.1	0.1	0.1	0.1
Nontax revenue	5.8	5.2	6.2	7.8	8.4	11.1
Government services[1]	4.6	3.9	4.3	5.6	5.3	5.8
Rents and investment income	0.9	0.9	1.5	1.8	2.3	3.4
Other[2]	0.3	0.4	0.4	0.4	0.8	1.9
Total	17.8	17.6	22.0	26.3	29.5	35.9

Sources: Data provided by the Tongan authorities; and Fund staff estimates.

[1]Excludes gross income from the post office.

[2]Includes net income from the post office and transfers from duty-free shops.

Table 5. Tonga: Central Government Current Expenditure, Fiscal Years 1982/83–1987/88

(In millions of pa'anga)

	1982/83	1983/84	1984/85	1985/86	1986/87	1987/88
Public administration	5.1	6.0	7.0	9.2	12.2	12.3
General administration	2.9	3.6	4.3	5.9	8.2	8.1
Fiscal administration	0.5	0.6	0.5	0.7	0.9	1.1
Law and order	1.7	1.8	2.2	2.6	3.0	3.1
Social and community services	5.0	5.3	6.1	7.6	8.5	9.8
Education	2.3	2.4	2.9	3.7	4.2	5.2
Health	2.2	2.3	2.6	3.2	3.3	3.6
Pensions and gratuities	0.4	0.4	0.4	0.5	0.6	0.7
Other	0.1	0.2	0.2	0.3	0.3	0.3
Economic services	5.5	5.0	6.0	7.1	7.4	7.7
Agriculture, forestry, and fishing	1.5	1.5	1.7	2.0	2.1	2.3
Tourism	0.2	0.2	0.2	0.2	0.2	0.3
Transport and works	3.2	2.8	3.9	4.7	5.0	5.1
Communications[1]	0.6	0.6	0.2	0.2	0.1	0.1
Other[2]	0.2	0.4	0.8	1.6	1.7	2.5
Total	15.8	16.7	19.9	25.6	29.7	32.3

Sources: Data provided by the Tongan authorities; and Fund staff estimates.

[1] Excludes post office expenditures.

[2] Includes STABEX transfers to the Commodities Board; excludes amortization on public debt and appropriations for the development budget and sinking funds.

Table 6. Tonga: Monetary Survey, Fiscal Years 1982/83–1987/88

(In millions of pa'anga; end of period)

	1982/83	1983/84	1984/85	1985/86	1986/87	1987/88
Net foreign assets	15.2	21.6	25.1	25.2	36.9	34.7
Domestic credit	7.8	6.4	8.9	13.0	12.1	17.7
Government (net)[1]	−2.2	−4.0	−2.3	−1.6	−4.9	−8.0
Private sector[2]	10.0	10.4	11.2	14.6	17.0	25.7
Other items (net)[3]	6.9	8.6	9.9	11.2	13.0	17.2
Total liquidity	16.1	19.4	24.1	27.0	36.0	35.2
Currency	2.5	2.8	2.9	4.2	4.4	5.6
Demand deposits	4.1	6.2	7.3	7.1	9.9	9.9
Savings deposits	4.7	5.0	7.1	8.2	10.5	11.3
Time deposits	4.8	5.4	6.8	7.5	11.3	8.5
			(Annual percentage change)			
Memorandum items:						
Private credit	20.2	3.9	7.7	30.2	16.2	51.3
Total liquidity	2.5	21.0	23.9	12.1	33.6	−2.2

Sources: Data provided by the Tongan authorities; and Fund staff estimates.

[1] Includes aircraft loan to the Government.
[2] Includes public enterprises.
[3] Includes bills payable.

Table 7. Tonga: Interest Rate Structure, Fiscal Years 1982/83–1987/88

(In percent per annum; end of period)

	1982/83	1983/84	1984/85	1985/86	1986/87	1987/88
Bank of Tonga deposits						
Savings deposits[1]	5.00	5.00	5.00	5.00	5.00	5.00
Time deposits[2]						
3 months	5.25	5.25	5.25	5.25	5.25	5.25
6 months	5.50	5.50	5.50	5.50	5.50	5.50
12 months	5.75	5.75	5.75	5.75	5.75	5.75
24 months	6.00	6.00	6.00	6.00	6.00	6.00
36 months	6.50	6.50	6.50	6.50	6.50	6.50
Bank of Tonga loans						
Housing						
Residence	7.50	7.50	7.50	8.50	8.50	8.50
Investment property	10.00	10.00	10.00	10.00	10.00	10.00
Personal[3]	8.50–10.00	8.50–10.00	8.50–10.00	10.00	10.00	10.00
Commercial	8.50–10.00	8.50–10.00	8.50–10.00	10.00	10.00	10.00
Investment	10.00	10.00	10.00	10.00	10.00	10.00
Tonga Development Bank loans						
Agriculture	6.00	6.00	6.00	6.00	8.00	8.00
Export industries	8.00	8.00	8.00	8.00	8.00	8.00
Other	10.00	10.00	10.00	10.00	10.00	10.00

Source: Data provided by the Tongan authorities.
[1]The minimum balance to earn interest is T$15, and the maximum balance on which interest is payable is T$15,000 for personal accounts and T$50,000 for charitable organizations.
[2]For deposits under T$100,000; for deposits of T$100,000 and over, the interest rates are 6.0 percent for 3 months, 6.25 percent for 6 months, 6.5 percent for 12 months, 6.5 percent for 24 months, and 6.75 percent for 36 months.
[3]Including a loan fee of 0.5 percent.

Table 8. Tonga: Balance of Payments, Fiscal Years 1982/83–1987/88
(In millions of SDRs)

	1982/83	1983/84	1984/85	1985/86	1986/87	1987/88
Trade balance	–31.1	–27.3	–28.2	–30.1	–28.6	–33.9
Exports, f.o.b.[1]	3.5	7.2	8.8	5.3	5.5	4.3
Imports, f.o.b.[1]	–34.6	–34.5	–37.0	–35.4	–34.1	–38.2
Services, net	1.7	2.1	2.0	–0.4	2.6	2.6
Receipts	12.8	18.1	18.5	16.2	17.6	18.1
Payments	11.1	16.1	16.5	16.7	15.0	15.5
Private transfers, net	17.7	16.7	16.7	20.5	18.0	17.3
Receipts	21.7	19.8	18.9	22.8	20.5	19.7
Payments	4.0	3.1	2.2	2.3	2.6	2.4
Official transfers	13.9	14.0	12.5	10.2	11.4	11.0
Current account	2.3	5.5	3.0	0.1	3.4	–3.0
Official capital, net	0.3	0.7	0.9	–0.1	4.1	0.9
Receipts	0.5	1.0	1.4	0.4	4.4	1.9
Payments	0.2	0.3	0.6	0.5	0.4	1.0
Errors and omissions[2]	–3.4	–0.7	–5.2	–2.3	–1.1	2.2
Overall balance	–0.8	5.5	–1.3	–2.3	6.4	0.1
Memorandum items:						
Current account (in percent of GDP)	3.9	8.6	4.7	0.1	5.8	–4.5
Pa'anga per SDR (period average)	1.15	1.15	1.28	1.56	1.85	1.82

Sources: Data provided by the Tongan authorities; and Fund staff estimates.
[1]Including re-exports.
[2]Including the counterpart to valuation changes and net private capital flows.

Table 9. Tonga: Exports by Commodity, Fiscal Years 1982/83–1987/88

(Value in thousands of SDRs, volume in metric tons, unit value in SDRs per metric ton)

	1982/83	1983/84	1984/85	1985/86	1986/87	1987/88
Copra meal						
Value	8	74	67	43	44	2
Volume	58	709	355	1,321	1,671	68
Unit value	134	104	190	32	26	24
Coconut oil						
Value	405	2,835	4,131	1,338	1,000	718
Volume	1,096	3,281	4,262	4,253	4,108	2,001
Unit value	370	864	969	315	244	359
Desiccated coconut						
Value	170	506	531	378	373	252
Volume	232	532	463	575	875	400
Unit value	732	951	1,147	657	426	631
Bananas						
Value	188	423	589	666	995	431
Volume	845	1,558	2,381	3,149	4,974	1,852
Unit value	222	271	247	211	200	233
Vanilla beans						
Value	513	489	882	755	759	466
Volume	11	8	13	13	15	9
Unit value[1]	48	60	66	59	52	51
Root crops[2]						
Value	152	168	324	123	140	191
Watermelons						
Value	224	529	357	125	2	2
Fish						
Value	271	337	448	415	669	731
Other (value)[3]	1,592	1,859	1,501	1,417	1,568	1,466
Total (value)	3,523	7,219	8,830	5,258	5,550	4,259

Sources: Data provided by the Tongan authorities; and Fund staff estimates.
[1]Per kilo.
[2]Root crops comprise taro, yams, and cassava.
[3]Including re-exports.

Table 10. Tonga: Imports by Commodity Group, Fiscal Years 1982/83–1987/88

(In millions of SDRs)

	1982/83	1983/84	1984/85	1985/86	1986/87	1987/88
Food	7.2	7.3	8.4	7.8	7.8	10.3
Beverages and tobacco	1.9	1.7	2.2	2.0	2.0	1.8
Raw materials	2.3	2.0	1.9	1.8	2.0	1.6
Mineral fuels	4.8	4.5	3.9	3.9	3.3	3.4
Oils and fats	0.1	0.1	0.1	0.1	0.1	0.1
Chemicals	2.0	1.8	2.0	2.7	2.4	2.2
Manufactured goods	6.7	6.2	7.0	6.0	5.6	5.1
Machinery and transport equipment	6.7	7.6	8.5	7.4	7.2	9.9
Other	2.9	3.3	3.0	3.7	3.8	3.8
Total	34.6	34.5	37.0	35.4	34.1	38.2

Sources: Data provided by the Tongan authorities; and Fund staff estimates.

Table 11. Tonga: External Debt and Debt Service, Fiscal Years 1982/83–1987/88

(In millions of SDRs)

	1982/83	1983/84	1984/85	1985/86	1986/87	1987/88
External debt (end of period)	20.3	19.9	20.7	22.3	27.6	28.9
United Kingdom	4.2	3.1	2.8	2.7	2.4	3.1
Germany, Federal Republic of	10.1	9.7	9.3	11.2	12.6	11.4
Asian Development Bank	4.4	5.2	6.4	6.1	6.2	6.9
European Investment Bank	0.6	0.9	1.1	1.1	1.3	1.5
International Development Association	—	—	—	—	—	0.3
International Fund for Agricultural Development	—	—	0.2	0.6	0.6	1.0
OPEC Fund	1.0	1.0	0.9	0.6	0.6	0.3
Commercial loans	—	—	—	—	3.9	4.5
Debt service	0.5	0.5	0.9	0.8	0.7	1.6
Amortization	0.2	0.3	0.5	0.4	0.4	1.0
Interest	0.3	0.2	0.4	0.4	0.3	0.6
Memorandum items:						
External debt (in percent of GDP)	34.8	30.9	33.0	35.2	46.8	44.3
Debt service (in percent of exports of goods, services, and private transfers)	1.4	1.1	2.0	1.9	1.6	3.8

Source: Data provided by the Tongan authorities.

Table 12. Tonga: International Reserves, Fiscal Years 1982/83–1987/88

(In millions of SDRs; end of period)

	1982/83	1983/84	1984/85	1985/86	1986/87	1987/88
Assets	12.9	18.2	17.1	15.2	21.4	21.3
Government	1.1	1.3	1.4	1.1	1.5	1.5
Treasury	0.5	0.4	0.5	0.4	0.6	0.5
Currency Commissioners	0.6	0.9	0.9	0.7	0.9	1.0
Reserve position in IMF	—	—	—	0.7	0.8	0.7
Bank of Tonga	11.8	16.9	15.7	13.4	19.1	19.1
Bank of Tonga liabilities	0.3	0.1	0.3	0.8	0.5	0.3
Net total reserves	12.6	18.1	16.8	14.5	20.9	21.0
Memorandum items:						
Assets (in months of imports)	3.8	5.2	4.6	4.2	6.1	5.5
Pa'anga per SDR (end of period)	1.22	1.19	1.49	1.72	1.79	1.64

Source: Data provided by the Tongan authorities.

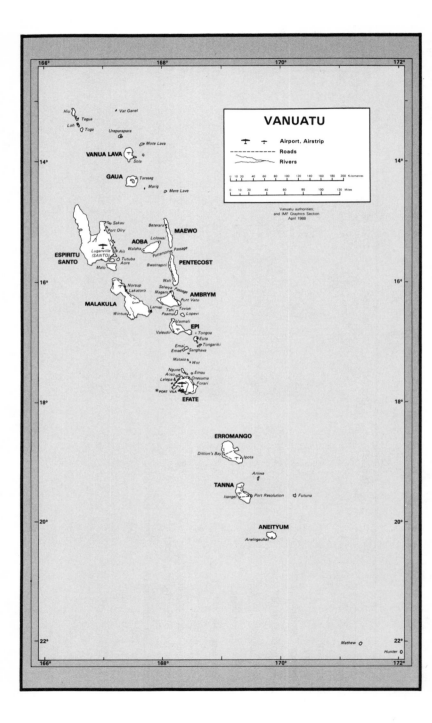

VANUATU

Airport, Airstrip
- - - - - - - - Roads
Rivers

0 10 20   40   60   80   100   120 140 160 180 200 Kilometres

0 10 20   40   60   80   100   120 Miles

Vanuatu authorities,
and IMF Graphics Section
April 1988

Hiu
Tegua
Loh
Toga
Vat Ganel
Ureparapara
Mote Lava
VANUA LAVA
Sola
GAUA   Tarasag
Marig
Mere Lave

Sakau
Port Olry
Beterara
MAEWO
AOBA   Lolowai
Luganville   Ais   Walaha   Patterson
(SANTO)
Tutuba
ESPIRITU   Aore
SANTO   Malo
Bwatnapni   PENTECOST
Passage

Wali
Norsup   Selwya Passage
Lakatoro   Magam
MALAKULA   Port Vato   AMBRYM
Lamap   Tahi   Taviak
Wintua   Paama   Lopevi

Vasmali
Valesdir   EPI   Tongoa
Euta
Emae   Tongariki
Emae   Sanghava
Mataso   Wot

Ngune   Emau
Aroso   Onesuma
Lelepa   Forari
PORT VILA
EFATE

ERROMANGO

Dillon's Bay   Ipota

Aniwa

TANNA
Isangel   Port Resolution   Futuna

ANEITYUM
Aneingauhat

Mathew

Hunter

7

Vanuatu

The Republic of Vanuatu, previously known as the New Hebrides, is an archipelago of some 80 small islands, with a land area of 12,000 square kilometers. The population of 140,000 is 94 percent Melanesian; the expatriate community consists mainly of Europeans, Chinese, and Vietnamese. Population growth has exceeded 3 percent annually in recent years. Most people live on the coastal plains where the soil is fertile and the rainfall predictable. The largest concentration of population is in the capital, Port Vila. Cultivation of the interior is difficult because of the mountainous terrain. There are more than 100 different languages. The traditional society is characterized by strong clan affinities and religious beliefs. Education indicators are below the regional average, including high illiteracy rates and low primary school enrollment.

The first contacts with Europeans were through explorers, whalers, and traders. In the second half of the nineteenth century, planters settled in increasing numbers, while many Melanesians were recruited to work on sugar plantations in Fiji and Australia. The United Kingdom and France set up a joint naval commission in 1888 to maintain order in the islands, an arrangement that was strengthened with the formation of the Anglo-French Condominium in 1906. Over the next 75 years, a complex administrative structure was built, featuring parallel British, French, and joint services. There was no integrated public expenditure program, as each administration financed and administered projects according to its own priorities and special interests. In a move that would have repercussions to this day, titles covering approximately one fifth of the total land area were granted to European settlers.

Vanuatu became independent in 1980. Legislative functions are entrusted to a single-chamber Parliament of 46 members elected every four years, and executive powers are held by the Prime Minister and Council of Ministers. Under the Constitution, indigenous citizens have an unalienable right to all land, except that the Government may hold or acquire land in the public interest. Following independence, land granted to European settlers reverted to custom ownership, but many disputes arose between rival claimants. Adjudication by the courts has been slow, and there is a large backlog of unresolved cases. The Government has the authority to lease disputed land for up to 75 years, but has used this power sparingly. The resolution of land tenure issues would aid agricultural development.

Annual per capita GDP is SDR 750, somewhat above the average for the Pacific region, partly reflecting the relatively high expatriate incomes. Although the economy is heavily dependent on a few traditional agricultural commodities, it has achieved an important degree of diversification into tourism and offshore banking services since the early 1970s. After a brief period of social and economic disruption surrounding independence, Vanuatu sustained a satisfactory rate of growth for several years. Assisted by large receipts of concessional aid and cautious demand management, the external position was sound and inflation was moderate. However, the economy remained vulnerable to adverse external developments, as shown in 1985–87, when declining prices of primary exports contributed to a weakening in the growth and balance of payments performance.

Economic Structure

Production and Prices

Agriculture accounts for about 40 percent of GDP. The main cash crop is copra; cocoa cultivation and beef production are other important activities. Subsistence agriculture is the principal means of livelihood for 80 percent of the population, although its contribution to GDP is only 25 percent. The relative importance of plantation agriculture has declined during the past 20 years as a result of aging trees, lack of investment, and a strong preference of the rural population for subsistence farming rather than plantation employment. The problems have been compounded since independence by land tenure issues and the lack of trained management. Rehabilitation of plantations is feasible, however, in most areas.

Fish and forestry resources appear to have potential, but exploitation has been minimal. The fish cannery halted operations in 1986 because of inadequate supplies. Mining activity ceased in 1980 with the depletion of manganese deposits. Manufacturing, which is mainly agro-based and includes the processing of beef for export, accounts for only 5 percent of GDP. Obstacles to development include inadequate transport facilities and the small size and fragmented nature of the domestic market. In light of these constraints, the Government favors export-oriented industries and places little emphasis on import substitution, except in a few carefully chosen areas that promote the use of local raw materials.

The economy is dominated by service activities, which account for more than 50 percent of GDP. Long-established functions include trading and shipping, which were originally associated closely with the operations of the plantations. The fastest growing areas in recent years have been public administration, tourism, financial and banking services, and flag-of-convenience registration of ships. While their number has declined since independence, foreign experts are welcome in positions requiring special skills, as they are considered critical for further economic development.

Consumer prices are determined primarily by import prices, especially of goods imported from Australia. Price controls are applied to a few basic food items. Wages are influenced strongly by trends in the public sector, where a relatively high wage structure was inherited at independence. With the shortage of skilled labor and the large number of expatriates, attempts to reduce real wages have been firmly resisted by employees. However, restraint in public sector salaries has recently become an important element in the policies to moderate growth in public current expenditure. Income disparities between the modern and subsistence sectors are large by regional standards, partly reflecting the cost of expatriate services.

Balance of Payments

Exports consist of a small range of goods with copra representing three fourths of the total. Export earnings fluctuate widely but average only 10–15 percent of GDP. Imports are equivalent to 40 percent of GDP, reflecting the limited variety of domestic production, substantial amounts of foreign aid, and the large tourist sector. Food and other consumer goods comprise about 40 percent of the total. Major categories of imports also include construction materials and capital equipment, particularly aid-financed goods for government projects. The direction of trade has not changed substantially since independence. While exports to Japan have grown, most exports continue to be destined for Western Europe. Imports are supplied predominantly by Australia, New Zealand, and Japan.

The external current account (including grants) has normally recorded surpluses. Large trade deficits have been more than offset by receipts from tourism and financial services, private transfers in the form of expenditure by foreign residents, and official grants from the United Kingdom, France, Australia, and New Zealand. Net outflows have normally been registered on the capital account, especially during 1980–81 when substantial private funds were transferred abroad. Relatively large official international reserves have been maintained, because of the volatility of export earnings and the large foreign currency deposits held by residents. External commercial borrowing has been avoided, which in part accounts for the low external debt service ratio of 3 percent of current receipts. The vatu has been fixed in relation to a basket of currencies since February 1988; previously, since 1981, the vatu had been fixed in relation to the SDR.

Public Sector

The public sector comprises the central government, 11 regional governments, and 12 public enterprises. The central government budget, which covers the calendar year, is organized through nine ministries. The Budget Office in the Ministry of Finance, assisted by the Budget Committee that includes representatives of the Central Bank, the National Planning and Statistics Office, and the Public Service Commission, oversees the formulation of the current revenue and expenditure estimates. Following approval of the Council of Ministers, a draft budget is submitted to Parliament in October for review and discussion; final approval is usually granted in December. Supplementary budgets must also be approved by the Council of Ministers and Parliament.

Development projects and technical assistance expenditure, which are mainly financed with cash grants from abroad, are administered jointly with the donor countries through the Development Fund. Consolidated public sector accounts are not available, as data relating to local government and public enterprise activities are scarce. Public enterprises operate on a commercial basis and generally do not require budgetary support from the Government.

The central government plays a preponderant role in the economy, with total expenditure amounting to over 50 percent of GDP. Domestic revenue is about 25 percent of GDP, with foreign trade taxes representing well over half of the total. There are no individual and corporate income taxes, capital gains taxes, or estate and gift duties. Foreign grants have declined from 50 percent of GDP at independence to 20 percent, as a result of the gradual withdrawal of budgetary support from the United Kingdom and France, and reductions in technical assistance from abroad. Current expenditure is about 25 percent of GDP, with approximately two fifths attributable to general public services. Technical and development assistance account for about 10 percent of GDP each. However, development expenditure is constrained by shortages of expertise and locally trained labor.

Financial Sector

The financial sector embraces the Central Bank; three commercial banks, which are subsidiaries or branch offices of foreign banks; the Development Bank of Vanuatu; and the Vanuatu Cooperative Savings Bank. The Central Bank of Vanuatu was established in 1980. The domestic currency, the vatu, was introduced in 1981. The New Hebrides franc ceased to be legal tender in 1983. The Central Bank does not use reserve requirements to influence bank liquidity. Interest rates are market determined. Reflecting the absence of exchange controls, the commercial banks may transact deposit and loan business in both domestic and foreign currencies. Residents are free to hold bank deposits denominated in any currency; in 1987, about two thirds of the total were held in foreign currency.

The Development Bank of Vanuatu was established in 1979 to promote rural and industrial development, with emphasis on the processing of raw materials; to provide employment and training; and to improve the balance of payments. The financial resources of the Bank come mainly from foreign grants and concessionary loans. The principal goal of the Savings Bank is to mobilize rural savings. In addition to accepting deposits from villagers, the bank collects loan installment payments on behalf of the Development Bank, makes salary payments for the Government, and arranges for money transfers. A National Provident Fund was established in 1987. Employers and employees are each required to contribute 3 percent of wages and salaries to the Fund.

The Finance Center was established in 1971 by the British authorities, with the tacit approval of the French authorities, as an offshore financial center and tax haven. Banks, law firms, accountants, and trust companies provide services to over 1,000 registered companies. While these enterprises pay a registration fee, they are not subject to taxes and are guaranteed secrecy about their business activities; however, they are prohibited from engaging in local operations. The center is estimated to contribute about 10 percent of GDP, and is an important source of employment and training.

Developments in the 1970s

Steady economic growth was achieved in the 1970s. Copra output of smallholders and beef production increased in response to stronger world demand. However, mainly because of insufficient investment and maintenance on plantations, coffee and cocoa output declined. Tourism benefited from improved airline connections and hotel facilities and from increased visits by cruise ships. Financial activities expanded after the establishment of the offshore center. Government services were largely financed by assistance from France and the United Kingdom. The public accounts consistently showed surpluses and the Government maintained a net creditor position with the banking system. Little credit was extended to the private sector and most assets of the commercial banks were invested abroad. With growing earnings from exports of goods and services and inflows of foreign aid, Vanuatu recorded external current account and overall balance of payments surpluses.

In preparation for independence, the colonial powers drew up a series of development proposals during the 1970s. They identified the main structural problems as the duplication of government services by the French and British administrations; the shortage of skilled manpower with over 80 percent of the population illiterate and only 10 percent having completed six or more years of education; and the poor transport system, which inhibited the distribution of economic opportunities throughout the country. However, little progress was made in tackling these issues. At independence, infrastructure remained inadequate, particularly with regard to transport and communications.

Developments in the 1980s

The Government's development strategy for the 1980s has emphasized better utilization of available natural and human resources, balanced regional and rural growth, and the preservation of the cultural and environmental heritage of Vanuatu. It has sought to gradually reduce dependence on external aid through the mobilization of domestic resources. A larger role was envisaged for the private sector because, with lower external assistance, the size of the public sector would exceed the country's ability to support it. Foreign direct investment is generally welcomed.

Disruption and Recovery in 1980–84

In 1980, the economy faced severe problems from the civil disruptions that accompanied independence and from a serious deterioration in the external terms of trade. Real GDP dropped by 10 percent while supply shortages and the higher cost of imports prompted a sharp increase in consumer prices. Agricultural output and exports fell because of the sudden departure of expatriates who had held managerial positions in the plantation sector. In addition, tourist arrivals declined, investment came to a halt, and private capital outflows increased. In 1981–82, although real GDP grew by 1–2 percent annually, Vanuatu was affected by the decline in copra prices, which fell by more than the price of most other primary commodities in this period. Moreover, in contrast to most other Pacific island economies that received increased aid at independence, Vanuatu experienced declining assistance.

Despite these difficulties, the external current account recorded surpluses in 1980–82. Imports initially fell with the departure of expatriates and the weak economy. With a return to political stability, tourism and offshore banking expanded. Agriculture recovered more slowly, partly because of depressed export prices. To limit fluctuations in the incomes of copra producers and thereby encourage greater output, the Vanuatu Commodities Marketing Board was established in 1982. The Board took over the procurement and export of copra from foreign-owned trading companies, and its price support operations helped to limit the decline in production. With the recovery in import demand as the economy gathered strength, the trade deficit increased and the current account surplus was reduced. However, with renewed capital inflows, the balance of payments recorded an overall surplus in 1982.

During 1983–84, the growth rate picked up and the balance of payments strengthened. The rate of real GDP growth accelerated to 3 percent in 1983 and to 7 percent in 1984. Exports rebounded strongly mainly because of higher world copra prices. While the Commodities Board allocated a substantial part of the increased earnings to reserves, procurement prices were raised several times. The trade deficit fell sharply, although import demand expanded because of buoyant export income, higher wages and salaries in the public sector, increased investment, and growth in tourism. The downward trend in official transfers was temporarily halted. Compensatory grants were received from the European Community for earlier low export prices and the grants were made by the United Kingdom to help meet claims on the Government arising from the civil disturbances at independence. In view of the strength of the external accounts, the vatu was revalued by 5.6 percent against the SDR in March 1984.

With the large drop in external cash support, the Government budget shifted into deficit in 1982–83, but a surplus was restored in 1984. Domestic revenue increased from 17 percent of GDP in 1982 to 21 percent in 1984. The Government placed greater reliance on import duties, raising rates in successive years on various goods, principally coffee, beer, spirits, tobacco, gasoline, and motor vehicles. It also introduced measures to broaden the tax base, including an airport departure tax, a turnover tax on hotel rooms and restaurant services, and work permit fees for nonresidents. However, the ability to mobilize revenue was constrained because the tax base was narrow and the effectiveness of higher import duties was undermined by frequent exemptions.

The Government reduced current expenditure from 28 percent of GDP in 1982 to 25 percent in 1984 and made progress in streamlining the public administration by eliminating overlapping services inherited from the condominium powers. To this end, it abolished several ministries and merged a number of functions. Tight controls were maintained on government employment, including the periodic imposition of hiring freezes. However, pronounced pressures for additional expenditure included demands for a wider range of facilities than had existed prior to independence, steps to strengthen project implementation capacity, and efforts to maintain the growing capital stock. Education needs absorbed one fourth of the current budget and one third of the salaried work force.

Development spending averaged 10 percent of GDP during this period. Agriculture, land, and natural resources received about one half of the total. The next largest categories were transport and communi-

cations, primarily in the form of improved interisland port and telephone services, and education, including school buildings. The allocation of funds was broadly consistent with longer-term objectives, although the recurrent costs of new projects were not always fully
appraised prior to implementation.

Liquidity grew rapidly during 1981–84, chiefly because of the
balance of payments surpluses. Its impact on domestic prices was
limited, because of the strong demand for financial savings. Interest
rates were largely market determined on both vatu and foreign currency deposits. Depositors chose to maintain an increasing proportion
of their assets in foreign accounts, particularly since higher interest
rates were available in international markets. Deposits in vatu also
grew steadily, but despite ample bank liquidity and firm support from
the Government for more domestic lending to the private sector, the
growth of domestic credit was small. The banks adopted a cautious
attitude toward private sector lending because of the high servicing
costs of small loans, especially in rural areas, and the shortage of
qualified staff. The Government maintained a net creditor position with
the banking system.

Less Favorable Developments in 1985–87

Real GDP remained more or less unchanged in 1985–87. Two
cyclones caused a decline in agricultural output in 1985, and a downturn
in the Australian economy and a depreciation of the Australian dollar
led to a fall in tourist arrivals. Agricultural production rebounded in
1986, but tourism continued to decline, partly because the national
airline ceased operations following the termination of its management
contract with a foreign airline. Another severe cyclone struck Vanuatu
in early 1987, causing loss of life and extensive property damage to the
capital. Despite rehabilitation expenditure, especially on the reconstruction of buildings, economic activity remained depressed in 1987.

The balance of payments was affected by the lower world price of
copra. While the support operations of the Commodities Marketing
Board helped to maintain the volume of output, the value of exports fell
in 1986. The value of imports increased in 1985 but fell sharply in 1986,
as a result of lower oil prices, lower requirements in the tourist sector,
and weak domestic demand. Official transfers declined, despite additional grants for cyclone rehabilitation. After the large surpluses of

preceding years, the current account and the overall balance of payments recorded deficits in 1985–86, which were financed by drawing down the net foreign assets of the commercial banks. The external position strengthened in 1987, mainly because of temporarily high grants from the European Community's STABEX facility and cyclone-related insurance claims and concessional aid.

The central government budget moved into deficit in 1985 and the deficit reached 6–7 percent in 1986–87. Although import duties and license fees were increased, budgetary receipts declined in relation to GDP because of the lower official grants. Current expenditure rose because of wage and salary increases and measures to repair cyclone damage. Fiscal adjustment was implemented in 1987. Revenue was boosted by further increases in import duties and royalty payments from the U.S.S.R. under a one-year fishing agreement. Additional inflows of foreign aid were received for cyclone reconstruction. The Government also decided that STABEX compensation received from the European Community consequent upon the fall in export prices would not be fully transferred to the Commodities Board, as had been done in the past. However, expenditure continued to grow strongly, despite a freeze on recruitment.

Liquidity growth was modest in 1985–87, mainly because of the smaller expansionary impact of external factors. Although the Government drew down its deposits for most of the period to help finance the budget deficit, private sector credit demand was generally weak because of depressed economic activity. With the less restrictive stance of fiscal policy, the authorities adopted a more flexible exchange rate policy in order to help strengthen competitiveness and protect the external position. The vatu was depreciated by a total of 29 percent in three stages during 1985–86. Subsequently, exchange rate policy has continued to be directed toward protecting the external position, with close attention focused on the competitiveness of the tourist industry.

Table 1. Vanuatu: Gross Domestic Product by Sectoral Origin, 1983–87

(In millions of vatu at 1983 prices)

	1983	1984	1985	1986	1987
Agriculture, forestry, and fisheries	2,649	2,831	2,771	2,648	2,591
Manufacturing	311	419	466	466	588
Energy	158	191	192	190	180
Construction	303	293	282	368	514
Transport and communications	757	808	770	741	762
Wholesale and retail trade, hotels, and restaurants	3,627	3,740	3,753	3,518	3,599
Finance center	819	772	967	1,128	1,087
Real estate and business services	526	587	611	591	534
Government services	1,393	1,542	1,629	1,721	1,614
Community and personal services	72	72	74	76	79
Less: bank service charges	–465	–410	–548	–654	–721
GDP at constant market prices	10,150	10,846	10,966	10,751	10,821
Memorandum items:					
GDP at current market prices	10,150	12,339	12,534	12,150	13,143
Change in real GDP (in percent)	3.0	6.9	1.1	–2.0	0.7

Source: Data provided by the Vanuatu authorities.

Table 2. Vanuatu: Output of Main Commodities, 1980–87

(In metric tons)

	1980	1981	1982	1983	1984	1985	1986	1987
Copra	33,500	46,500	34,300	37,900	47,800	38,300	41,800	36,300
Cocoa	723	868	528	1,297	782	982	1,281	1,168
Coffee	...	61	21	38	25	49	57	53
Beef	...	2,051	1,940	2,208	2,246	2,259	2,009	2,720

Source: Data provided by the Vanuatu authorities.

Table 3. Vanuatu: Consumer Price Index, 1980–87

(Annual average percentage change)

	Weights¹	1980	1981	1982	1983	1984	1985	1986	1987
Food	46.5	13.0	35.6	0.8	-2.6	1.2	-2.5	5.6	16.0
Beverages and tobacco	10.2	15.2	28.7	12.0	3.4	10.5	5.3	5.2	15.8
Clothing and footwear	14.1	3.1	12.6	8.6	11.5	12.7	0.3	1.1	5.4
Rent, water, fuel, and electricity	2.1	15.4	31.2	24.4	11.8	5.2	2.7	-1.3	6.6
Household articles	7.9	6.8	18.5	12.5	6.0	12.2	6.6	5.7	12.2
Transport and communications	9.7	19.7	24.3	13.7	2.5	6.5	4.3	6.1	23.2
Recreation, health, and education	9.5	2.6	13.1	7.4	2.3	4.7	3.9	4.7	14.1
Overall index	100.0	11.1	27.5	6.2	1.7	5.5	1.1	4.8	14.8
				(End-of-period percentage change)					
Memorandum item:									
Overall index	100.0	18.4	26.7	-1.2	4.8	3.2	0.9	6.5	17.2

Source: Data provided by the Vanuatu authorities.
¹Low-income groups in Port Vila, March 31, 1976 = 100.

Table 4. Vanuatu: Central Government Budget, 1980–87

(In millions of vatu)

	1980	1981	1982	1983	1984	1985	1986	1987
Revenue and grants	4,902	5,301	4,958	4,493	5,625	5,710	5,263	6,504
Tax revenue	943	1,021	1,265	1,467	2,038	2,298	2,241	2,685
Nontax revenue	320	346	343	425	466	672	679	962
External grants	3,639	3,934	3,350	2,601	3,121	2,740	2,343	2,859
Budgetary	1,033	899	743	559	437	279	134	75
Nonbudgetary	2,606	3,035	2,607	2,042	2,684	2,461	2,210	2,782
Total expenditure	4,441	4,786	5,296	4,570	5,155	5,822	6,045	7,480
Current expenditure	1,870	2,104	2,728	2,438	2,952	3,191	3,432	3,600
Technical assistance	1,693	1,635	1,497	1,050	1,270	1,362	1,362	1,310
Development expenditure	879	1,047	1,071	1,082	933	1,269	1,251	2,570
Overall balance	460	515	–338	–78	470	–112	–782	–976
Financing, net	–460	–515	338	78	–470	112	782	976
External	–21	–23	–26	38	83	88	89	338
Domestic banking system	–439	–492	435	89	–568	–130	557	656
Other domestic	—	—	–71	–49	15	154	136	–18
				(In percent of GDP)				
Memorandum items:								
Revenue and grants	66.4	61.0	51.7	44.3	45.6	45.6	43.3	49.5
Tax revenue	12.8	11.7	13.2	14.5	16.5	18.3	18.4	20.4
Nontax revenue	4.3	4.0	3.6	4.2	3.8	5.4	5.6	7.3
External grants	49.3	45.2	35.0	25.6	25.3	21.9	19.3	21.7
Total expenditure	60.1	55.0	55.3	45.0	41.8	46.5	49.8	56.9
Current expenditure	25.3	24.2	28.5	24.0	23.9	25.5	28.2	27.4
Technical assistance	22.8	18.8	15.6	10.3	10.3	10.9	11.2	10.0
Development expenditure	11.9	12.0	11.2	10.7	7.6	10.1	10.3	19.6
Overall balance	6.2	5.9	–3.5	–0.8	3.8	–0.9	–6.4	–7.4

Sources: Data provided by the Vanuatu authorities; and Fund staff estimates.

Table 5. Vanuatu: Central Government Revenue, 1980–87

(In millions of vatu)

	1980	1981	1982	1983	1984	1985	1986	1987
Tax revenue	943	1,021	1,265	1,467	2,038	2,298	2,241	2,685
Goods and services	124	151	247	317	460	489	576	521
Tourist services	—	—	63	93	105	94	70	68
Licenses	61	95	115	136	170	213	282	224
Registration fees	63	53	66	82	162	157	192	196
Work permit fees	—	3	3	6	23	25	32	33
International transactions	791	840	992	1,100	1,522	1,724	1,595	2,042
Import duties	712	710	901	974	1,245	1,491	1,523	1,969
Export duties	79	130	91	126	277	233	72	73
Airport tax	—	13	15	23	25	43	34	32
Other	28	17	11	26	31	42	36	90
Nontax revenue	320	346	343	425	466	672	679	962
Public enterprises	77	80	84	136	129	276	306	334
Rents and interest	125	157	139	154	159	160	146	74
Fines and fees	30	26	28	37	50	83	92	117
Other	88	83	92	98	128	153	135	437
Total	1,263	1,367	1,608	1,891	2,504	2,970	2,920	3,647

Sources: Data provided by the Vanuatu authorities; and Fund staff estimates.

Table 6. Vanuatu: Central Government Current Expenditure by Economic Classification, 1981–87

(In millions of vatu)

	1981	1982	1983	1984	1985	1986	1987
Wages and salaries	1,171	1,306	1,362	1,544	1,735	1,865	1,970
Purchases of goods and services	857	923	952	960	990	1,143	1,094
Interest payments	28	25	19	23	33	26	41
Other[1]	48	474	105	425	433	398	495
Total	2,104	2,728	2,438	2,952	3,191	3,432	3,600

Sources: Data provided by the Vanuatu authorities; and Fund staff estimates.
[1]Includes transfers of STABEX funds.

Table 7. Vanuatu: Monetary Survey, 1981–87

(In billions of vatu; end of period)

	1981	1982	1983	1984	1985	1986	1987
Net foreign assets	2.3	4.3	6.0	9.3	9.9	11.2	11.7
Domestic credit	1.8	2.4	2.9	2.2	1.9	2.7	2.0
Government, net[1]	-1.3	-0.9	-0.7	-1.3	-1.4	-0.9	-2.2
Private sector[2]	3.1	3.3	3.6	3.5	3.3	3.6	4.1
Other items, net	-0.3	-0.8	-1.6	-0.9	-0.7	-1.2	-0.9
Total liquidity	3.8	5.9	7.3	10.6	11.1	12.7	12.8
Money supply	1.3	1.5	1.8	2.1	2.2	2.2	2.8
Currency outside banks	0.6	0.6	0.7	0.9	1.0	0.9	1.0
Demand deposits (vatu)	0.7	0.9	1.1	1.2	1.2	1.3	1.8
Quasi-money	2.5	4.4	5.5	8.5	8.9	10.5	10.1
Time and savings deposits (vatu)	0.7	1.5	1.9	2.2	1.8	2.7	2.0
Time and savings deposits (foreign currency)	1.6	2.6	3.3	4.8	6.1	6.8	6.7
Demand deposits (foreign currency)	0.2	0.3	0.3	1.5	1.0	1.0	1.4
Memorandum item:							
Deposits of the Vanuatu Commodities Marketing Board	—	—	0.5	1.4	1.2	0.7	0.5
Total liquidity (annual percentage change)	...	55.3	23.7	45.2	4.7	14.4	0.8

Sources: Data provided by the Vanuatu authorities; and Fund staff estimates.
[1]Includes government foreign currency deposits with commercial banks.
[2]Includes public enterprises.

Table 8. Vanuatu: Interest Rate Structure, 1981–87

(In percent per annum; end of period)

	1981	1982	1983	1984	1985	1986	1987
Vatu savings deposits	4.00–8.00	4.00–6.00	4.00–6.00	4.00–6.50	4.00–6.50	4.00–4.50	2.00–4.00
Vatu time deposits							
1 month	8.75–10.75	7.50–10.25	6.75–9.00	5.75–8.50	6.13–8.00	4.50–7.50	3.00–4.50
2–6 months	8.75–11.00	8.00–11.00	8.00–10.00	6.75–9.00	6.38–8.50	4.50–8.79	3.00–6.00
Above 6 months	8.50–11.00	8.50–11.25	8.50–11.50	7.00–9.50	6.00–9.00	4.85–8.50	3.00–6.75
Australian dollar deposits							
1 month	8.70–9.20	8.10–11.00	6.00–8.00	8.00–9.00	12.00–17.38	12.00–14.00	5.00–9.00
Vatu loans							
Commercial	12.00–18.00	12.00–18.00	12.00–18.00	12.00–16.00	12.00–16.00	12.00–16.00	8.00–16.00
Personal	15.00–18.00	15.00–18.00	14.00–18.00	14.00–21.00	14.00–19.50	14.00–16.50	8.00–17.00
Housing	11.50–18.00	11.50–18.00	11.50–18.00	11.50–16.00	11.50–16.00	11.50–16.00	7.00–16.00

Source: Data provided by the Vanuatu authorities.

Table 9. Vanuatu: Balance of Payments, 1980–87

(In millions of SDRs)

	1980	1981	1982	1983	1984	1985	1986	1987
Trade balance	–24.4	–17.9	–29.5	–26.1	–18.6	–33.0	–32.4	–33.6
Exports, f.o.b.	9.9	13.5	9.7	16.8	31.7	18.4	7.5	10.6
Imports, f.o.b.	–34.3	–31.4	–39.2	–42.9	–50.3	–51.4	–39.9	–44.2
Services, net	–0.5	8.5	3.9	5.2	5.1	8.2	4.8	0.1
Receipts	29.8	32.7	47.1	54.7	65.1	63.7	62.0	50.6
Payments	30.3	24.2	43.2	49.3	59.9	55.5	57.2	50.5
Private transfers, net	2.3	3.0	7.4	5.6	6.8	6.6	6.0	4.4
Official transfers, net	40.0	35.2	31.8	24.5	31.4	25.2	19.1	35.0
Budgetary support	11.6	8.9	7.0	5.3	4.3	2.6	1.1	0.3
Development grants	10.6	9.7	10.2	9.3	9.4	9.9	6.8	8.7
Technical assistance	17.8	15.7	14.1	9.9	12.5	12.7	10.9	9.2
STABEX grants and other	—	0.9	0.5	—	5.2	0.1	0.3	16.8
Current account	17.4	28.8	13.6	9.2	24.7	7.0	–2.5	5.9
Nonmonetary capital, net	...	...	7.8	5.9	8.3	5.4	5.1	10.8
Official	...	...	1.5	0.4	0.8	0.8	0.6	0.7
Private	...	...	6.3	5.5	7.5	4.6	4.5	10.1
Errors and omissions	...	...	–4.7	1.4	5.2	–15.5	–13.8	–12.5
Overall balance	...	...	16.7	16.5	38.0	–3.1	–11.2	4.3
Memorandum items:								
Current account (in percent of GDP)	20.9	34.5	15.1	9.6	21.2	7.2	–2.7	6.5
Vatu per SDR (period average)	88.8	103.0	106.2	106.2	101.6	107.5	124.1	141.9

Sources: Data provided by the Vanuatu authorities; and Fund staff estimates.

Table 10. Vanuatu: Exports by Commodity, 1980–87

(Value in thousands of SDRs, volume in metric tons, unit value in SDRs per metric ton)

	1980	1981	1982	1983	1984	1985	1986	1987
Copra								
Value	6,659	10,278	6,685	12,316	26,883	12,943	3,570	5,066
Volume	26,732	47,070	34,798	38,538	46,682	34,930	40,612	31,846
Unit value	249	218	192	320	576	371	88	159
Cocoa								
Value	1,057	1,123	537	1,723	1,327	1,235	1,579	1,458
Volume	723	944	548	1,232	791	814	1,197	1,243
Unit value	1,462	1,189	979	1,399	1,678	1,517	1,319	1,173
Beef, canned								
Value	517	470	556	480	236	9	24	7
Volume	188	132	152	179	115	4	13	7
Unit value	2,752	3,562	3,655	2,683	2,052	2,321	1,855	1,006
Beef, fresh and frozen								
Value	326	1,065	1,177	1,337	1,160	1,829	1,021	1,761
Volume	178	672	624	875	566	1,130	489	1,037
Unit value	1,833	1,585	1,886	1,528	2,050	1,619	2,088	1,698
Sawn timber								
Value	11	202	207	122	49	102	152	129
Logs								
Value		—	—	179	1,396	1,161	352	1,340
Other (value)	1,845	787	1,064	1,092	855	1,140	836	821
Total (value)	9,899	13,455	9,670	16,770	31,672	18,419	7,534	10,582

Source: Data provided by the Vanuatu authorities.

Table 11. Vanuatu: Imports by Commodity Group, 1980–87

(In thousands of SDRs)

	1980	1981	1982	1983	1984	1985	1986	1987
Imports for domestic consumption	40,450	37,687	43,606	49,237	57,276	60,093	47,468	52,487
Food and beverages	11,170	10,681	10,763	11,516	13,805	13,612	10,378	8,243
Consumer goods	7,379	8,464	10,885	12,175	14,661	13,287	9,727	10,089
Industrial materials	6,839	6,084	7,966	8,945	9,066	10,891	9,325	14,534
Fuels and lubricants	5,714	4,760	5,876	5,235	6,755	5,989	4,558	3,783
Machinery	3,948	4,107	3,550	5,433	6,745	6,964	7,588	7,581
Transport equipment	3,937	3,052	3,324	4,331	5,900	6,425	4,590	6,362
Other	1,462	537	1,243	1,601	344	2,925	1,302	1,895
Imports for re-export[1]	14,916	11,488	9,718	10,104	9,695	9,889	1,608	1,325
Total	55,366	49,175	53,324	59,341	66,971	66,981	49,076	53,811

Sources: Data provided by the Vanuatu authorities; and Fund staff estimates.
[1] Mainly tuna fish for processing. The cannery was closed during 1986.

Table 12. Vanuatu: Public Sector External Debt and Debt Service, 1980–87

(In millions of SDRs)

	1980	1981	1982	1983	1984	1985	1986	1987
External debt (end of period)								
Beginning-of-period stock	3.7	3.2	2.6	3.7	3.5	4.0	4.6	5.4
Net inflow	—	—	1.4	0.3	0.8	0.8	0.5	0.8
Valuation adjustment	-0.5	-0.6	-0.3	-0.5	-0.3	-0.2	0.3	0.4
End-of-period stock	3.2	2.6	3.7	3.5	4.0	4.6	5.4	6.3
Debt service	0.7	0.5	0.5	0.5	0.5	0.7	0.7	0.7
Amortization	0.5	0.3	0.3	0.3	0.3	0.4	0.4	0.4
Interest	0.2	0.2	0.2	0.2	0.2	0.3	0.3	0.3
Memorandum items:								
External debt (in percent of GDP)	4.0	3.2	4.1	3.6	3.3	3.9	5.5	6.8
Debt service (in percent of current receipts)	1.8	1.1	1.7	1.3	0.9	1.7	3.1	2.9

Sources: Data provided by the Vanuatu authorities; and Fund staff estimates.

Table 13. Vanuatu: International Reserves, 1980–87

(In millions of SDRs; end of period)

	1980	1981	1982	1983	1984	1985	1986	1987
Official assets	9.6	15.8	12.4	10.4	15.2	20.2	20.3	28.8
Central Bank	6.3	6.1	6.6	7.3	8.6	13.1	19.8	28.0
Reserve position in IMF	—	—	1.0	1.6	1.6	1.6	1.6	1.6
SDRs	—	—	—	—	0.1	0.2	0.2	0.3
Foreign exchange	6.3	6.1	5.6	5.7	6.9	11.3	18.0	26.1
Government	3.3	9.7	5.8	3.1	6.6	7.1	0.5	0.8
Central bank liabilities	—	—	0.4	0.2	0.1	0.2	0.2	—
Net official reserves	9.6	15.8	12.0	10.1	15.1	20.0	20.1	28.8
Memorandum items:								
Official assets (in months of imports)	3.4	6.0	3.8	2.9	3.6	4.7	6.1	7.8
Commercial banks	...	...	32.5	48.8	84.9	80.6	61.6	54.8
Assets	...	...	184.1	163.5	205.2	265.6	227.4	201.5
Liabilities	...	...	151.6	114.7	120.3	185.0	165.8	146.7
Vatu per SDR (end of period)	93.1	106.2	106.1	106.6	100.5	110.1	142.2	142.7

Sources: Data provided by the Vanuatu authorities; and Fund staff estimates.

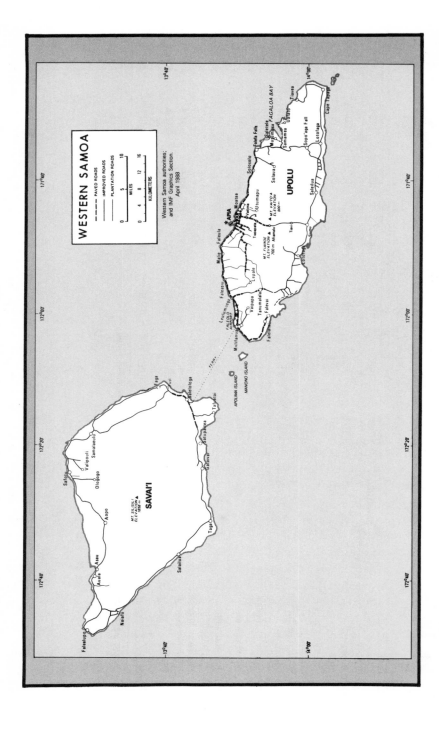

WESTERN SAMOA

PAVED ROADS
IMPROVED ROADS
PLANTATION ROADS

MILES
0   5   10

KILOMETERS
0   4   8   12   16

Western Samoa authorities;
and IMF Graphics Section
April 1988

SAVAI'I

MT. SILISILI
ELEVATION ▲
1858 m

Falealupo
Neiafu
Auala
Asau
Satuiatua
Taga
Puapua
Gataivai
Sili
Sapulega
Salelologa
Taumai
Salailua
Fagamalo
Samalaeulu
Velepoui
Olobogo
Aopo
Safotu

Tafua
Salelologa
Talamai
Apolima Island
Manono Island

APOLIMA ISLAND
MANONO ISLAND

FALEOLO AIRPORT

Mulifanua
Luatuanuu
Faleasiu
Faleolo
Apia
Saleula
Malie
Moataa
Matautu
Faleata
Tuanaimato
Siumu
Lepale
Tanumalala
Faleasiu
Falesea
Vaiusu
Faleasiu
Aleipata
MT. VAITOA
ELEVATION ▲
500 m
MT. FIAMOE
ELEVATION ▲
700 m
Solaua
Solosolo
Falefa Falls
Falefa
Muamausu
Saletele
Samamea
Uafato
Tiavea
Sono'aga Fall
Lotofaga
Cape Tapaga

UPOLU
Salelua
Saleaaumua
Tiavi

FAGALOA BAY

APIA

8

Western Samoa

Western Samoa, with a land area of 2,800 square kilometers, consists of nine islands that are volcanic in origin, tropical in climate, and centrally situated in the South Pacific. Virtually all of the population of 160,000 is of Polynesian origin and resides in settlements along the coastline of the two main islands. Life expectancy is 65 years and health and education standards are above the regional norm. Despite a relatively high birth rate, population growth has averaged less than 1 percent annually during the 1970s and 1980s. Slow growth of output and employment problems have resulted in steady emigration, mainly to New Zealand but also to Australia and the United States. While this emigration has forestalled serious unemployment and pressures on cultivatable land, shortages of skilled labor are evident throughout the country.

The first European settlers, who came to Western Samoa in the nineteenth century, were missionaries, British and U.S. traders, and German businessmen who established large copra plantations that exist to this day. Attempts by each group to further its economic interests through political alliances with local chiefs resulted in considerable friction and the navies of the main powers gathered near the capital, Apia, in 1889. After the ships were dispersed by a hurricane, an agreement was signed under which Germany would control what is now Western Samoa; the United States gained the islands to the east, which are now American Samoa; and the United Kingdom established a protectorate over Tonga. In 1914, New Zealand occupied Western Samoa and subsequently administered the territory in various capacities, including under a trusteeship of the United Nations, until 1962 when the country became the first South Pacific nation to gain independence from colonial authority. Parliamentary elections are held every three years; the right to vote is restricted to about 20,000 village chiefs and about 2,000 registered voters in Apia.

GDP per capita, which is at present SDR 500 annually, increased little in real terms over the past two decades. Economic growth was constrained mainly by the slow growth of output in the plantation sector. As a result, exports declined steadily in relation to GDP and their coverage of imports fell from four fifths to only one fifth. The economy became heavily dependent on private transfers to finance consumption and official transfers to finance investment. Despite the growth in these receipts, severe balance of payments pressures were encountered in the late 1970s and early 1980s, principally because of a large expansion in public expenditure. In the past few years, the external position strengthened because of the adoption of less expansionary financial policies.

Economic Structure

Production and Prices

Agriculture is the mainstay of the economy, accounting for one half of GDP and the bulk of exports. The major cash crops are coconuts and cocoa, which account for about two thirds of agricultural output. Over the years, production has been adversely affected by disease and the aging of trees. Although rehabilitation is feasible, replanting at the commercial and smallholding levels has so far not been very effective. Production of bananas, which was traditionally a major export, has virtually ceased. Taro is the only crop to have shown persistent growth in recent years. Passion fruit, coffee, and mangos are grown in small quantities and mostly for domestic consumption.

A substantial portion of output originates in the traditional subsistence-oriented sector, which comprises 80 percent of the area under cultivation. Villages are normally made up of 40–50 households, presided over by a council of chiefs, who may help to organize the cultivation of land and redistribute part of the villagers' earnings to help needy households. The land tenure system is not conducive to agricultural development. Land allocations among families may be changed at the discretion of the chief, so that the system tends to work as a disincentive for family financed capital improvement. The area outside communal ownership is held in large part by the Western Samoa Trust Estates Corporation, a statutory body that controls the main coconut and cocoa plantations. The remainder of the land, mostly located in and near the capital, is privately owned and used mainly for housing and commercial enterprises.

Development of the nonagricultural primary sector, industry, and private services has been modest. The seas surrounding Western Samoa have potential for commercial fishing, but these resources are largely untapped. Growth of the livestock industry is hampered by animal disease and the shortage of skilled management. The once-abundant forestry resources have been depleted by logging and land clearing. The industrial sector, which contributes 10 percent of GDP, includes hydroelectric power facilities, a crushing mill for the production of coconut oil and copra meal, a brewery, and processed food factories. Government policy focuses on assisting those industries that utilize local materials and have potential for exports and import substitution. The largest component of the services sector is government administration. The possibilities of increasing tourism are being exploited, following recent investment in airport and hotel facilities.

The economy is very open and consumer prices are influenced strongly by the price of imports, especially consumer goods from Australia and New Zealand. Domestic factors, including the size of wage settlements, are also important. During 1976–83, the inflation rate was higher than that in other countries of the region because of excess demand pressure. Employees in the public sector were normally compensated in full for price rises and workers in the private sector usually obtained similar wage adjustments. In this period, the value of the Western Samoa tala was depreciated considerably against the New Zealand dollar, although the change in the real effective rate was not pronounced. More recently, rates of price increase have moved closer to the regional average as a result of weaker domestic demand and greater flexibility in wage settlements, which has helped to achieve greater stability of the exchange rate in nominal terms.

Balance of Payments

The balance of payments is characterized by large foreign trade deficits. Exports fluctuate within a range of 10–15 percent of GDP, with coconut products representing about half of the total; cocoa, taro, and a range of agro-based manufactured items account for most of the other half. The largest export market is New Zealand, followed by Australia, the Federal Republic of Germany, and the United States. Developments in imports are strongly influenced by materials and capital goods associated with projects financed by external aid and by demand for consumer goods supported largely by inflows of private remittances. The sources of imports are more diversified than export markets. New Zealand and Australia account for about half of total imports; Fiji and Japan each account for about 15 percent.

The external current account (including grants) is usually in surplus. The services account shows a small surplus. The largest source of receipts is tourism, and the largest category of payments is interest on external debt. Remittances from Western Samoans living abroad, primarily used to finance consumption by relatives at home, have long been a major element in the balance of payments. They are presently equivalent to about 30 percent of GDP. Official external grant assistance, which comes mainly from Australia, China, the European Community, the Federal Republic of Germany, Japan, and New Zealand, is equivalent to about 15 percent of GDP.

Capital transactions are relatively small and approximately in balance. Inflows are mainly in the form of concessionary loans from multilateral financial institutions. Outflows are mainly repayments of principal on public sector borrowing. External debt is equivalent to 75 percent of GDP, although only a small proportion is on commercial terms. External debt service is 13 percent of exports of goods, services, and private remittances. Official international reserves are equivalent to seven months of imports. The exchange rate, which is determined in relation to a basket of currencies of Western Samoa's major trading partners, is managed flexibly.

Public Sector

The public sector consists of the central government and 20 public enterprises. The administration is organized through eight ministries, except for a few local public services in rural areas that are carried out by the village councils. The central government budget, which covers the calendar year, includes all receipts and expenditures of departments, receipts of cash and commodity grants, and expenditures financed by project grants and loans. Budget estimates are prepared in a conservative manner, but supplementary expenditure requests are normally submitted to the Legislative Assembly during the fiscal year. The public enterprise sector receives considerable financial support from the Government in the form of advances, low interest loans, and capital transfers. Consolidated public sector accounts are not available.

The central government plays a major role in the economy, with receipts and expenditure each equivalent to about 50 percent of GDP.

Tax revenue is equal to more than 30 percent of GDP, a higher ratio than in other Pacific island countries. Import duties account for over half of revenue, and their importance has increased in recent years because of tariff reforms. Income tax is the next largest source of revenue. A recently imposed indirect tax on certain services brought more tourist spending into the tax net. Nontax revenue is 7 percent of GDP, comprising mainly fees and charges, the surpluses of departmentally organized commercial undertakings, and rent on government property. External grants are 15 percent of GDP, in the form of project assistance and cash from the European Community's STABEX facility.

The central government budget is generally in surplus. Current expenditure is about 22 percent of GDP, of which more than half represents wages and salaries. Development expenditure is about 26 percent of GDP, of which about two thirds is financed by external grants and concessionary loans. Net lending primarily reflects subsidies and capital transfers to the public enterprises. Domestic financing of the budget, when required, mainly involves transactions with the banking system and purchases of government securities by the National Provident Fund.

The nonfinancial public enterprises play an important role in the economy. The main areas of operation are tree crop plantations, manufacturing, marketing and distribution of agricultural production, construction of infrastructure, and public utilities. In recent years, strong efforts have been made to improve the financial position of this sector through management restructuring, staff reductions, flexible pricing policies, and the privatization of some construction, trading, and manufacturing activities. Privatized assets are absorbed mainly by funds made available to resident investors through the publicly owned nonbank financial institutions.

Financial Sector

The financial system consists of the central bank, two commercial banks, and several nonbank financial institutions. Western Samoa has issued its own currency through the Treasury or a commercial bank for several decades but, until recently, monetary instruments were undeveloped. A Monetary Board, comprising the Minister of Finance, the Financial Secretary, and four other members appointed by the Government, carried out a very limited range of central banking functions during 1975–83, but exercised almost no role in the regulation of credit. The Central Bank of Samoa commenced operations in 1984, assuming most monetary authority functions, including the issue of currency, partial management of the foreign reserves, the regulation of commercial banks, and implementation of monetary and exchange rate policies. Monetary policy is now exercised mainly through reserve requirements, a system of credit control by which allowable increases in credit are linked to the growth of longer-term deposits and the partial regulation of interest rates. The Government issues medium- and long-term bonds, but there is no active secondary market; there are no issues of treasury bills or central bank short-term paper.

Both commercial banks are under foreign management; one is owned equally by a New Zealand bank and the Government, and the other is owned by an Australian bank, a U.S. bank, and domestic investors. The National Provident Fund, which was established in 1972, collects contributions equivalent to 10 percent of the wage and salary bill from all employers who may reclaim up to half of this amount from their employees. It is an important source of finance for the central government budget. The Development Bank of Western Samoa, which was established in 1974, is primarily a conduit for channeling external grants and concessional loans to agriculture and industry.

Developments in the 1970s

Western Samoa entered the 1970s with a typical economic structure for a small Pacific island country at an early stage of development. In the decade after independence, conservative financial policies ensured the preservation of budget balance. However, efforts to expand investment and growth were constrained by shortages of foreign exchange. The availability of external aid was limited. Exports were stagnant, reflecting the dependence on plantation agriculture, which had suffered from inadequate investment. A foreign exchange allocation system was in effect to allocate and limit private sector imports.

During 1972–75, balance of payments difficulties emerged when more expansionary expenditure policies were implemented in an attempt to accelerate growth. Increased public expenditure led to large overall budget deficits and rapid credit expansion. Inflation accelerated and most wage earners received full compensation for price rises. The external pressures were compounded after the first round of oil price increases and the subsequent international recession, when import prices increased, export prices declined, and remittances from families living abroad fell. The current account deficits were largely financed by commercial borrowing in the New Zealand market and a drawdown in official reserves from nine months' imports in 1971 to two and a half months' imports in 1975.

In the second half of the 1970s, a series of economic adjustment programs were adopted, supported often by Fund stand-by arrangements, but they generally fell short of their objectives. The growth in foreign exchange earnings was weak. Exports from plantations were depressed owing to the aging of trees and management difficulties. Prices paid to small copra and cocoa producers followed those in world markets. The resulting instability in incomes and low average rates of return were not conducive to increased production. With a lack of buoyancy in budget revenue and strong growth in expenditure, including wages and salaries, public sector deficits and recourse to the banking system remained large. Monetary policy instruments had little capacity to help constrain demand for imports; balance of payments pressures were fended off by tight exchange controls. Exchange rate adjustments contributed to rising domestic prices of imports, but were not supported adequately by demand management policies and thus were inadequate to strengthen the competitiveness of Western Samoan producers.

Adjustment Policies During 1975–79

The first stabilization program designed to correct domestic and external imbalances was introduced in late 1975. The program aimed to tighten fiscal policy by increased rates of taxation and improved administration of income taxes and customs duties. The tala was depreciated by 20 percent on a trade-weighted basis in order to improve export profitability. However, domestic financial policies did not support external adjustment. The targeted reduction in the budget deficit was not achieved because of shortfalls in revenue, lack of current expenditure restraint, and lower-than-projected aid disbursements. Public enterprise deficits also increased in this period. The required supply response from the traded goods sector was not forthcoming because prices rose to such a degree that there was little depreciation in real terms.

A further program of demand restraint was planned in 1977. It emphasized the need to limit bank borrowing by the public sector in order to help contain domestic credit and improve the external position. A pronounced increase in export prices, as well as higher concessionary assistance, caused the balance of payments to strengthen. However, the external surplus contributed to a faster rate of monetary expansion and inflation. Bank deposit and lending rates that were highly negative in real terms discouraged private savings, and stimulated private sector demand for credit.

The authorities recognized that longer-term external viability depended on the growth and diversification of agricultural production and related industries. Another economic adjustment program was initiated in 1978, with the focus switched toward increased domestic public sector resource mobilization and the use of concessionary external assistance to finance an expanded public investment program. However, increased imports weakened the balance of payments, particularly since neither additional domestic nor external resources were generated on the expected scale. The use of advance accounts to prefinance projects pending the disbursement of external aid added to the borrowing needs of the public sector. The increase in imports helped hold down the rate of inflation, but external debt rose sharply and official international reserves were reduced to the equivalent of one month's imports.

A fourth attempt was made in mid-1979 to correct the underlying domestic and external imbalances. This program used fiscal restraint to promote public savings and raised most bank interest rates to stimulate private savings. The currency was depreciated by 19 percent on a tradeweighted basis to offset the appreciation in real terms that had occurred since 1976. The potential benefit of the exchange rate change was eroded by reductions in import duties and compensatory wage increases in the public sector; budget expenditure continued to grow strongly; and public enterprise finances deteriorated. With expanded commercial borrowing, external debt reached the equivalent of 45 percent of GDP at the end of 1979. In view of the difficult external position, additional restrictions on foreign exchange transactions for imports were imposed.

Developments in the 1980s

The rate of real GDP growth averaged 1–2 percent annually during 1980–87. Economic performance deteriorated further in the early

1980s, when the second round of oil price increases and the world recession had a profound impact because of the fundamental weakness of Western Samoa's balance of payments. However, the long period of economic decline was finally reversed during 1983–85 through the firm implementation of comprehensive adjustment policies, supported by two stand-by arrangements with the Fund. The adjustment measures relied primarily on fiscal and monetary restraint, combined with the active use of the exchange rate to improve the external position, and increases in interest rates to encourage financial savings. The pursuit of restrictive demand management policies consolidated these gains during 1986–87.

Continued Imbalances in 1980–82

During 1980–82, Western Samoa experienced a sizable fall in real income together with high rates of inflation and severe external financing problems. The difficulties stemmed partly from the deterioration in the terms of trade, reflecting lower copra export prices and higher import prices, on a scale similar to that experienced by most other Pacific island economies. Adverse weather compounded this setback, leading to several poor harvests of major export commodities. The adjustment of domestic economic policies to the worsened external environment initially proved insufficient. Fiscal measures and higher bank interest rates had little impact on dampening domestic demand, and inflation remained high. With only modest increases in workers' remittances and external grants, the external current account recorded unsustainable deficits.

During this period, the tala was held largely unchanged against the New Zealand dollar. This policy resulted in a sizable appreciation in real effective terms, mainly because of the high rate of domestic inflation. In view of the continued weak export performance, price stabilization schemes for cocoa and copra were instituted in early 1982. However, incentives for increased production in the short run remained inadequate. Demand continued to be high for imports of consumer goods, energy, and capital equipment. By the end of 1982, the external borrowing capacity had been exhausted, with debt equivalent to 80 percent of GDP and external payments arrears equivalent to one year's exports. The lack of foreign exchange severely reduced the availability of imports, and the external current account deficit fell sharply.

The overall budget deficit averaged 15 percent of GDP during 1980–82. While total expenditure continued to rise strongly, the shortage of imports on which duties could be levied, the failure to change tax rates and government charges, the lack of measures to broaden the tax base, and weak revenue collection procedures constrained the growth of receipts. In addition, the consolidated deficit of public enterprises averaged 7 percent of GDP, reflecting in part the inflexible pricing policies. Largely because of the public sector's financing needs, domestic credit expanded rapidly. Although low imports depressed private sector demand for bank credit for trade financing, the rate of monetary expansion contributed to high rates of inflation. Interest rates were substantially negative in real terms, and a wide differential emerged between domestic rates and those prevailing in the United States, Australia, and New Zealand.

Successful Adjustment in 1983–85

The economic and financial programs adopted during 1983–85, which coincided with a change in government, were the first stage of a medium-term adjustment process intended to achieve a sustainable balance of payments. Domestic spending was brought into line with available resources and the critical external financing position was eased, primarily through curbing public and private consumption. Measures to improve resource allocation and mobilize domestic savings laid the foundation for a resumption of growth. Actions were taken to strengthen public finances, reduce the growth of credit, dismantle the foreign exchange allocation system, and pursue flexible interest and exchange rate policies. The programs helped to moderate the rate of price increase and move the internal terms of trade in favor of the traded goods sector.

The country achieved an impressive degree of fiscal adjustment. The overall central government budget deficit moved into surplus by 1985. Revenue measures yielded the equivalent of 4 percent of GDP in 1983 and nearly 2 percent of GDP in 1984, including an import surcharge, increased excise duties, the collection of income tax arrears, and higher government fees and charges. A change in the basis of assessment of customs duties facilitated collection, and revised rates provided more uniform levels of effective protection within the import competing sector. Public sector imports were made subject to duty, and most excise duties were converted from a specific to an ad valorem basis.

Curbs on the growth of public sector employment, wages, and salaries, the postponement of lower priority projects, and the transfer of other projects to the private sector reduced current expenditure in relation to GDP. The Government also introduced an improved system of expenditure control, with intensified monitoring and quarterly discussions between the Treasury and departments to review trends in revenue and expenditure and, if necessary, impose reductions on future spending. The overall deficit of the public enterprises was reduced by the equivalent of 5 percent of GDP during 1983–85 by controlling costs and adjusting prices more frequently. This resulted in a considerable reduction in the rate of growth of domestic credit.

Interest and exchange rate adjustments were implemented early in the adjustment process. The Government raised bank deposit rates by 5–6 percentage points and lending rates by an average of 4 percentage points in early 1983, thereby establishing positive real rates on deposits of one year and longer and on commercial and personal loans, and eliminating the interest differential with neighboring countries. It maintained positive real interest rates and depreciated the tala on a trade-weighted basis by 18 percent in mid-1983, reversing the appreciation that had occurred since 1979. However, the rate of price increase accelerated to 24 percent during 1983. The erosion of competitiveness that occurred as a result of the rise in inflation was more than offset by a further depreciation of 12 percent in mid-1984. The rate of inflation slowed to 7 percent during 1984. With exchange rate flexibility subsequently maintained, international competitiveness continued to improve.

The external current account recorded surpluses in 1983–85 for the first time in more than ten years. A strong recovery in international commodity prices, which enabled the copra and cocoa marketing boards to raise procurement prices, recover earlier losses, and accumulate reserves for use in future price support operations, aided the adjustment effort. Manufactured exports benefited from the completion of a copra crushing mill and timber and tropical fruit processing facilities. A surge in workers' remittances followed the improvement in the world economy and the depreciation of the tala. Aid flows benefited from the restoration of confidence of foreign donors. The restrictive policies brought import demand under control, and the dismantling of the foreign exchange allocation system proceeded without disruption. More entrepreneurs were encouraged to participate in importing, thus generating greater price competition in this sector. The rate of inflation dropped steadily.

The Government gave priority to the elimination of external payments arrears, because of their negative impact on the country's ability to attract capital and service its debt; it achieved this goal by the end of 1985. Commercial arrears, which represented two thirds of the total and had been incurred largely on oil imports, were repaid over 18 months. Arrears of interest and principal on government and government-guaranteed debt were partly repaid within six months and the remaining amount was rescheduled in agreement with major creditors over a three-year period. At the request of one foreign creditor government, part of the debt was converted into equity investment. The external debt service ratio, including repayments of arrears, declined; gross official reserves were restored to three months of imports by the end of 1985.

Consolidation of Gains in 1986–87

The overall budget remained in surplus during 1986–87, despite measures providing lower corporate and personal income tax rates, some exemptions from excise taxes, and the temporary suspension of gift and estate duties. The Government controlled current spending and limited development spending to the availability of external assistance. Net lending increased, reflecting budgetary support for the restructuring of plantations and the financing of the commodity marketing boards. The Government undertook further repayment of indebtedness to the domestic banking system.

The Central Bank played an active role in containing the expansionary impact of the balance of payments surpluses. Direct credit controls to limit bank lending were supplemented by the introduction of reserve requirements in early 1986. High positive real interest rates were maintained, although nominal rates were reduced to reflect the lower rate of inflation. Banks were permitted to negotiate their own rates on deposits of 12 months and longer from late-1986. However, in order to encourage competition for funds among banks and to alleviate the rigidities inherent in credit ceilings, the permitted growth in each bank's lending was linked to their deposit growth from early 1987.

Despite the difficulties created by the sharp decline in world prices of coconut products, the external current account continued to register surpluses in 1986–87. Underlying the further improvement was a drop in imports that resulted from lower petroleum prices, increased domestic energy production, and restrained domestic demand. Although real GDP growth was small, the rate of inflation continued to decline. With the substantial gains in competitiveness and the strengthening of the external position in recent years, the gradual depreciation of the exchange rate was halted. Using a cautious external borrowing policy, Western Samoa continued to reduce the debt service ratio, while gross official reserves rose further in relation to imports.

Table 1. Western Samoa: Gross Domestic Product
by Expenditure, 1983–87[1]

(In millions of tala)

	1983	1984	1985	1986	1987
	(At current prices)				
Consumption	158.1	185.2	207.0	221.7	242.5
Private sector	136.2	155.1	172.5	184.4	201.6
Central government	21.9	30.1	34.5	37.3	40.9
Gross investment	42.3	53.5	54.3	51.2	62.6
Private sector	9.2	11.2	13.5	14.4	21.4
Central government	33.1	42.3	40.8	36.8	41.2
Domestic demand	200.4	238.7	261.3	272.9	305.1
External balance[2]	−46.0	−57.5	−70.1	−71.8	−83.9
Exports	41.6	50.0	59.4	53.3	57.2
Imports	−87.6	−107.5	−129.5	−125.1	−151.1
GDP at market prices	154.4	181.2	191.2	201.1	211.2
	(At 1984 prices)				
Consumption	173.6	185.2	184.1	180.8	193.0
Private sector	149.1	155.1	152.5	148.4	158.7
Central government	24.5	30.1	31.6	32.4	34.3
Gross investment	47.9	53.5	50.0	45.1	53.4
Private sector	8.4	11.2	12.4	12.7	183
Central government	39.5	42.3	37.5	32.5	352
Domestic demand	221.5	238.7	234.1	225.9	246.4
External balance[2]	−42.7	−57.5	−42.0	−32.8	−51.4
Exports	59.5	50.0	71.8	79.0	79.4
Imports	−102.2	−107.5	−113.8	−111.8	−130.8
GDP at market prices	178.8	181.2	192.1	193.1	195.0
Memorandum items:					
Investment (in percent of GDP)	27.4	29.5	28.4	25.5	29.6
Private sector	6.0	6.2	7.1	7.2	10.1
Central government	21.4	23.3	21.3	18.3	19.5
Changes in real GDP					
(in percent)	0.5	1.3	6.0	0.5	1.0

Sources: Data provided by the Western Samoan authorities; and Fund staff estimates.

[1]There are no official national accounts. Total GDP is derived from available data for agricultural production, industrial production, central government expenditure, and information on the construction and services sectors. The expenditure components incorporate balance of payments data for exports and imports of goods and services and available information on investment spending and government consumption; private consumption is derived as a residual.

[2]Goods and nonfactor services.

Table 2. Western Samoa: Output of Main Commodities, 1980–87

(In thousands of long tons)

	1980	1981	1982	1983	1984	1985	1986	1987
Copra	30.10	23.10	43.10	38.10	27.70	36.00	30.20	28.00
Cocoa	0.88	0.81	1.13	0.94	0.66	0.83	0.66	0.29
Bananas	14.80	11.80	10.30	9.40	9.70	8.00	8.00	8.00
Taro	8.42	16.66	15.16	15.18	16.18	16.50	16.81	18.43
Passion fruit	0.33	0.39	0.45	1.14	3.30	1.50	1.25	1.20
Beef	0.51	0.66	0.61	0.57	0.53	0.43	0.30	0.55
Pork	0.07	0.06	0.17	0.18	0.20	0.27	0.38	0.25
Poultry	0.15	0.15	0.15	0.15	0.09	0.03	0.04	0.05
Fish	3.20	3.17	3.12	3.52	3.84	3.64	3.72	3.43

Source: Data provided by the Western Samoan authorities.

Table 3. Western Samoa: Consumer Price Index, 1975–87

(Annual average percentage change)

	Weights[1]	1975	1976	1977	1978	1979	1980	1981	1982	1983	1984	1985	1986	1987
Food	58.8	–3.1	4.7	12.1	–0.1	19.0	21.8	20.2	21.1	15.1	8.8	9.8	6.5	2.8
Clothing and footwear	19.3	3.8	5.7	6.5	0.4	19.3	17.0	23.6	14.5	19.2	15.8	7.7	8.5	3.1
Household operations	31.3	0.9	7.0	42.9	7.2	31.3	13.0	35.2	20.5	13.3	13.6	4.7	2.0	1.4
Transport and communications	9.0	...	...	...	...	29.7	31.8	12.2	14.1	13.7	1.5	5.6	–0.9	6.4
Miscellaneous	16.0	6.6	3.2	16.3	11.1	21.6	16.7	14.7	8.6	26.3	24.9	12.1	8.2	12.4
Overall index	100.0	–0.8	5.0	14.8	2.0	21.7	20.5	20.5	18.3	16.6	11.6	9.1	5.7	4.6
						(End-of-period percentage change)								
Memorandum item:														
Overall index	100.0	–0.9	14.0	8.3	4.2	23.5	29.6	19.1	11.0	23.9	7.3	6.1	2.7	11.6

Source: Data provided by the Western Samoan authorities.
[1] Weights for 1979–87 are derived from the Household Expenditure Survey, 1976–77. Estimates for 1975–78 are based on slightly different weights.

Table 4. Western Samoa: Central Government Budget, 1975–87

(In millions of tala)

	1975	1976	1977	1978	1979	1980	1981	1982	1983	1984	1985	1986	1987
Revenue and grants	13.6	15.9	23.0	27.0	38.5	37.8	39.2	42.6	67.2	84.3	98.0	110.8	120.3
Tax revenue	8.0	8.7	12.2	14.6	16.6	20.4	20.3	23.9	34.1	49.9	58.5	59.7	69.1
Nontax revenue	2.1	2.7	2.6	3.5	4.2	4.5	4.0	4.4	6.9	9.1	13.0	14.4	18.4
External grants	3.4	4.5	8.2	8.9	17.7	12.9	14.9	14.3	26.3	25.3	26.5	36.7	32.8
Expenditure and net lending	17.8	21.7	26.5	39.6	48.7	52.5	56.8	61.7	69.3	101.8	92.1	94.3	108.4
Current expenditure	8.7	10.1	12.5	14.5	17.2	21.1	25.1	31.7	29.0	35.3	41.3	43.4	46.4
Development expenditure	9.1	11.6	14.0	23.6	30.5	26.5	26.9	27.2	39.0	53.9	49.8	45.9	54.9
Net lending[1]	...	...	...	1.5	1.0	4.9	4.7	2.8	1.3	12.6	0.9	5.0	6.9
Overall balance	-4.2	-5.8	-3.5	-12.5	-10.2	-14.7	-17.6	-19.1	-2.1	-17.5	-5.9	-16.5	11.9
Financing, net	4.2	5.8	3.5	12.5	10.2	14.7	17.6	19.1	2.1	17.5	-5.9	-16.5	-11.9
External	2.3	4.0	3.1	8.5	6.5	7.3	7.9	8.2	3.2	11.9	-6.1	-4.0	-6.6
Domestic	1.9	1.8	0.4	4.0	3.7	7.4	9.7	10.9	-1.1	5.6	0.2	-12.5	-5.3
Memorandum items:													
External arrears (increase +)	—	—	—	—	—	0.1	1.4	3.1	-1.8	-2.0	-1.5	—	—
(In percent of GDP)													
Revenue and grants	27.6	28.7	38.4	42.9	42.8	36.7	36.0	32.7	43.5	46.5	51.3	55.1	56.9
Tax revenue	16.3	15.7	20.4	23.2	18.4	19.8	18.6	18.3	22.1	27.5	30.6	29.7	32.7
Nontax revenue	4.3	4.8	4.3	5.6	4.7	4.4	3.7	3.4	4.5	5.0	6.8	7.2	8.7
External grants	6.9	8.1	13.7	14.1	19.7	12.5	13.7	11.0	17.0	14.0	13.9	18.2	15.5
Expenditure and net lending	36.2	39.2	44.2	63.0	54.1	51.0	52.0	47.4	44.9	56.2	48.2	46.9	51.4
Current expenditure	17.7	18.2	20.9	23.0	19.1	20.5	23.0	24.3	18.8	19.5	21.6	21.6	22.1
Development expenditure	18.5	20.9	23.4	37.5	33.9	25.7	24.7	20.9	25.2	29.7	26.1	22.8	26.0
Net lending	...	...	...	2.4	1.1	4.8	4.3	2.1	0.8	6.9	0.5	2.5	3.3
Overall balance	-8.5	-10.5	-5.8	-19.9	-11.3	-14.3	-16.0	-14.6	-1.3	-9.7	3.1	8.2	5.6

Sources: Data provided by the Western Samoan authorities; and Fund staff estimates.

[1]Including net loans and advances to public enterprises, capital subscriptions, and land purchases.

Table 5. Western Samoa: Central Government Revenue and Grants, 1975–87

(In millions of tala)

	1975	1976	1977	1978	1979	1980	1981	1982	1983	1984	1985	1986	1987
Tax revenue	8.0	8.7	12.2	14.6	16.6	20.4	20.3	23.9	34.1	49.9	58.5	59.7	69.1
Income and profits	2.2	1.9	2.7	3.8	4.1	6.0	6.6	8.4	11.0	12.7	12.6	16.0	14.9
Excise duties	—	—	—	0.1	0.8	2.8	2.6	3.5	3.9	6.9	9.7	10.6	12.1
International transactions	5.8	6.7	9.4	10.6	11.5	11.3	10.9	11.8	18.5	29.3	35.2	32.4	40.8
Import duties	5.8	6.7	9.3	9.9	10.4	10.1	10.1	11.0	17.5	27.9	32.5	30.4	38.7
Export duties	—	—	0.1	0.3	0.6	0.6	0.2	0.2	0.3	0.3	1.3	0.7	0.6
Foreign exchange levies	—	—	—	0.4	0.5	0.6	0.5	0.6	0.8	1.1	1.3	1.3	1.5
Other	—	0.1	0.1	0.2	0.1	0.3	0.1	0.3	0.7	1.0	1.0	0.7	1.3
Nontax revenue	2.1	2.7	2.6	3.5	4.5	4.5	4.0	4.4	6.9	9.1	13.0	14.5	18.4
Fees and service charges	0.8	0.9	1.2	1.3	1.8	1.5	1.5	1.8	2.0	1.6	2.7	2.6	3.3
Departmental enterprises	0.8	1.2	0.7	1.3	1.0	1.2	1.0	1.5	3.2	2.2	4.6	6.4	7.3
Rents, royalties, and interest	0.4	0.4	0.4	0.6	0.4	1.0	1.2	0.5	1.3	3.2	2.6	4.0	5.2
Sales of government supplies	—	0.1	0.1	0.1	0.2	0.1	0.1	0.2	0.1	0.1	0.2	0.2	0.1
Other	0.1	0.1	0.2	0.3	0.7	0.6	0.2	0.5	0.4	1.0	2.9	1.3	2.5
Total grants	3.5	4.5	8.2	8.9	17.7	12.9	14.9	14.3	26.3	25.3	26.5	36.7	32.8
Cash and commodity	0.3	0.2	2.3	0.3	1.4	0.3	2.8	0.7	2.0	1.7	0.3	9.4	11.0
STABEX	—	0.2	1.8	—	0.8	—	2.1	0.7	2.0	—	0.3	8.8	8.3
Commodity grants	0.3	—	0.5	0.3	0.5	0.3	0.7	—	—	1.7	—	0.6	2.7
Project aid grants	3.2	4.3	5.9	8.6	16.3	12.6	12.1	13.6	24.3	23.6	26.2	27.3	21.8
Total revenue and grants	13.6	15.9	23.0	27.0	38.5	37.8	39.2	42.6	67.2	84.3	98.0	110.8	120.3

Sources: Data provided by the Western Samoan authorities; and Fund staff estimates.

Table 6. Western Samoa: Central Government Expenditure, 1975–87

(In millions of tala)

	1975	1976	1977	1978	1979	1980	1981	1982	1983	1984	1985	1986	1987
Current expenditure	8.7	10.1	12.5	14.5	17.2	21.1	25.1	31.7	29.0	35.3	41.3	43.4	46.6
Wages and salaries	...	...	...	8.0	9.7	10.9	12.9	13.3	14.8	16.1	18.4	24.1	24.4
Interest payments	0.5	0.6	1.0	1.1	1.5	2.3	2.9	3.0	4.5	5.6	6.9	6.1	6.9
External	...	...	...	0.3	0.7	1.3	1.3	1.3	1.9	2.8	3.5	3.5	4.1
Domestic	...	...	...	0.8	0.8	1.0	1.6	1.7	2.7	2.8	3.4	2.6	2.8
Other[1]	...	...	...	5.4	6.0	7.9	9.3	15.4	9.7	13.5	16.1	13.1	15.3
Development expenditure	9.0	11.6	14.0	23.6	30.5	26.5	26.9	27.2	39.0	54.0	49.8	45.9	54.9
Domestically financed[2]	3.8	4.2	6.8	8.5	9.1	7.6	8.3	8.9	7.1	14.3	17.8	14.0	20.2
Project loan financed	1.7	2.6	3.3	6.5	5.1	6.3	6.5	5.2	7.6	16.1	5.8	4.7	12.9
Project grant financed	3.1	4.3	4.9	8.6	16.3	12.6	12.1	13.1	24.3	23.6	26.2	27.3	21.8
Net lending	—	—	—	1.5	1.0	4.9	4.7	2.8	1.3	12.6	0.9	5.0	6.9
Total	17.8	21.7	26.5	39.6	48.7	52.5	56.8	61.7	69.3	101.8	92.1	94.3	108.4

Sources: Data provided by the Western Samoan authorities; and Fund staff estimates.
[1]Derived as a residual. Includes mostly purchases of goods and services.
[2]Data for 1984 onward include government payments of import duties.

Table 7. Western Samoa: Monetary Survey, 1975–87
(In millions of tala; end of period)

	1975	1976	1977	1978	1979	1980	1981	1982	1983	1984	1985	1986	1987
Net foreign assets	4.7	3.0	7.0	1.9	-1.7	-9.0	-19.1	-25.9	-1.3	1.2	6.4	31.1	56.7
Domestic credit	4.8	8.3	6.2	13.7	21.3	27.1	41.9	57.9	48.4	50.3	54.8	43.8	30.2
Public sector	1.0	2.4	-0.9	3.9	10.6	15.8	29.9	43.7	32.5	31.2	32.4	17.2	-2.6
Government (net)	0.6	1.8	-1.5	2.0	6.2	9.6	19.9	31.5	22.0	21.1	20.3	4.9	-13.1
Public enterprises	0.4	0.6	0.5	1.9	4.4	6.2	10.0	12.3	10.5	10.1	12.1	12.3	9.9
Private sector	3.9	6.9	7.2	9.8	10.7	11.3	12.0	14.2	15.9	19.1	22.4	26.6	32.8
Other items (net)	-2.6	-2.1	-2.3	-2.9	-1.6	0.1	0.2	-0.8	-5.6	-8.7	-9.2	-11.7	6.3
Broad money	7.5	9.2	10.9	12.7	18.1	18.2	23.1	31.2	41.5	42.8	52.0	63.2	80.7
Money supply	4.4	4.8	5.8	6.8	9.1	9.2	14.0	16.5	16.5	18.6	19.5	21.6	28.7
Quasi-money	3.1	4.4	5.1	5.9	9.0	9.1	9.1	14.7	25.0	24.2	32.5	41.6	52.0
(Annual percentage change)													
Memorandum items:													
Domestic credit	50.0	72.9	-25.3	121.0	42.5	26.9	54.5	38.1	-9.0	3.9	8.9	-20.1	-31.1
Public sector	...	140.0	...	...	271.8	45.0	89.5	46.2	-16.8	-4.0	3.8	-46.9	-15.1
Private sector	-4.9	51.3	22.0	36.1	9.2	5.6	5.8	18.2	12.5	20.1	17.3	18.7	23.3
Broad money	5.6	22.7	18.5	16.5	42.5	1.0	26.4	35.3	-3.3	3.1	21.5	21.5	27.7
Money supply	2.3	9.1	20.8	17.2	33.8	1.5	52.3	18.1	-0.2	12.7	4.9	10.8	32.9
Quasi-money	14.8	41.9	15.9	15.7	52.5	0.5	—	62.0	-5.3	-3.2	34.3	28.0	25.0

Sources: Data provided by the Western Samoan authorities; and Fund staff estimates.

Table 8. Western Samoa: Interest Rate Structure, 1975–87
(In percent per annum; end of period)

	1975–78	1979	1980	1981	1982	1983	1984	1985	1986	1987
Commercial bank deposit rates										
Savings deposits	4.0	4.0	4.0	5.0	6.0	8.0	8.0	7.0	7.5	7.5
Time deposits										
3-month	5.0	6.5	6.5	8.5	9.0	14.0	14.0	12.0	11.0	10.25
6-month	5.5	7.0	7.0	9.0	10.0	15.0	15.0	13.0	12.0	12.00
12-month	6.0	8.0	8.0	10.0	11.0	17.0	17.0	15.0	Negotiable	Negotiable
14-month	6.5	8.5	8.5	10.5	11.5	17.0	17.0	15.0	Negotiable	Negotiable
Commercial bank lending rates										
Government[1]	7.0	9.0	9.0	9.0	12.5	15.0	15.0	15.0–18.0	14.0–17.5	14.0–17.5
Agriculture	8.0	9.0	9.0	10.0	12.0	14.0	14.0	15.0–18.0	14.0–17.5	14.0–17.5
Manufacturing	8.0	10.5–12.0	10.5–12.0	11.5–13.0	12.5–13.5	16.0	16.0	15.0–18.0	14.0–17.5	14.0–17.5
Commerce	8.5	10.5–12.0	10.5–12.0	11.5–15.0	12.5–15.0	18.0	18.0	15.0–18.0	14.0–17.5	14.0–17.5
Personal	9.5	10.5–12.5	10.5–12.0	10.5–15.0	14.0–16.0	20.0	20.0	15.0–18.0	14.0–17.5	14.0–17.5
Development Bank loans										
Agricultural loans	10.0–12.0	10.0–12.0	8.0	8.0	8.0	8.0	8.0	10.0–16.0	8.0–16.0	8.0–16.0
Industrial and other loans	10.0–12.0	10.0–12.0	12.0	12.0–14.0	12.0–14.0	12.0–17.0	10.0–17.0	10.0–16.0	8.0–16.0	8.0–17.0
Government securities										
5 years	7.0	7.0	7.0	11.00	12.00	17.50	17.50	14.0–12.75	13.0	10.5[2]
10 years	7.5	7.5	7.5	11.25	12.25	12.25	12.25	15.0–14.0[3]	13.0	11.0[4]
18–20 years	8.0	8.0	8.0	11.50	12.50	12.50	12.50	—	—	—

Source: Data provided by the Western Samoan authorities.
[1] Includes lending to public enterprises.
[2] On loans of 6 years' maturity.
[3] On loans of 5–7 years' maturity.
[4] On loans of 8 years' maturity.

Table 9. Western Samoa: Balance of Payments, 1975–87
(In millions of SDRs)

	1975	1976	1977	1978	1979	1980	1981	1982	1983	1984	1985	1986	1987
Trade balance	-24.3	-19.9	-20.3	-33.0	-43.3	-34.3	-38.4	-33.0	-29.0	-31.3	-34.6	-31.2	-37.8
Exports	5.9	5.8	12.7	8.9	14.2	13.5	9.5	12.2	16.6	18.1	15.9	9.0	9.0
Imports	-30.2	-25.7	-33.0	-41.9	-57.5	-47.8	-47.9	-45.2	-45.6	-49.4	-50.5	-40.2	-46.8
Services, net	2.1	2.3	2.2	1.2	-0.8	-0.1	-1.5	-1.8	-1.1	-1.1	2.0	2.9	5.6
Receipts	6.5	4.5	6.1	7.8	8.4	8.6	5.8	7.5	8.7	8.8	10.9	12.5	15.1
Payments	-4.4	-2.2	-3.9	-6.6	-7.6	-8.7	-7.3	-9.3	-9.8	-9.9	-8.9	-9.5	-9.5
Private transfers, net	4.7	4.5	5.0	9.7	10.5	14.4	15.7	16.9	19.1	20.0	23.3	24.2	27.8
Official transfers	4.8	6.1	6.4	9.6	16.7	10.8	12.2	12.4	15.3	13.0	11.3	13.4	11.9
Current account	-12.7	-7.0	-6.7	-12.5	-16.9	-9.2	-12.0	-5.5	4.3	0.6	2.0	9.4	7.5
Nonmonetary capital, net	10.7	5.0	11.3	6.8	15.3	2.7	4.5	1.3	-1.6	0.6	-0.1	-0.3	1.9
Official	4.6	7.1	6.0	9.7	7.1	5.1	4.4	2.8	3.1	4.2	-0.4	-1.4	2.4
Private[1]	6.1	-2.1	5.3	-2.9	8.2	-2.4	0.1	-1.5	-4.7	-3.6	0.3	1.1	-0.5
Allocation of SDRs	—	—	—	—	0.4	0.3	0.3	—	—	—	—	—	—
Overall balance	-2.1	-2.0	4.6	-5.7	-1.2	-6.2	-7.2	-4.1	2.7	1.3	2.0	9.0	9.2
Memorandum items:													
Current account (in percent of GDP)													
Including official transfers	-19.7	-11.6	-10.3	-18.3	-19.9	-10.7	-13.5	-3.8	4.6	0.6	2.4	12.3	9.6
Excluding official transfers	-27.1	-21.8	-20.1	-32.4	-39.5	-23.2	-27.2	-18.3	-11.7	-12.9	-11.1	-5.2	-5.6
Tala per SDR (period average)	0.76	0.92	0.92	0.92	1.06	1.20	1.22	1.33	1.65	1.88	2.28	2.62	2.74

Sources: Data provided by the Western Samoan authorities; and Fund staff estimates.
[1]Includes private capital flows, errors and omissions, and valuation adjustments.

Table 10. Western Samoa: Exports by Commodity, 1975–87

(Value in millions of SDRs, volume in thousands of metric tons, unit value in SDRs per metric ton)

	1975	1976	1977	1978	1979	1980	1981	1982	1983	1984	1985	1986	1987
Copra													
Value	3.4	2.1	5.1	3.9	8.3	7.0	3.5	2.1	0.8	—	0.4	0.6	—
Volume	19.4	11.8	17.8	13.8	18.5	25.3	16.1	10.4	4.8	—	2.8	3.2	—
Unit value	176	174	284	283	445	276	215	200	177	—	152	121	—
Coconut oil													
Value	—	—	—	—	—	—	—	3.1	6.7	11.0	6.9	2.5	3.1
Volume	—	—	—	—	—	—	—	8.0	12.2	10.7	10.9	12.6	11.5
Unit value	—	—	—	—	—	—	—	260	551	1,030	628	199	272
Copra meal													
Value	—	—	—	—	—	—	—	0.3	0.4	0.3	0.2	0.3	0.2
Volume	—	—	—	—	—	—	—	4.0	5.2	4.3	5.9	6.2	4.1
Unit value	—	—	—	—	—	—	—	72	78	73	41	40	54
Coconut cream													
Value	—	—	—	0.3	0.4	0.5	0.5	0.6	0.7	0.9	1.2	1.1	1.1
Cocoa													
Value	1.5	2.4	6.4	2.8	3.4	1.5	1.1	0.7	2.8	1.2	1.0	1.2	0.9
Volume	1.5	1.6	2.2	1.1	1.4	1.6	1.0	0.8	2.1	0.7	0.6	0.9	0.7
Unit value	1,056	1,473	2,957	2,577	2,449	1,627	1,073	962	1,320	1,834	1,780	1,374	1,213
Bananas													
Value	0.1	0.2	0.1	0.1	1.3	0.4	0.3	0.2	0.2	0.1	0.1	0.2	0.1
Taro													
Value	0.1	0.4	0.4	1.4	0.2	1.1	1.8	1.6	1.4	1.5	2.2	1.7	1.8
Timber													
Value	0.2	0.7	0.2	0.3	0.2	0.4	0.5	1.0	0.3	0.7	0.4	0.2	0.1
Volume[1]	1.2	0.5	1.5	2.2	1.5	1.7	1.7	2.6	1.4	1.7	1.3	0.6	0.3
Unit value	160	160	140	140	160	212	261	364	233	387	281	369	462
Other (value)	0.5	0.6	0.5	0.4	0.3	1.2	1.3	1.2	1.9	1.9	1.8	1.2	1.1
Re-exports	0.2	0.1	0.1	—	—	0.4	0.7	0.9	1.2	0.8	1.7	0.4	0.7
Total, including re-exports	5.9	5.9	12.7	8.9	14.2	13.5	9.5	12.2	16.6	18.1	15.9	9.0	9.0

Sources: Data provided by the Western Samoan authorities; and Fund staff estimates.
[1] In millions of board feet.

Table 11. Western Samoa: External Grants, 1980–87

(In millions of SDRs)

	1980	1981	1982	1983	1984	1985	1986	1987
Project grants	13.1	11.2	12.1	14.8	12.5	11.5	10.4	9.6
Australia	4.0	1.6	4.4	6.8	4.8	4.0	1.6	3.1
Germany, Federal Republic of	1.5	0.8	0.4	0.1	0.8	0.4	1.0	1.2
Japan	1.5	2.9	2.4	1.2	0.2	1.8	4.9	2.3
Netherlands	0.2	0.5	0.1	0.1	0.2	0.2	—	—
New Zealand	3.3	3.4	2.1	2.3	2.9	3.3	2.4	1.8
European Development Fund	1.5	0.7	1.5	3.9	1.9	0.7	0.1	0.5
United Nations Development Programme	0.8	1.2	0.1	0.1	0.8	0.7	0.2	0.5
Other	0.3	0.1	0.1	0.3	0.8	0.4	0.2	0.2
Expenditure abroad[1]	-2.6	-1.3	-1.9	-2.1	-1.6	-1.6	-1.5	-1.7
Net total	10.5	9.9	10.2	12.6	10.9	9.9	8.9	7.9
Cash and commodity grants	0.3	2.3	0.5	1.2	0.9	0.1	3.7	4.0
European Community—STABEX	—	1.7	0.5	1.2	—	0.1	3.4	3.0
Other	0.3	0.6	—	—	0.9	—	0.2	1.0
Total grants	10.8	12.2	10.7	13.8	11.8	10.1	12.5	11.9

Sources: Data provided by the Western Samoan authorities; and Fund staff estimates.

[1]Mainly technical assistance in the form of scholarships for Western Samoans to study abroad and that part of the salaries for foreign experts that is not spent in Western Samoa.

Table 12. Western Samoa: External Debt and Debt Service, 1975–87

(In millions of SDRs)

	1975	1976	1977	1978	1979	1980	1981	1982	1983	1984	1985	1986	1987
External debt (end of period)	13.6	18.8	24.0	33.0	38.3	44.4	63.3	69.8	75.0	76.0	65.7	61.6	60.7
Government debt	8.5	12.4	16.3	24.2	27.6	34.2	43.4	46.3	52.6	58.3	51.2	48.9	51.8
Bilateral	2.3	2.2	2.3	2.4	5.1	4.9	5.1	5.6	5.6	6.2	4.8	4.1	4.8
New Zealand	2.1	1.9	1.3	2.0	1.8	1.8	1.7	1.6	1.4	1.0	0.9	0.4	0.4
Germany, Federal Republic of	—	—	—	—	3.3	3.1	2.9	2.9	2.3	2.0	2.4	2.5	2.2
China	—	—	—	0.4	—	—	0.4	1.1	1.9	3.1	1.6	1.2	2.2
Multilateral	3.5	6.1	10.1	16.4	17.6	24.5	33.5	36.5	43.3	49.4	43.4	42.3	42.9
Asian Development Bank	3.5	4.5	6.7	10.3	11.3	14.4	19.2	19.9	25.2	30.4	24.9	25.2	26.8
International Development Association	—	0.9	1.9	3.4	2.6	4.2	6.6	7.9	8.9	9.7	9.2	9.0	9.2
OPEC	—	0.7	1.3	2.0	1.9	2.6	3.7	4.8	4.8	5.2	4.6	3.7	2.7
IMF Trust Fund	—	—	0.2	0.8	1.4	1.9	2.0	1.9	1.9	1.7	1.4	1.0	0.6
European Community	—	—	—	—	0.5	1.4	2.0	1.9	2.4	1.9	2.7	2.9	2.9
IFAD[1]	—	—	—	—	—	—	—	—	0.1	0.4	0.6	0.6	0.7
Other	2.7	4.1	4.0	5.3	4.9	4.8	4.9	4.2	3.7	2.7	3.0	2.5	4.1
Bank of New Zealand	0.3	0.3	0.3	0.2	0.1	0.1	0.1	0.1	—	—	—	—	—
New Zealand money market	2.2	2.9	2.9	2.9	2.6	2.6	2.5	2.2	2.1	1.6	1.5	1.0	1.1
Eurodollar loans	—	—	—	1.5	1.5	1.4	1.3	1.1	1.2	0.9	1.5	1.0	0.6
Suppliers' credits	0.1	0.8	0.8	0.7	—	0.2	0.2	—	—	—	—	—	—
Government of Nauru	—	—	—	—	0.7	0.7	0.8	0.8	0.4	0.2	—	—	0.5
Saudi Fund	—	—	—	—	—	—	—	—	—	—	—	0.5	1.9
Government-guaranteed debt	3.5	4.1	6.1	6.1	7.3	6.4	6.7	6.8	8.8	6.5	5.5	5.0	3.7
Use of Fund credit	1.6	2.3	1.6	2.7	3.3	2.6	4.5	3.8	5.7	8.3	8.6	7.3	5.2
External payments arrears	—	—	—	—	—	1.2	8.8	13.0	3.9	2.0	0.4	—	—
Rescheduled arrears	—	—	—	—	—	—	—	—	4.1	1.0	0.1	0.4	—
Debt service	0.9	0.8	1.6	2.8	2.5	3.6	4.1	6.4	5.4	8.5	7.3	6.4	6.5
Amortization	0.4	0.4	0.7	1.6	1.2	1.7	2.4	4.5	3.3	6.4	5.0	4.5	4.8
Interest	0.5	0.4	0.9	1.2	1.3	1.9	1.6	1.9	2.1	2.1	2.3	1.8	1.7
Memorandum items:													
External debt (in percent of GDP)	21.1	31.2	36.8	48.3	45.1	51.6	71.0	71.3	80.0	79.2	78.3	80.3	77.7
Debt service (in percent of exports of goods, services, and private remittances)	5.3	5.4	6.7	10.6	7.6	9.9	12.9	17.5	12.2	18.2	14.6	13.9	12.5

Sources: Data provided by the Western Samoan authorities; and Fund staff estimates.
[1]International Fund for Agricultural Development.

Table 13. Western Samoa: International Reserves, 1975–87

(In millions of SDRs; end of period)

	1975	1976	1977	1978	1979	1980	1981	1982	1983	1984	1985	1986	1987
Assets	6.2	5.2	7.7	3.9	4.0	2.3	2.9	3.3	7.0	10.8	12.8	20.0	26.2
Official assets	0.8	0.5	1.3	0.6	0.5	0.4	0.2	0.4	1.2	3.7	9.5	14.5	18.2
SDRs	—	—	—	—	—	—	—	—	0.4	0.2	—	0.8	1.3
Treasury foreign exchange	0.8	0.5	1.3	0.6	0.5	0.4	0.2	0.4	0.8	1.4	2.3	1.7	1.4
Central Bank of Samoa	—	—	—	—	—	—	—	—	—	2.2	7.2	12.0	15.5
Other assets	5.4	4.7	6.4	3.3	3.5	1.9	2.7	2.9	5.9	7.0	3.3	5.4	8.0
Sinking fund	0.2	0.2	0.3	0.3	0.3	0.1	0.1	0.1	0.1	—	1.4	2.6	4.4
Commercial banks	5.2	4.5	6.1	3.0	3.2	1.8	2.6	2.8	5.8	7.0	1.8	2.9	3.6
Liabilities													
Official liabilities	1.6	2.3	1.8	3.5	5.2	6.9	7.0	6.8	7.8	10.2	10.2	8.4	6.3
Use of Fund credit	1.6	2.3	1.8	3.5	4.7	4.5	6.3	5.8	7.6	10.0	10.0	8.3	5.8
IMF Trust Fund loans	1.6	2.3	1.6	2.7	3.3	2.6	4.4	3.8	5.7	8.3	8.6	7.3	5.2
Treasury overdraft[1]	—	—	0.2	0.8	1.4	1.9	1.9	1.9	1.9	1.7	1.4	1.0	0.6
Commercial banks	—	—	—	—	0.5	2.4	0.7	1.0	0.2	0.2	0.3	0.1	0.5
Net total reserves	4.6	2.9	5.9	0.4	–1.2	–4.6	–4.1	–3.5	–0.8	0.6	2.5	11.6	19.9
Memorandum items:													
Official assets (in months of imports)	2.5	2.4	2.8	1.1	0.8	0.6	0.7	0.9	1.8	2.6	3.0	6.0	6.7
Tala per SDR (end of period)	0.90	0.93	0.91	0.93	1.20	1.19	1.28	1.36	1.70	2.14	2.53	2.69	2.85

Sources: Data provided by the Western Samoan authorities; and Fund staff estimates.

[1]Including any other government foreign borrowing with a maturity of less than 12 months.

Multilateral and Bilateral Economic Assistance Programs in the Pacific Region

Regional Bodies

The South Pacific Bureau for Economic Cooperation was established in 1973 by the members of the South Pacific Forum, which comprises the leaders of the Governments of Australia, New Zealand, and 13 self-governing or independent island countries in the region, including the 7 Fund members. The Bureau, with headquarters in Fiji, promotes regional cooperation in the formulation of economic policies and in relations with industrial countries. Its work program is grouped around trade and industry; shipping, civil aviation, and communications; economic research and planning; and energy matters. The Bureau was active in the establishment of the Pacific Forum Line to operate regional shipping services; the Forum Fisheries Agency to enhance regional cooperation in fisheries and maximize benefits for member countries from the exploitation of the 200-mile exclusive economic zones; and the negotiation of the South Pacific Regional Trade and Economic Cooperation Agreement to provide preferential access for island exports to Australia and New Zealand.

The South Pacific Commission was established in 1947 by Australia, France, the Netherlands, New Zealand, the United Kingdom, and the United States, with membership extended to 22 territories in the region as they became independent or self-governing, including the seven Fund members. The Commission, with headquarters in New Caledonia, provides advice and training principally in the fields of food and marine resources, rural management and technology, education and community services, and environmental protection. It is the executive arm of the South Pacific Conference, which meets annually at the ministerial level and adopts the work program and budget for the coming year.

Multilateral Organizations

The Economic and Social Commission for Asia and the Pacific is the umbrella organization for UN agency activities in the region. Fiji, Papua New Guinea, Solomon Islands, Tonga, Vanuatu, and Western Samoa are full members. Kiribati, which has not joined the United Nations, is an associate member. Its work program includes economic planning; research and statistics, including national accounts; transport and communications; development of natural resources, trade and industry; and human environment. A regional operations center is based in Vanuatu. The United Nations Development Programme, with headquarters in New York, has multiyear programs for each of the seven Fund member countries in the region, under which grant assistance is provided for development projects. It also plays a leadership role in aid coordination activities. Resident representative offices are based in Fiji, Papua New Guinea, and Western Samoa.

The World Bank membership includes the seven island countries that are members of the Fund. The Bank provides financial assistance to these countries primarily by cofinancing loans with the Asian Development Bank. Fiji and Papua New Guinea are assisted exclusively by World Bank loans, while the other five countries are eligible for concessional credits from the International Development Association. Financing is provided for development finance, agriculture, and a wide range of infrastructure, with emphasis on increasing the productivity of exports and diversifying agriculture. Reflecting the special measures needed to assist these economies, the World Bank also provides multiproject loans. These loans are extended to individual countries to cover a number of projects that are viable but too small in scale to merit independent consideration. Lending operations are complemented by economic and sector work and technical assistance to improve absorptive capacity.

The Asian Development Bank, with headquarters in Manila, aims principally to promote investment of public and private capital in the Pacific region for development; to finance especially those projects that are not adequately financed through existing sources; and to act as a focal point and stimulus for regional economic cooperation. All of the regional Fund members, except Fiji, are eligible to receive concessional loans from the Asian Development Fund. In earlier years, loans generally supported the development of infrastructure, but direct assistance has increasingly been provided for productive activities, the energy sector, and development finance institutions. Policies and practices are applied flexibly in recognition of the limited administrative capacity of the countries and include simplified loan documentation and implementation procedures, high local cost recovery, modified procurement tendering, and special training facilities. A regional office is based in Vanuatu.

The European Community conducts trade and promotes economic cooperation with the seven Fund members of the Pacific region in the context of the Lomé Convention, which covers relations with African, Caribbean, and Pacific states. Its financial assistance is provided in the context of medium-term country programs, primarily for infrastructural projects including roads, airstrips, jetties, and harbors, and rural development and emergency relief. Another major source of assistance is the STABEX facility, which provides grants as compensation for declines in the export prices of primary commodities, including copra, coffee, and cocoa. Delegations are based in Fiji and Papua New Guinea and representative offices are maintained in Solomon Islands, Vanuatu, and Western Samoa.

Bilateral Donors

Australia devotes about three fourths of its total bilateral economic assistance program to the seven Fund member countries in the region. While Papua New Guinea receives a high proportion of the total, Australia is also the largest bilateral donor in several of the other islands. Virtually all assistance is provided in grant form, with projects concentrated in agricultural and livestock development, coconut processing facilities, water and sewerage supply, port development, telecommunications, and education.

Japan's involvement in the Pacific, which was relatively limited until the early 1960s, has grown considerably in the past few years as a result of the rapid growth in its aid budget. In promoting economic development, it focuses on areas that have potential for foreign private investment. Bilateral programs are in effect with the seven Fund member countries, and in most cases Japan is the second or third largest source of assistance. Grants and technical cooperation in fisheries, agriculture, transportation, and education account for the majority of aid.

New Zealand's economic assistance program is heavily concentrated in the Pacific region, including its special responsibilities for the

Cook Islands, Niue, and other dependencies. Among the seven Fund member countries, it has especially close links with Tonga and Western Samoa, for historical reasons and because of the large-scale emigration from these countries to New Zealand. It directs economic assistance toward the development of agriculture, livestock, and forestry resources and the provision of health facilities; substantial contributions are also furnished for the regional shipping services.

France primarily aids Vanuatu among the seven Fund member countries, in addition to its support for French Polynesia, New Caledonia, and other dependent territories. While British aid for the region has declined since the expiration of the financial agreements negotiated at independence with several countries, bilateral programs exist with most of the Fund member countries and a development team is located in Fiji to assist with their implementation. U.S. aid in the region was traditionally directed toward American Samoa and the former UN Trust Territories of the Pacific Islands in Micronesia, but the United States is now expanding its economic assistance program to other countries in the region. Other donors in the region include Canada, China, the Federal Republic of Germany, and numerous nongovernmental organizations.

Fund Relations with the Pacific Island Countries

Fund relations with the countries reviewed in this study date from the early 1970s. Fiji was the first of the island countries to become a member, joining in 1971 shortly after attaining independence. Western Samoa, which had been independent for almost a decade, joined the same year. During 1975–81, Papua New Guinea, Solomon Islands, and Vanuatu joined shortly after attaining their independence. During 1985–86 Tonga and Kiribati joined, after reflecting on the obligations and benefits of membership for some years. The combined quotas of the seven countries are equivalent to 0.14 percent of Fund quotas, with Fiji and Papua New Guinea representing four fifths of the group total.

The Fund generally holds annual consultations with each of the Pacific member countries. Discussions between a staff team and officials of the ministry of finance, other departments, the central bank, financial institutions, and public enterprises are normally held in the country concerned over a two-week period. A staff report that reviews recent economic developments, analyzes current policy issues, and assesses short-term and medium-term prospects is prepared for discussion by the Fund's Executive Board. To ensure regular contact without absorbing excessive resources, the Fund and country officials recently decided to conduct full consultations every two years with these members, with interim discussions and less comprehensive reports in alternate years.

With the exception of Western Samoa, which had six stand-by arrangements during 1975–84, and Solomon Islands, which had two stand-by arrangements during 1981–83, the regional members have not borrowed from the Fund to support adjustment programs. However, regular use has been made of the compensatory financing facility to cover temporary export shortfalls. Fiji, Papua New Guinea, Solomon Islands, and Western Samoa made a total of 14 purchases under this facility during 1976–83. Solomon Islands obtained emergency assistance after the cyclone in 1986. Kiribati, Tonga, and Vanuatu have not made use of Fund credit. The lack of extensive use of Fund resources reflects, in some cases, the smallness of the members' quotas in relation to their financing needs and, in most cases, their ample access to alternative sources of finance on concessional terms. All the island members, except Fiji and Papua New Guinea, are on the list of those countries eligible to use the structural adjustment facilities, which are designed to provide balance of payments assistance—in conjunction with the World Bank and other lenders—to lower-income members facing protracted balance of payments problems. Fiji, Papua New Guinea, Solomon Islands, and Western Samoa have received SDR allocations.

The Pacific island members have made extensive use of technical assistance from the Fund in the central banking, fiscal, legal, and statistical fields. During 1980–87, long-term assignments of experts provided by the Fund totaled 95 man-years, and were chiefly concentrated in the area of central banking. Fund staff and consultants made 74 short-term visits ranging in length from a few days to six months. Central banking assistance has been geared mainly to the establishment and operation of central monetary institutions, including the development of appropriate instruments of monetary policy, management of foreign exchange reserves, supervision of commercial banks and nonbank financial institutions, and research and statistical activities. Most experts have been engaged for periods of about two years to act as policy advisors within the monetary authority although, in some instances, they have occupied executive positions as chief and deputy chief executive officers and department heads.

Fiscal assistance has been designed mainly to strengthen public sector financial and economic management capability. With respect to budgetary procedures, assignments have been directed to the requirements for project analysis and evaluation, the criteria for including spending proposals in the budget, the classification of expenditure items, the basis for revenue and expenditure projections, and the integration of macroeconomic analysis and policy advice into the budget process. On the revenue side, the assignments have included advice on widening the tax base, strengthening the customs and excise administration, and computerizing income tax administration. On the machinery of expenditure control, weaknesses in monitoring and reporting have been identified and changes in accounting practices have been suggested. For the public enterprises, a policy framework to govern their operations has been proposed in several cases, including the generation of financial information for their own use and for the government, and the establishment of a unit within the ministry of finance to monitor their activities and advise on policy.

The Fund has provided legal assistance to several countries, primarily for the drafting of legislation in connection with the establishment of a central monetary institution, the supervision of other financial institutions, and the revision of customs tariffs and the income tax system. It has provided statistical assistance to all seven Pacific island member countries, in such areas as output and prices, money and banking, government finance, and the balance of payments.

For long-term technical assistance assignments, counterparts are normally identified; they are expected to subsequently assume the expert's responsibility. Most countries have made satisfactory progress toward localization. Officials of all seven Pacific island member countries have participated in the courses of the IMF Institute in Washington, D.C.; the Fund has also organized seminars on economic and financial management in the region. A Fund resident representative has been stationed in one island country for a number of years.

Table 1. Pacific Island Countries: Relations with the Fund

	Year of independence	Year of membership	Quota in millions of SDRs at end-1987	Consultation cycle[1]	Number of utilized stand-by arrangements	Number of purchases under the compensatory financing facility	Eligibility for structural adjustment facilities	Short-term technical assistance visits 1980–87	Long-term technical assistance in man-years 1980–87
Fiji	1970	1971	36.5	Bicyclic	—	3	No	25	15
Kiribati	1979	1986	2.5	Bicyclic	—	—	Yes	3	—
Papua New Guinea	1975	1975	65.9	Bicyclic	—	2	No	7	21
Solomon Islands	1978	1978	5.0	Bicyclic	2	2	Yes	15	24
Tonga	1970	1985	3.3	Bicyclic	—	—	Yes	4	1
Vanuatu	1980	1981	9.0	Bicyclic	—	—	Yes	4	24
Western Samoa	1962	1971	6.0	Bicyclic	4	6	Yes	15	10

Source: International Monetary Fund.
[1] Under the bicyclic procedure, full consultations are held every two years, with interim discussions and less comprehensive reports in alternate years.

Table 2. Pacific Island Countries: Use of Fund Credit

Country[1]	Type of credit	Date of arrangement	Amount (in millions of SDRs)	Percent of quota
Fiji	Oil facility	Sept. 1974	0.34	3
	Compensatory financing	July 1977	6.50	50
	Compensatory financing	Feb. 1982	13.50	50
	Compensatory financing	Jan. 1985	4.75	13
Papua New Guinea	Oil facility	Mar. 1976	14.80	74
	Compensatory financing	June 1976	10.00	50
	Compensatory financing	Nov. 1981	45.00	100
Solomon Islands	Compensatory financing	Apr. 1979	1.05	50
	Stand-by arrangement	May 1981	0.80	25
	Compensatory financing	Oct. 1982	1.60	50
	Stand-by arrangement	June 1983	0.96	30
	Emergency assistance	Sept. 1986	1.25	25
Western Samoa	Stand-by arrangement	Nov. 1975	0.50	25
	Compensatory financing	Nov. 1975	0.50	25
	Oil facility	Nov. 1975	0.26	13
	Oil facility	Mar. 1976	0.16	8
	Compensatory financing	Nov. 1976	0.50	25
	Compensatory financing	Feb. 1977	0.50	25
	Stand-by arrangement	Feb. 1978	0.73	36
	Compensatory financing	Nov. 1978	1.25	42
	First credit tranche	Apr. 1981	0.75	17
	Compensatory financing	Apr. 1981	2.00	44
	Stand-by arrangement	June 1983	3.38	75
	Compensatory financing	June 1983	1.15	25
	Stand-by arrangement	July 1984	3.38	56

Source: International Monetary Fund.

[1] No use of Fund credit has been made by Kiribati, Tonga, and Vanuatu. Trust Fund loans were made during 1977–81 to Papua New Guinea (SDR 19.55 million) and Western Samoa (SDR 1.95 million). Drawings were not made under stand-by arrangements approved with Fiji in November 1974 (SDR 3.25 million), and with Western Samoa in January 1977 (SDR 0.59 million) and in August 1979 (SDR 0.75 million). Partial drawings were made under stand-by arrangements that were approved with Solomon Islands in May 1981 (SDR 0.80 million was drawn out of SDR 1.60 million) and in June 1983 (SDR 0.96 million was drawn out of SDR 2.40 million).

Table 3. SDR Rates Against the U.S. Dollar, 1975–87

Year	Period Average	End of Period
1975	1.21	1.17
1976	1.15	1.16
1977	1.17	1.21
1978	1.25	1.30
1979	1.29	1.32
1980	1.30	1.28
1981	1.18	1.16
1982	1.10	1.10
1983	1.07	1.05
1984	1.03	0.98
1985	1.02	1.10
1986	1.17	1.22
1987	1.29	1.42

Source: International Monetary Fund.

List of Tables

Western Samoa

Annex: Fund Relations with the Pacific Island Countries

The following symbols have been used throughout this book:

...   to indicate that data are not available;

—   to indicate that the figure is zero or less than half the final digit shown, or that the item does not exist;

–   between years or months (e.g., 1984–85 or January–June) to indicate the years or months covered, including the beginning and ending years or months;

/   between years (e.g., 1985/86) to indicate a crop or fiscal (financial) year.

"Billion" means a thousand million.

One square kilometer = 0.3861 square mile.

Minor discrepancies between constituent figures and totals are due to rounding.

Economic Development in Seven Pacific Island Countries

Designed and composed by the Composition Unit of the International Monetary Fund.

The text was set using Linotype Century Old Style and tabular matter was set in Helvetica.

Cover design by Philip Torsani.
The cover type is Oliver Bold.

Printed and bound by Kirby Lithographic Company in Arlington, Virginia, U.S.A.

2053   3290